Saturday Morning Censors

CONSOLE-ING PASSIONS Television and Cultural Power
A series edited by Lynn Spigel

Saturday Morning Censors

Television Regulation before the V-Chip

HEATHER HENDERSHOT

Duke University Press   Durham and London   1998

 1998 Duke University Press
All rights reserved
Printed in the United States of America on acid-free paper ⊛
Typeset in Quadraat by Tseng Information Systems, Inc.
Library of Congress Cataloging-in-Publication Data appear
on the last printed page of this book.

Contents

Acknowledgments

Many people and institutions helped me research and write this book. The staff of the University of Rochester Interlibrary Loan Department found innumerable books and articles for me, and archivists and librarians at other institutions were also helpful above and beyond the call of duty. Thanks to the staffs of the Action for Children's Television Archive at Harvard University's Gutman Library, the Margaret Herrick and American Film Institute Libraries in Los Angeles, the University of California, Los Angeles, Film and Television Archive, the Museum of Television and Radio in New York, and the University of Massachusetts Special Collections.

At the University of Rochester, Nancy Hall, Rosemary Hattman, Patty Neill, Lucy Peck, and Cindy Warner helped me endure the daily trials and red tape as the book was initially taking shape. Thanks are also due to the Susan B. Anthony Center for Women's Studies, which provided funding on numerous occasions. Michelle Balzé, Jeanette Delamoir, Amanda Howell, and Anna Williams carefully read early drafts of several chapters. Over the years, Mark Betz's relentless acumen has contributed crucially to my own intellectual development. Jan-Christopher Horak was always a scrupulous and helpful reader, D. N. Rodowick offered professional savoir faire, and Constance Penley provided professional support and several fine meals that linger in memory. I thank Lisa Cartwright for reading closely and giving advice and encouragement. At Vassar College, the Henry Luce Foundation provided funding for a year of teaching and book revisions. Sarah Kozloff, Bill Hoynes, and Jim Steerman were all supportive Vassar colleagues. Thanks also to Marsha Kinder for her feedback and to Henry Jenkins for his valuable help with the manuscript and his ongoing support.

When I was at wit's end, a number of students sustained my energy and made me feel like my teaching and research really mattered. I extend my gratitude to Jay Bartow, Jamie Bradshaw, Danté Bruno, Michelle Eden, Caroline Hanni, Kevin Maher, Sheila Murphy, and Rob Sosin, among many others. I owe a particular debt to the students in my Hampshire College classes on media censorship and animation history and aesthetics. The

Paper Tiger Television collective also played a crucial role in reinvigorating my interest in this project.

In my salad days, Joyce Ackermann taught me how to read books. Lew Hendershot inspired an early interest in the pleasures of movies and cartoons; Peggy Hendershot and Ethel Gallagher enabled a healthy genetic disposition to writerly stubbornness. Special thanks are due to Eric Smoodin, a good friend who spurred me on and had confidence in my work, even at its earliest and most tenuous stage. Myrtle was the best e-mail pal a girl could ask for; Siobhan supplied the necessary tarts and roasts; and Lynn helped me wig out. Finally, I thank John Palattella. His companionship, perspicacity, and eggplant parmigiana provided sustenance.

Adults, Children, and Censorship

> Debates on censorship invariably see it as a prohibitive
> process, assuming that a censored text, by distorting
> "reality" or in some other sense falling short of it, is in
> some sense partial in its representation. . . . This view
> is grounded in a distinction between a "real" world of
> social action on the one hand, and texts and represen-
> tations on the other. It assumes, moreover, that the
> "real" constitutes a kind of self-evident truth, a truth
> that should—or in certain circumstances should not—
> be reflected in representations; and that censorship
> stands, rightly or wrongly, in the way of this process of
> reflection.—Annette Kuhn, *Cinema, Censorship, Sexuality,*
> *1909-1925* [1]

Censorship is usually understood as prohibition: censorship forbids, ob-
structs, denies vision. It functions like a blindfold or a pair of scissors.
This conception of censorship is misleading. In actuality, censorship does
not just cut out images, sounds, or texts whose politics censors object to.
The act of censorship is a *social process* through which the politics of class,
race, gender, violence, and other potentially "problematic" issues are de-
constructed and reconstructed, articulated and scotomized. Censorship is
a social process that both prohibits and produces meanings.

Feminist film scholars Annette Kuhn and Lea Jacobs have shown, for example, that censorship does not simply eliminate genres censors object to.
Some generic conventions (indeed, entire genres) owe their existence to
censorship as a social force. In her study of early twentieth-century British
cinema, Kuhn explains that "the union of cinema and [censorious] public morality . . . produced a new cinematic genre," the propaganda film.[2]

Likewise, Jacobs has shown that Hollywood censorship during the early thirties resulted in a reworking of the conventions of nineteenth-century literary melodrama into the "fallen woman" film.[3] In this book, I argue, like Kuhn and Jacobs, that censorship should be seen not as a reified, prohibitory force but as a dynamic, productive force. By studying censorship, we can decipher some of the conundrums of our culture's deepest fears about sexism, violence, and racism. Censorship does not hide these fears; it reveals them. Unlike Jacobs and Kuhn, I take not film but children's television as the subject of my study. Whereas the history of film censorship has been extensively studied, the history of television censorship, to date, has been largely unexamined.

Saturday Morning Censors studies the regulation of children's television at the industrial (self-regulatory), government (Federal Communications Commission [FCC], Federal Trade Commission), and public (activist) levels in order to produce a social history of the adult reception of children's television. This interdisciplinary study of censorship draws on a wide variety of resources that includes government documents, studio archival material, social scientific scholarship, and oral history. This research forms the groundwork for both close textual readings (strongly informed by feminist work in cultural studies) and historical accounts of the roles pressure groups, the state, and the TV industry play in the regulation of "dangerous" images. Through textual and historical readings of programs such as *Strawberry Shortcake*, *Sesame Street*, and *Fat Albert*, I examine how the meanings of the violence, sexism, and racism of children's programs are defined differently at different historical moments and across disciplines and institutions. This approach diverges from much previous social scientific children's television research in that it tries to address the social world outside of the laboratory.

Rather than focusing on child viewers, this book constructs a history of the reception of children's television by examining *adult* interpretive communities: the FCC, network censors, reform groups, social scientists, children's television producers, and the popular press. I strive to understand why and how these adult readers of children's programs interpret the interaction between child and television program to be dangerous. This entails arguing, like Jacqueline Rose in her study of *Peter Pan*, that "children's" entertainment is impossible: that is, impossible to understand as something that merely responds to the needs and desires of children.[4] Debates around children's entertainment inevitably reveal what *adults* need or desire *for* themselves and *of* children.

Censorship and Childlike Subjectivity

Although the focus of *Saturday Morning Censors* is the regulation and censorship of children's television, my conclusions are relevant to other censorship debates since censors of many different kinds of texts strive to "protect" both the victims of dangerous texts and the potential victims of those victims. Methodologically, my separation of children's television from other censored media is, on the one hand, an artificial and arbitrary separation because censorship knows no generic boundaries. On the other hand, focusing on children's television to study censorship is absolutely logical and absolutely necessary because censorship tends to infantilize all endangered consumers. For example, although most pornography readers are not children, in antiporn discourses they are assumed to think and act *like* children. Many antiporn crusaders infantilize the corruptible/corrupted adult; they believe the person who reads pornography for pleasure has an easily influenced, childlike mind while the government-funded investigator who (ostensibly) reads only for investigative purposes is a mature, level-headed adult. Thus, President Ronald Reagan's Meese Commission could willfully expose itself to vast amounts of dangerous pornography without endangering itself because the commission was composed of upper-middle-class, mature, adult researchers who saw themselves as utterly unlike the stereotypical uneducated, lower-class porn aficionado. The Meese Commission presumed to "know better" than to reenact a pornographic image. Although children's television is censored in unique ways, the imagined *childish* child viewer whom TV censors want to protect is not so conceptually different from the imagined *childlike* adult consumers of porn that Reagan's cronies hoped to impede.

The saga of the Meese Commission is a recent installment in the long-playing drama of media censorship in the United States. In the course of such debates, reformist voices often sound strikingly similar, regardless of political affiliation. Since television's proliferation in the fifties, liberal and conservative reform groups have voiced similar concerns about the possible dangers of television to children's physical and psychological health. In this unofficial coalition of left and right, debates about the censorship of children's television are analogous to debates about the censorship of pornography. The right-wing Meese Commission and the left-wing Women Against Pornography found they shared certain political goals in 1986; similarly, the right-wing Focus on the Family organization finds it has goals in common with the Democratic Clinton administration, which supports the Children's Television Act of 1990.[5]

It seems that similar underlying assumptions about subjectivity inform reformist concerns across the political spectrum and across genres of "dangerous" media. In the eyes of reformers, adult consumers of pornography and child viewers of children's television have much in common. Would-be censors imagine spongelike viewers easily provoked by images to commit copycat crimes ranging from rape to hitting someone over the head with a mallet, Tom-and-Jerry style. In her Meese Commission testimony, antipornography feminist Andrea Dworkin implied an indisputable causality between pornographic photos of bound Asian women hanging from trees and a *New York Times* report of the rape and murder of a Chinese girl whose body was left hanging from a tree. The narrator of the filmstrip *Children and Television* similarly elides the complexities of representation and effects: "Can children distinguish between the fantasy world of television and the reality of their own lives? How many children believe there really is a person named Gilligan who lives on some remote island in the Pacific? How many believe they can be bionically rebuilt if they're in an accident? . . . How many children have seriously injured themselves trying to re-create the stunts of Evel Knevil?"[6] In these accounts, the adult rapist and the child couch potato react to images in the same way: monkey see, monkey do.

Both kidvid reformists and porn prohibitionists tend to explain subjectivity in essentialist terms. Many antipornography feminists, in imagining a utopian world free of patriarchy, rely on normative assumptions about female sexuality; they imagine a sexuality that without patriarchy could be gentle and power-free. Yet few antipornography feminists are as oblivious to the role culture plays in the formation of gender identity as some anti-antipornography feminists would like to believe. In *Only Words*, antiporn crusader and lawyer Catharine MacKinnon asserts that the "physical response to pornography is nearly a universal *conditioned* male reaction" (my emphasis).[7] In this antiporn, procensorship argument, the pornography reader/rapist is a fully "conditioned" consumer. Although much antipornography writing focuses on the apparently essential evils of the penis, without some notion of male sexuality as socially constructed, campaigns against pornography would be futile.[8] In other words, if men (or their metonymic organ) were inherently evil, eliminating pornography (the rape-conditioner) would do little to reduce violence against women.

Like pornography readers, child TV viewers can be "conditioned" to be aggressive, yet the TV reformer's essentialist model of innocent child subjectivity is (arguably) even more intransigent than the antiporn activist's essentialist model of male subjectivity. In debates over children's television, societal conditioning is acknowledged and feared, but essential innocence or goodness is never in doubt. TV reformers see culture as something that is merely added onto an inherently innocent child. From this perspective, children are tabulae rasae, and any writing on these youthful slates is potentially dangerous and potentially indelible. (Needless to say, this model does not allow for a psychoanalytic theory of infantile sexuality, wherein the child is a sexualized being from the very beginning.) Reformers label children's programs "bad" or "good" (unhealthy or healthy) based on the paradox that inherently innocent children, if exposed to the wrong images, are capable of wreaking havoc. The seemingly innocuous program *The Care Bears* plays out this narrative logic repeatedly: good children who do not know how to share their feelings are corrupted by bad guys with unbelievable ease, as if for children good/evil were a light switch. Following this light-switch logic, many reformers conceive of television as endangering its potentially dangerous viewers: innocent children will imitate whatever sexism, racism, and violence they see on "bad" shows, or they will copy the good behavior broadcast on "good" shows.

Diverging from the more common approach,[9] this study does not embrace the naturally innocent model of the child. This does not mean that I see children as inherently corrupted or that I think parents should not be concerned about their children's well-being. Of course parents want to instill their own ethics in their children, and they recognize that the media often promote ethical systems at odds with their own values. One can be sympathetic to this kind of parental anxiety while also recognizing that the need to protect child television viewers is a symptom of a relatively recent social idea that childhood is, as Stephen Kline explains, "a stage of growth that in the long-term interests of civilized society [has] to be isolated and guarded from an abusive world."[10] It is the abusive world of the censorious adults who concern themselves with children's television that *Saturday Morning Censors* studies.

Beyond the Plug-In Drug

It is difficult to talk about children's television without talking about children. Because many adults consider children's television to be dangerously sexist, racist, violent, commercial, or even sinful, discussion inevitably turns to possible effects. Concerned adults have a tendency to conceive of child viewers as passive, imperiled consumers. The passive kiddy couch potato is represented over and over again in newspaper cartoons, childrearing manuals, women's magazines, and even the *Congressional Record*, where reformers and politicians frequently debate the possible effects of television violence.

The impressionable child viewer is also the subject of much scientific debate. The bulk of social scientific research on children and television has been "effects research," which seeks to understand how TV viewing changes children. It is important to question how media may change our lives. The problem, however, with much effects research is that it strives to answer a question with profound *social* implications—How may TV change us?—but in pursuing the answer, it often isolates TV viewing from its social context. Much effects research strives to factor out the child viewer's cultural baggage, distilling him/her into a cognitive processor.[11]

Cultural studies researchers, conversely, are more likely to conceptualize a child viewer who is inseparable from the social world. Taking an approach to child viewers that suffers neither from the biological determinism evident in much social scientific TV research nor from the censorious demagoguery of moral reformers, Ellen Seiter, Henry Jenkins, Patricia Palmer, and David Buckingham, among others, have suggested that children *use* TV in their daily lives rather than being merely used (or abused) by TV.[12]

This book is sympathetic to both the idea that children are culturally embedded readers of media texts and to the desire to examine how children may be affected by television's representations. Yet the book approaches children's television from a different angle, addressing how *adult* readers make meanings out of so-called children's television and how they *anticipate* child reception. That is, *Saturday Morning Censors* examines the adult production of the industrial, social scientific, and activist discourses that circulate around children's TV. I contend that adults constitute a large segment of the audience for children's programs. Adults both produce and censor TV for children, and they speak to and for children through such activities. By examining that process, we can see how adults use television to reinforce their own ideas about what constitutes childhood innocence and how that innocence is (according to reformers, censors, and some parents) or is not (according to TV producers, free market advocates, and some parents) imperiled.

In *Sold Separately: Children and Parents in Consumer Culture*, Ellen Seiter has challenged the child-centeredness of the study of children's television by arguing that parents are consumers targeted by the children's media industry. Her research has broadened our understanding of how parents' and children's desires are spoken to differently by marketers, but this intergenerational approach to the study of children's media is far from typical. Marie Winn and Neil Postman exemplify more common approaches to children's media. Winn's glassy-eyed zombies and Postman's infantile sexpots are typical images our culture holds of children tainted by television. In *The Plug-In Drug*, Winn argues that TV harms essentially innocent children; the very title of the book suggests that the "boob tube" is a pusher, its viewers junkies. Winn uses scientific evidence to prove that watching TV is as addictive and dangerous as taking drugs, and she accuses TV of destroying the family. According to her, before TV existed, family members happily talked and played together, whereas now their lives are dictated by *TV Guide*; when they are together, they stare at the screen like zombies. Winn deemphasizes TV content. To her, what you view is unimportant. The damage comes from the mere *act* of viewing, which is inherently pacifying. The inherently innocent child and potentially happy family are ineluctably thwarted by the TV "drug" experience.

In *The Disappearance of Childhood*, Postman, unlike Winn, recognizes the very concept of childhood as historically specific and variable. He argues that childhood grew out of the separation of adult and child worlds that the printing press engendered by introducing literacy, which served to keep adult knowledge from children. The invention of electronic communication, beginning with the telegraph, led to the disappearance of childhood because, unlike books, electronically disseminated information was available to all, regardless of age. Postman argues that TV harms child viewers, in part, because viewers of all ages watch the same shows. The sordid secrets of adult life are thereby revealed to children. Television destroys childhood because it shows too much to children—adult secrets about life, death, sex, and violence that children should be guarded from.

As in Winn's argument, the child is central to Postman's account yet paradoxically absent. The child does not speak but is spoken for and defended by grown-ups. When, as recounted in the preface to the 1994 edition of *The Disappearance of Childhood*, children write angrily to Postman and tell him that TV has not destroyed childhood, he takes their protests not as a challenge to his thesis but as evidence that children are valiantly fighting against all odds to retain the concept of childhood. Despite their philosophical and methodological differences, Winn and Postman are typical critics of children's television; they speak in defense of a mythical imperiled child.

By examining how adults construct such myths and how censorship strives to maintain an ideal, archetypically innocent child, this book shows how children's TV is a cipher for adult desires. Chapter 1 examines one of the largest groups to speak for children, the children's television industry. This chapter explains the history of broadcast self-censorship, the censors' belief that children's television censorship emerged as a response to cultural anxieties about violence, and the differences (and similarities) between regulation and censorship. The focus is on the adults who read programs before, during, and after their production, the behind-the-scenes, corporate audience of animators and network employees who determine what images are safe for child viewers.[13]

Network children's programs are the scrupulously censored products of a multitude of adult readers. These readers are particularly concerned that sexism be censored from cartoons, yet the popular and industrial documents examined in chapter 2 indicate the presence of sexism at the industrial level, where predominantly male cartoon producers and female network censors of children's programs find themselves in constant conflict with one another. Whereas the industry sees sexism as something to excise during preproduction, racism is not seen as a preproduction issue because nonwhite cartoon characters are tokens or nonexistent. By looking at what happens after preproduction censorship, chapter 2 examines sexism and racism at the level of cartoon manufacture, where the bulk of cartoon labor is performed by poorly paid men and women of color abroad and by poorly paid women in the United States.[14]

Analyzing the gender and race dynamics of cartoon production and censorship illustrates that television programs are not merely, as many reformers and scientists would have us believe, *causes* of violence, sexism, or racism among viewers; they are also products of sexist and racist production practices. In this sense, censoring programs is like censoring hate speech. To censor TV content is to attack manifestations of attitudes without necessarily affecting the enunciators' beliefs or self-justification. In other words, silencing a racist TV producer makes him/her a quiet racist. Likewise, inking over cleavage or forbidding racist caricatures does not alter sexism and racism within the animation industry; such censorship/regulation alters symptoms without addressing structural inequities.

Chapter 2 shows that different types of documents yield different interpretations of what censorship is and how it operates. The documents examined render legible what animation historian Eric Smoodin, following Jackie Stacey, calls a "rhetoric of reception":[15] sources of reception history (documents, oral accounts) do not enable historians access to original audiences, but they do allow them to read the discourses of multiple audiences. In other words, reception documents can be read as narratives that follow certain generic conventions. In Stacey's study of British female spectators of the forties and fifties, the fan letter is not merely a "real" letter written (or supposedly written) by a fan; it is also a genre of writing whose conventions are recognized by letter writers and readers. Rather than seeing reception documents as "mediated" or "distorted" by their own narrative conventions, I would agree with Stacey that "audience researchers must deal inevitably with the question of representation, but not as a *barrier* to meaning, but rather as *the form* of that meaning."[16] Bearing Stacey's words in mind, chapter 2 examines different kinds of documents and oral accounts to see how different adult audiences understand the censorship of children's television. The goal is not to synthesize these different narratives in order to produce the single, true story of children's television censorship but rather to explore how various adult readers represent children's television censorship differently.

Turning away from television producers, in chapters 3 and 4, I look at media activists as viewers of children's TV. These chapters focus on the public pressure group Action for Children's Television and the controversial product-based programs of the eighties. Although anticommercialism fueled both ACT's antisugar drive of the seventies and its eighties attack on He-Man, Teenage Mutant Ninja Turtles, and other licensed characters, the two campaigns were quite different. First, ACT's seventies activism took place in the context of a widespread liberal (and sometimes radical) media reform movement, whereas its eighties activism operated in the shadow of the Reagan FCC's deregulation of the television industry. Second, in the eighties, ACT's focus shifted from attacking commercials to attacking shows it claimed were commercials.

Chapters 5, 6, and 7 turn from the so-called dross of children's television to examine more prestigious, seemingly "uncensorable" TV shows. Chapter 5 explains the history of criticisms of *Sesame Street*. Although *Sesame Street* now symbolizes the epitome of "high-quality" TV, when the show premiered, some adults protested that it was too fast paced and would overstimulate children and even condition them to use drugs; others criticized the show for its integrated cast and "Commie" politics. Chapter 6 offers a new critique of *Sesame Street* by examining the program's child-testing practices and its international production and distribution policies. Chapter 7 explains why and how Bill Cosby's widely praised cartoon *Fat Albert and the Cosby Kids* served various adult interests; in particular, the show helped CBS defend itself against the censorious congressional attacks on the TV industry that followed the 1972 release of the surgeon general's report on television violence. This chapter also examines the role *Fat Albert* played in Cosby's dissertation and how his educational image sealed the program's educational image.

Taken together, the chapters of this book do not focus on whether children's television should or should not be censored. Questioning whether censorship should or should not be can profoundly limit critical debate. As Michael Holquist explains, "[A]ll too often [censorship] is still treated through a crude axiology, as an absolute choice between prohibition and freedom. This position denies the reality of interdiction and masks the necessity of choosing the myriad specific conditions that embody censorship's fatedness. To be for or against censorship is to assume a freedom no one has. Censorship *is*. One can only discriminate among its more and less repressive effects" (original emphasis).[17] Just as, historically, the question of whether or not pornography should exist has occluded the study of what pornography actually is,[18] the question of whether or not censorship should exist has often occluded the study of what it is. But, as Holquist observes, censorship *is*. The question is, *how*, *when*, and *why* does it function? *Saturday Morning Censors* takes children's television as a lens through which to scrutinize these questions. The book provides a historical context for understanding current debates surrounding both children's television and censorship in general.

Attacking (TV?) Violence

1

> If you have any doubt about the influence MTV wishes
> to exert on today's adolescents, watch their popular
> program *Beavis and Butthead*. It will chill your soul. . . .
> Beavis and Butthead are animated characters, about
> 14 years of age. They use crude words, fondle them-
> selves, do horribly cruel things to animals (like using
> frogs for baseballs), laugh at women's private parts,
> and sit around watching heavy-metal videos as bright
> green stuff runs from their noses. They are profane, ni-
> hilistic and sick. But to a generation of children, they
> are hilariously funny. Butthead is obsessed with fire.
> "I like to burn stuff," he says. In one episode, Beavis and
> Butthead took a trip to a rifle range where they acci-
> dentally shot down an airplane. They had difficulty open-
> ing the door of the wrecked plane, so they left women
> and children to die inside. *This* is the fare served up to
> preteens and adolescents by the company that seeks
> to shape an entire generation. — Dr. James C. Dobson,
> Focus on the Family Newsletter [1]

Focus on the Family fears Beavis and Butthead. Why? Beavis and Butthead represent values abhorrent to the right-wing Christian fundamentalist group, and Dr. James C. Dobson, the group's founder, assumes that
children will be shaped by the representation of such values. Dobson fears
that kid viewers will engage in copycat behavior. Network children's television executives also fear imitation; if children injure themselves or others
by imitating an act shown on a children's program, the network showing the program can be held liable. Whereas the networks seek only to
turn a profit, Focus on the Family seeks Christian spiritual redemption

for our "morally bankrupt society." Yet both imagine child viewers in remarkably similar ways: child viewers are both dangerous to society and endangered by television because of their proclivity for imitation. This fantasy construction of the child viewer as a mimetic machine often appears in popular discourses. When a small-town American child burned down his trailer home in 1994, killing his baby sister, his mother said the child had done so because he had watched *Beavis and Butthead*. Hoping to avoid legal trouble, MTV responded by moving *Beavis and Butthead* to a later time slot and shelving the episode in which Butthead plays with fire. MTV censored the episode so that no other parents could complain that their kids had imitated Butthead.

Focus on the Family and other foot soldiers in the right-wing war on culture claim that the contemporary media have reached an all-time moral low and that children's entertainment was wholesome before the sixties countercultural movement. The history of cultural anxieties about children's media is, however, much more convoluted than such moral crusaders would have us believe. In fact, rather than simply signaling the end of wholesome TV, the disruption of the sixties actually served as an impetus for network self-censorship of TV content. This chapter lays the groundwork necessary for understanding the historical conditions that brought about network self-censorship, explaining how TV censorship was modeled on film censorship and why TV censors themselves believe censorship/regulation increased in 1968. The story must be prefaced, however, by a brief explanation of the differences between censorship and regulation, both in principle and in practice.

Regulation versus Censorship

Regulation is legal, whereas censorship is illegal. If the Federal Communications Commission (FCC) penalizes a disc jockey for saying "fuck" on the air, it is practicing regulation. If the courts declare the FCC's action illegal, the "fuck" prohibition becomes censorship. Prices, technology, and content can all be subject to government regulation. Table 1 shows the FCC's August 1991 fine schedule. The FCC's very public deliberations over TV ratings, the v-chip, and other hot-button issues lead many people to think that the commission spends most of its time discussing TV content. But in actuality, as the list of regulatable items illustrates, content regula-

Table 1. FCC Fines, August 1991

Violation	Fine	Violation	Fine
Misrepresentation or lack of candor	$20,000	Use of unauthorized equipment	$10,000
Inadequate tower lighting and marking	$20,000	Violations of children's television rules	$10,000
Construction or operation without authorization	$20,000	Violation of main studio rule	$10,000
Unauthorized substantial transfer of control	$20,000	Operation of unauthorized location	$10,000
False distress broadcasts	$20,000	Inadequate frequency coordination	$10,000
Misuse of distress and safety frequencies	$20,000	Failure to file information	$7,500
Refusal to permit inspection	$18,750	Failure to maintain public files	$7,500
Malicious interference	$17,500	Failure to properly identify sponsors	$6,250
Failure to respond to FCC communications	$17,500	Violations of rules governing lotteries	$6,250
Exceeding authorized antenna height	$15,000	Failure to maintain technical logs	$5,000
Exceeding power limits	$12,500	Failure to maintain time-brokerage files	$5,000
Unauthorized emissions	$12,500	Broadcasting telephone calls without permission	$5,000
Use of unauthorized frequency	$12,500	Failure to make measurements and monitor	$2,500
Emergency Broadcasting System equipment not installed or operational	$12,500	Violations of enhanced underwriting requirements	$2,500
Broadcast of indecent programming	$12,500	Failure to identify station on air	$2,500
Failure to comply with Equal Employment Opportunity obligations	$12,500	Failure to maintain records	$2,500
Violations of political broadcasting rules	$12,500	Unauthorized pro forma transfer of control	$2,500
Unauthorized discontinuance of service	$10,000	Miscellaneous violations	$1,250

Source: Broadcasting 5 Aug. 1991: 24.

Note: Amounts given are the "base" fines for violations. Base fines are subject to adjustments up or down by 20% to 90%, based on specific criteria. Criteria for charging more than the base fine are (1) egregious misconduct (50%–90%); (2) ability to pay (50%–90%); (3) intentional violation (50%–90%); (4) substantial harm (40%–70%); (5) prior violation of same rule (40%–70%); (6) substantial economic gain (20%–50%); and (7) repeated or continuous violation (varies). Criteria for charging less than the base fine are (1) minor violation (50%–90%); (2) good faith or voluntary disclosure (30%–60%); (3) history of overall compliance (20%–50%); and (4) inability to pay (varies).

tion is not one of the highest FCC priorities. Whereas the 1991 base fine for inadequate tower lighting was $20,000, the fine was half as much for violating the Children's Television Act of 1990.[2] The fine for indecent programming was slightly higher, at $12,500.

Since they are illegal, both indecency and obscenity can be regulated. Obscenity is generally difficult to prove in a court of law, but indecency does not have to be proved, and therefore censorious politicians such as Jesse Helms find it very useful. Indecency is explicitly a value judgment that allows for government regulation of broadcasting. (Historically, the term has been applicable only to broadcasting, but the Telecommunications Decency Act, declared unconstitutional by the Supreme Court in 1997, would have extended indecency to other media: the Internet and the World Wide Web.) When the FCC fines "shock-jock" Howard Stern, it is because it has found the content of his broadcasts to be indecent. Technically, reference to genitals or excretory functions constitutes indecency, but in practice, indecency is a vague term that the FCC has described as "material that fails to conform to 'accepted standards of morality.' "[3] The conservative Ronald Reagan and George Bush FCCs championed the abolition of broadcast indecency, which ironically, in light of the conservative stance on reproductive choice, led to the censoring of a Pro-Life advertisement that featured a "graphic" image of an aborted fetus.

Indecency as a legal concept enabling government content regulation predates the Reagan-Bush era. In 1973, New York City radio station WBAI played a George Carlin monologue in which Carlin listed seven dirty words that he declared were not allowed on radio or TV: shit, piss, fuck, cunt, cocksucker, motherfucker, and tits. The FCC promptly proved that Carlin was right by chastising the station and banning the monologue from all but late-night broadcasting. In industry lingo, late-night provides a "safe-harbor for indecency." The Pacifica Foundation, WBAI's owner, appealed to the Washington, D.C., circuit court, which overturned the FCC ruling. Eventually, however, the Supreme Court reinstated the FCC's original decision.[4] At no point did the FCC try to prove that the monologue was censorable because it was legally obscene for, again, obscenity has proven difficult to substantiate. The FCC merely declared Carlin's words "indecent," thereby creating indecency as a legal category.[5] When indecent words or images are broadcast, they are not constitutionally protected speech. Although one might commonsensically conclude from the *Pacifica* case that indecent speech is censored in the United States, on the legal level, such speech is merely regulated.

The distinction between government censorship and industry self-regulation is a tenuous one. Indeed, the government censorship versus industry self-regulation binary easily breaks down in light of the fact that self-regulation often results from fear of government censorship. "Censorship" and "regulation" describe basically the same process: preventing the production or dissemination of meanings that are deemed dangerous, potentially dangerous, or even potentially controversial. If regulation and censorship have similar effects, why bother to differentiate between them at all? The networks, the government, and, generally, citizens who believe in the absolute existence (or possibility) of "freedom of speech" have much at stake in upholding the distinction between regulation and censorship. The difference between censorship and regulation is tightly bound up in the ideological process of constructing nationalism and patriotism. Both conservatives and liberals deem the very idea of media censorship to be "un-American." Patriotic conservatives and liberals argue that *other* countries have state-run media. Since the U.S. government does not have a censorship department per se that censors media in an *overt* way, the United States is free of censorship. Or, at the very least, following this line of reasoning, the United States may have censorship problems, but there is a consistent, ongoing effort to overcome censorship.

A standard introductory communications textbook, Sydney W. Head and Christopher H. Sterling's *Broadcasting in America*, aptly illustrates the common idea that the free market guarantees the absence of U.S. censorship. The authors argue for the freedom of the U.S. system by breaking down world broadcasting into three categories: the permissive, the paternalistic, and the authoritarian. These categories correspond to the First, Second, and Third Worlds, respectively, and the authors rank the countries in that order, evaluating the First World (that is, the United States) as best (most free) and the Third World as worst (least free). The fact that the free United States monopolizes information and technologies, limiting the freedom of Second and Third World communications systems, does not enter into Head and Sterling's hierarchical schema. In their argument, the commercial U.S. system "pays attention to what people *want* rather than what critics, experts, and government leaders think they *need*" (original emphasis).[6] Here, "people" means those who count in TV ratings, mostly white, middle- to upper-middle-class Nielsen families.[7] From this perspective, popular desires constitute a healthy, nonoppressive form of censorship, the only real censorship that exists in the United States.

While one might expect a pro-American-industry stance in a mainstream college communications textbook, it is perhaps more surprising to hear liberals in the alternative press make equally specious claims about American freedoms. In a *Nation* editorial on children and television violence, Robert Scheer argues against censorship. Citing *Beavis and Butthead* as an example of triumphant free enterprise (which it is, of course), Scheer concludes that if you do not like the program "because you think it represents the dumbing-down of American and world culture, then vote—by just turning the damn thing off."[8] Like the more mainstream *Broadcasting in America* authors, Scheer assumes that the freedom to turn off your set obviates the need for government regulation. Although he thinks *Beavis and Butthead* is a very bad show with the potential to produce ill effects (desensitization to violence), he argues that " 'we,' collectively, can't and should not do anything about it. We can't because we live in a market economy. . . . The 'we' as represented by the state should do nothing," except "vote" against the show. Again, the problem here is that if you are not a Nielsen family, turning off your set cannot conceivably affect broadcasting content. Not watching a program *is* a viable personal alternative to industry or government censorship. But it is *not* a vote. Broadcast content is decided by capitalist, not democratic, means. Although capitalist democracies do exist, capitalism and democracy are not the same thing. But the idea that viewers vote for and against programs constitutes a powerful fantasy that is created and reinforced by the rhetoric of consumer capitalism. Within this rhetoric (for example, "the marketplace of ideas"), consumption from a menu designed by someone else simultaneously affirms individuality and democracy.

Laissez-faire advocates argue that all externally imposed regulation is censorship and that altruistic American businesspeople do not need paternalistic government officials to tell them how to operate in the public interest. This free market approach to regulation assumes that self-regulation of content is adequate, inevitable, and benevolent because big business feels a sense of duty to consumers. Most of the time, we think of censorship as preventing access to information, but for the hard-core laissez-faire businessperson, government meat inspections or worker-safety regulations constitute censorship. You do not have to be Upton Sinclair to realize that such "censorship" is desirable. In fact, in spite of the rampant Reagan-Bush deregulatory drive, many potentially dangerous products remain subject to federal regulations. The American Society of Toy Manufacturers (ASTM), for example, abides by certain federal standards set by the U.S. Consumer Product Safety Commission. These standards imposed from the outside are censorious; they limit toy manufacturers' freedom in a way that benefits consumers.

The ASTM not only is regulated by the government but also engages in *self*-regulation. It proudly proclaims its adherence to a number of completely voluntary guidelines that include use of toy-safety labels, testing of toys, and limitation of toxin levels on toys children might ingest.[9] Clearly a basic desire for self-protection plays a role in self-regulation, for if children die from using a toy, a company's profits will be hurt. Indeed, the whole toy industry may be affected. Self-regulation may benefit consumers by preventing them from being harmed by products, but at the same time, self-regulation is a survival tactic for companies.

Broadcasters do not deal with a product that is as obviously and directly dangerous as a poisonous toy, but they do sometimes choose to self-regulate. By the terms of their contracts with the networks, local television affiliates may refuse any program in the name of local consumers/viewers, although the most profitable affiliates usually will not refuse programming because they are "O and Os," stations that are "owned and operated" by the networks. Local TV censorship is most often articulated as an issue of states' rights or "community standards" (which also happens to be a legal criterion for judging obscenity). So if a network affiliate refuses a program, it often justifies this refusal as a democratic expression that functions to protect the viewing community. Birmingham, Alabama, for example, was the only city in the United States that censored the 1997 *Ellen* coming-out episode; the local CBS affiliate reasoned that the show would not be acceptable to Birmingham's citizens if aired during "family viewing hours," and the network would not allow the program to be shown later. (A group of local gay and lesbian citizens set up a public satellite screening at a downtown auditorium, renting guards and metal detectors for the entrance.) Many CBS affiliates chose not to show the *Maude* episode in which the title character had an abortion. In 1991, many PBS stations decided not to show their communities *Tongues Untied* (1989), Marlon Riggs's video about gay African Americans. During the Civil Rights era, some affiliates refused to air news programs they thought viewers might find unpleasant or controversial. And some affiliates even deliberately disrupted broadcast-signal transmission. In 1955, a Jackson, Mississippi, station deliberately interrupted a speech on race relations by Thurgood Marshall with a message reading, "Sorry, Cable Trouble from New York."[10] These are all examples of self-regulation of broadcast content.

In general, the different players in the corporate entertainment industry impose regulation from within in hopes of avoiding censorship from without. To the broadcasting corporation, the local affiliate is a potential censor. To the producer selling his/her show to the broadcasting corporation, on the other hand, the corporation is exterior and therefore constitutes the censor. In other words, the producing company often regulates itself to placate network censors. The distinction between regulation and censorship is shaky, and clearly these slippery terms depend upon each other for their meaning.

Television coverage of the Gulf War aptly illustrates the interdependency of the concepts of regulation and censorship. Gulf War images were "censored" by the government and "regulated" by compliant television news producers. It has become something of a cliché to note that the Gulf War was a "television war" but in a different way from Vietnam. "Vietnam" was rhetorically prominent throughout the Gulf War. In their study of viewer perceptions of the war, Michael Morgan, Justin Lewis, and Sut Jhally explain that "in all the coverage, from August 1, 1990 through February 28, 1991, the word *Vietnam* appeared far more often than any other (7,299 times, about three times as often as the runner-up, *human shields*). Thus, far more than anything else, it appears as though news viewers had indeed learned the 'lesson' of Vietnam—at least as the media and the administration presented it."[11] President Bush persistently reiterated that Operation Desert Storm would not be another Vietnam, meaning that the United States would not fight the Gulf War "with one arm tied behind its back," that thousands of Americans would not die in the Gulf, and that he, the admonishing patriarch par excellence, hoped that Americans would not disappoint him by cruelly rejecting returning veterans as many had rejected Vietnam veterans. Importantly, Bush and the army were determined that the Gulf War would not be another Vietnam *televisually*. Whereas television had offered dirty images of Vietnam (although such images are more prominent in public memory than they were in actuality, according to content analyses), the Gulf War was absurdly clean.

Such cleanliness seemed strangely out of place, given the prevalence of down-and-dirty violent images elsewhere on TV, particularly on "reality-based" cop shows. Ironically, during the Gulf War, the news was among the least overtly violent programming on television. Such cleanliness reflects not only the level of government censorship but also the level of network self-regulation. Military censorship was overt in the Gulf, while back in the States, information about the Gulf War was intensely regulated by the news in order to manipulate public opinion. Media scholar George Gerbner gives one example of such self-regulation: "NBC first commissioned, then refused to broadcast, uncensored footage of heavy [Iraqi] civilian casualties. (The broadcast was vetoed by NBC President Michael Gartner, who led a media crusade for freedom of press in the 1980s.) The video was then offered to CBS. The night before it was to air on the CBS *Evening News*, the show's executive producer was fired and the report canceled." [12] Whether regulation/censorship was ordered by military officials or by network executives, the net result was an excess of propaganda, such as computer-generated images that simulated scud movements, and a dearth of information (civilian casualty figures).

Regulation and censorship are technically different: regulation is legal, whereas censorship is not (except when the president and the military say it is). But on a practical level, regulation and censorship are often indistinguishable. Perhaps the best way to characterize U.S. regulation/censorship is as both forbidden and tolerated. America is widely considered the land of the free, so officially censorship does not exist, yet regulation exists to ward off censorship. [13] Plainly put, if the networks gave details on foreign wars instead of regulating themselves, they would be censored. Many people would tolerate such censorship; it is seen as necessary by those who assume that the government only censors specific information about troop movements and fleet departures, all in the interest of national security.

Similarly, the regulation to avoid censorship of children's television is considered a necessary evil. Many concerned adults, from across the political spectrum, agree that child viewers need protection from "dangerous" images. Some adults would even go so far as to argue that the poisonous toy and the Saturday morning cartoon are equally pernicious. Congressional pressure on networks to self-regulate has been constant since the fifties, the threat consistently being that if the networks do not "choose" to regulate (by adopting a ratings system for v-chip users, for example), they will be punished either by overt censorship (a ratings system devised and enforced by the government) or by economic attack (antitrust suits). When network self-censorship departments were radically reduced in the eighties largely because of the Reagan administration's deregulatory policies, children's Standards departments were retained in part, I believe, because the networks felt that adults would not tolerate unregulated children's programming. Like TV news during wartime, children's TV regulation/censorship is widely considered acceptable in the name of a greater good: the safety of children.

History and Operation of Broadcast Standards

Cartoons were not deemed truly dangerous and therefore censorable until the fifties, when they became firmly labeled "children's" programming. Up until that point, theatrical cartoons were considered to be more for children than for adults, but with their double entendres, references to contemporary politics, and parodies of adult-oriented genres, cartoons were clearly also intended to be enjoyed as part of a film bill for adults.[14] Hollywood's self-censoring agency, the Production Code Administration (PCA), did not formally monitor theatrical cartoons as rigorously as it monitored live-action films. The very lack of PCA documentation of cartoon censorship illustrates that theatrical cartoons were considered less censorable—less potentially controversial or endangering to viewers—than live-action feature-length films, each of which has a file of PCA correspondence and evaluation reports.[15]

The pretelevision cartoon context is crucial background for understanding the regulation of television cartoons, since television shows are regulated in a way analogous to the PCA method for live-action films.[16] Producers submit scripts to network Standards departments, the television industry's PCA equivalent. Standards responds, producers revise their scripts, and so on, until a final script is shot; then the program is shown to Standards staff and approved, sometimes only after alterations. The PCA operated in much the same way. However, PCA methods were not simply neatly transferred to television; broadcast self-regulation has its own unique history.

In 1951, only 10 percent of U.S. households had televisions. Yet Kathryn Montgomery reports that "as early as 1952, the House of Representatives held hearings to investigate 'moral and otherwise offensive matter' in television programming. By 1954 the Senate had taken up the investigation, this time focusing on the possible contribution that television programming made to crime and juvenile delinquency." [17] Even when reception was limited by low ownership of sets, cultural anxieties surfaced about this medium that could so easily enter homes, possibly uniting families or, conversely, dividing them.[18] Ironically, it is this era of "classic" television programming that reformers and proregulation government officials often nostalgically evoke in their arguments against modern TV. They valorize the very TV that, in the fifties, members of Congress attacked for promoting juvenile delinquency.

Public and governmental debates in the fifties about the possible dangers of TV made the networks nervous. To protect against both public and governmental pressure, the industry's trade organization, the National Association of Broadcasters, devised a Code of Good Practice in 1952. The code lacked any real means of enforcement and was mostly effective as a public relations ploy. The 1959 quiz show scandal renewed industry fears of government regulation and public repudiation.[19] Largely as a result of the scandal and fear of the FCC, network self-regulation increased in 1959.

Sponsors stopped packaging programs, and single sponsorship was replaced with the magazine format in which, as in the print media, advertisers would buy commercial spots rather than sponsoring a whole program. Although the magazine format seemed like a safeguard against the possible unethical maneuverings a single sponsor might undertake to promote his/her product, the change to this format was not merely a response to the quiz show scandal. The magazine format benefited the industry by making sponsorship more appealing to potential advertisers. Spot ads were cheaper than total sponsorship, and, in addition, they made it more difficult for consumers to target advertisers for boycott. (In the fifties, anti-Communist boycotts were of particular concern to advertisers.) [20] The power of network censors was increased as Standards and Practices departments (also known as Continuity and Acceptance, Program Practices, or Broadcast Standards departments) formulated elaborate rules to guard against "plugola" and "payola."

Technically, broadcast "Standards" and "Practices" are not the same thing. "Practices" refers to departments concerned with "commercial clearance." Practices checks programs against state and federal commercial laws and keeps game shows honest (no "payola" or "plugola"). "Standards" refers to network self-regulatory departments concerned with "programming clearance." Standards reviews scripts, storyboards (pre-production sketches of key actions in cartoons), revisions, rough cuts, and final prints of programs, as well as handling public relations by responding to viewer complaints.[21] While Practices protects a network's legal concerns, Standards strives to eliminate material that might offend viewers.

Although broadcasters certainly maintain the public relations concerns that were the raison d'être of Standards departments, the departments now operate at decreased capacity. Standards departments gradually died out or were radically reduced in staff throughout the eighties, when Reagan's FCC deregulated the television industry. The Reagan and Bush administrations believed that the ratings should be the only content censor, so their free market approach served to undermine their "family values" agenda. The eighties marketplace mentality directly enabled the downsizing of broadcast Standards departments. *Children's* Standards departments still operate in full force, however. Broadcasters know that children's programming is a sensitive issue and that the money spent to maintain Standards personnel will pay off in the long run. By censoring children's television, networks hope to reduce complaints, avoid lawsuits, and generally maintain a benevolent image. Children's Standards departments, in other words, are good public relations.

Cartoon producers send their scripts, storyboards, and final cartoons to the Standards department of the network to which they are contracted. Producer and network exchange memos, haggle over details, and sometimes reach an equitable compromise. Standards criteria are constantly revised by individual networks; there is no single set of rules to which all networks adhere. Technically, only the networks (ABC, CBS, NBC, and Fox) need Standards departments, the reasoning being that the networks use the publicly owned broadcast spectrum and their programming is available to all, whereas cable is paid for, does not use the spectrum, and is not required by law to operate in "the public interest, convenience, and necessity."[22] In the name of public relations, however, cable venues that direct much of their programming to children, such as the Cartoon Network, do have their own internal Standards departments. Each Standards department upholds different criteria, and in fact, each person within each Standards department has a slightly different conception of how to regulate cartoons. Although the National Association of Broadcasters has periodically published guidelines for children's programs, there is no generally available code that television producers can refer to as they negotiate with networks. And although Standards departments have their own internal guidelines, these guidelines are not disseminated to cartoon producers, much less to researchers such as myself.

In any case, it is unlikely that access to internal censorship guidelines would actually prove very helpful in elucidating how censorship operates. Like film censorship, TV censorship cannot be adequately read using what Annette Kuhn calls a "legal model." That is, censorship rules are not simply applied like laws to representations. Sometimes censorship is thought to operate like a legal system, and the Production Code is understood as a positivist slide rule for censorship.[23] Yet in practice the Code was a malleable, somewhat amorphous document that producers and the PCA alternately tried to manipulate to their own ends or ignore completely. As PCA staffer Jack Vizzard recounts:

> Joe [Breen, PCA director] was arbitrary; there is no doubt about it. He did not feel himself limited to what was down in black and white in the Code. There were even occasions when we knew him to "quote" a Code clause he had invented on the spot. . . . But who ever examined the Code that exactly? And if, by some accident, a rare legal eagle challenged Joe with a claim that there was no Code clause to cover his objection, Joe would fire back, "I don't give a fiddler's fuck . . . whether it's in the Code or not. I won't pass your scene."[24]

Vizzard's PCA account is not an academic history but rather a series of loosely joined anecdotes. Yet the anecdote cited above throws a wrench into any attempt to study the PCA merely by reading PCA documents. The Code is commonly thought of as a static text, but Vizzard accounts for *revisions* in the Code. Vizzard explains, for example, that the Code shifted to allow for "miscegenation" and "sex perversion" (homosexuality), as well as to include a prohibition against kidnapping, apparently in response to public consternation over the Lindbergh baby's abduction. The PCA functioned like a machine in that its review process was standardized and it enabled the mass production of censored movies, but like children's Standards, the PCA did not merely enforce rigid rules in a precise, mechanical fashion.

PCA documents are available to researchers because the PCA has gone out of business. Standards departments, on the other hand, continue to function, albeit in a decreased capacity since eighties cutbacks. Unless one has "connections," gaining access to Standards documents is impossible. Standards departments only rarely surface in the popular press, and there is little public understanding of broadcast Standards. Given what little material is available, how can a history of Standards be written? And would having access to Standards documents make industrial censorship fully "knowable"? Paper documents can mislead: they say nothing about untranscribed business meetings, phone conversations, electronic messages that never existed on paper, and executives who, like Breen, didn't give a "fiddler's fuck" about written guidelines. Vizzard's account does not by any means imply that researchers should discount PCA documents and give up altogether on ever understanding Hollywood censorship. However, the "fiddler's fuck" factor should alert us to be cautious in examining PCA paper documents. Likewise, paper documents from Standards, if they were more readily available, would not necessarily answer all of our questions about children's television regulation. When I asked Action for Children's Television cofounder Peggy Charren if she had had much interaction with Standards departments, she laughed. Of course she had. Was any of that interaction written down in letters or memos? Charren responded (on the phone) that she preferred telephone communication because it helps "keep you out of trouble." [25] Charren has repeatedly influenced (or strong-armed) network censors, as chapter 3 will explain, but her interaction with Standards and Practices has left no paper trail. Perhaps the best way to explain how TV censorship operates is to turn to industry workers themselves. How do they explain TV censorship, and how do they see themselves as mirrors of society's anxieties? Interestingly, although TV phobia dates back to the fifties, the industry singles out 1968 as the most important date in TV censorship history.

Cultural Anxieties about (TV) Violence in 1968

Given the long history of concerns about the possible deleterious effects of entertainment on child viewers, it may seem rather arbitrary to begin a history of children's television censorship in 1968. Clearly, children's TV censorship did not suddenly begin in 1968. Adults have voiced concerns about protecting children from mass culture for over 100 years. Anthony Comstock, the famous moral purity crusader, attacked the dime novel throughout the 1880s, and later radio, film, and crime comics were brutally attacked by reformers fearing their ill effects on child consumers.[26] In the thirties, the Payne Fund Studies explained the "dangers" of child and adolescent filmgoing, which ranged from disrupted sleep patterns to heavy petting. Although not focused on children in particular, fear of television also existed as early as the thirties, a decade many people perceive as predating television. In 1930, documentary filmmaker Pare Lorentz ended his polemical book against state censorship of motion pictures by imagining a future dystopia in which war is nonchalantly declared on TV and funded by multinational corporations.[27] In the post–World War II years, Frederic Wertham's handbook of Cold War paranoia, *Seduction of the Innocent*, explored the perils of comic books, which could teach children to torture people with red-hot pokers and could even turn little girls into "lesbians" like Wonder Woman.[28] Wertham ends by warning that children who have been warped by reading comic books may find the same perversity in television; he worries that child viewers weaned on comic books will insist upon equally sadistic television fare, and producers will have to accommodate their desires.

TV phobia may have been expressed by Lorentz in the thirties and Wertham in the fifties, but industry insiders specify 1968, the year of Robert Kennedy's assassination, as the crucial TV censorship date.

> Saturday morning television programming for the 1966–1967 season [was] almost "totally a matter of cartoon superheroes beating the brains out of supervillains." . . . Television critic Neil Compton (1968) considered the Saturday morning children's cartoon shows an oasis of wit and sophistication in the earlier part of the 1960's, but says these shows were replaced by morally repellent pseudoscientific space fantasies by 1966. The nature of children's programming has changed radically once more since then. . . . Since the 1968 assassination of Robert Kennedy,

there has been an outcry against violence on television; as a result, content has shifted away from space shows and superhero stories. The networks have been especially careful not to buy shows whose basic premises are violent.[29]

Since the Robert Kennedy assassination, one network has assigned censors to accompany film crews on location, "to approve as they shoot—advise on the set." [30]

When Bobby Kennedy was assassinated, President Johnson wondered in a public speech, "Could it be because of television?," whereupon all three networks toughened their standards and stripped violence from films which were already made.[31]

To understand why industry insiders would assert that children's television censorship began with RFK's assassination, one must have a sense of Kennedy's mythic persona. Kennedy had been Joseph McCarthy's assistant counsel in the fifties, but a decade later, in the midst of Vietnam and Civil Rights protests, he became a media icon of liberal hope. He approved of blood donations to the Vietcong; he supported striking Mexican American grape pickers; he criticized the Justice Department for refusing to bury a Communist in Arlington National Cemetery; he raised public consciousness of the extremely poor living conditions in Native American reservations; and he suggested that inner city blacks should join whites in the suburbs.[32] Kennedy's assassination during his campaign to become the Democratic presidential nominee dashed the hopes of liberals who saw in him a cure for many of society's ills.

Yet Kennedy's death was not the only brutal and shocking event of 1968. Producers and network censors who say that the 1968 public was indignant about TV violence *only* because of Bobby Kennedy's death assert an overly simplistic causality. However, it is not overly simplistic to postulate that Kennedy's death might have served as an impetus for increased *children's* TV regulation for, in addition to having a liberal political image, Kennedy was seen as a devoted family man (with eleven children) who had high hopes for the improvement of children's television. In 1961, as attorney general, RFK threw his full support behind Newton Minow, President John F. Kennedy's New Frontier FCC commissioner. In his "vast wasteland" speech,

Minow identified children's television as one of his major concerns.[33] RFK responded:

> I was brought up with the idea that three things shape children growing up—family, church, and school. There is no question now that there are four things and the fourth is television. . . . My children know all the advertising slogans, westerns, gangsters, and I would hope that they will know more when they grow up. I am counting on Newt Minow. He cannot do it by himself as far as education is concerned, but what they [Kennedy's children] are going to be like twenty years from now depends a great deal on him and his success.[34]

RFK collaborated with Minow in devising the "rotating children's hour" plan, whereby the networks would share the financial burden of children's television by joining together in producing a series, and each network would air the show twice a week. Kennedy authorized Minow to tell the industry that the Justice Department would ignore the antitrust implications of such a noncompetitive merger. The plan fell through, but it did succeed in convincing the industry of RFK's strong-arm capabilities where broadcasting for children was concerned, and it is possible that RFK's violent death renewed broadcasters' anxieties about government regulation of violent children's television.

Although Bobby Kennedy had a large popular following, he was also criticized for his liberal causes and his political savvy, which some interpreted as crafty or even "ruthless." "Ruthless" was the anti-Kennedy buzzword shortly before his death, but after his death, many of the old critical voices faded away. A writer in the Washington Post commented on how quickly his image was revamped: "The old illusions about Robert Francis Kennedy have probably died with him—the illusions of ruthlessness, coldness, and cant. And the new illusions, as in the case of his dead brother John, may soon take their place—larger-than-life illusions of grandeur and gallantry."[35] Probably the least controversial aspect of RFK's persona was his excellent rapport with children. Journalists who had previously opposed Kennedy's politics eulogized him by telling about the time he visited kids in an inner city nursery school or the day he stopped on the way to an important meeting to watch teenage boys playing football. One newspaper cartoon from 1968 went so far as to mock the idea that Kennedy was ruthless by showing him surrounded by a horde of happy, admiring children. He carries an African American child piggyback style while resting his right hand on a white boy's head and cradling a white girl in his left arm. She points to him and says, "Sure, I know who you are! You're the nice man named Ruthless Opportunist!"[36] The contradictions inherent in praising Kennedy as a perfect hero immediately after his death could be smoothed over by emphasizing his indisputable love of children, and this explains, in part, why censors would link increased children's TV censorship to Kennedy's death. His stance on communism may not have been consistent, but his prochild persona was incontrovertible, and censoring in his name, for the good of child viewers, was like a tribute.

In her study of children's television producers, communications scholar Muriel Cantor remarks that producers commonly reported that after Bobby Kennedy's death mothers throughout the United States wrote letters to the networks protesting violent programs. Cantor describes the letters as "folklore"; although producers had not actually seen such letters, they believed the networks had received them.[37] Since historically the burden of "proper" childrearing—which includes the preservation of childhood innocence, uncorrupted by violence, both real and represented—has been placed squarely on the shoulders of mothers, it is understandable that children's TV producers believed that mothers were deluging the networks with angry antiviolence mail following Kennedy's assassination. Like the mythical idea that TV censorship increased because of the Kennedy assassination, the myth of hysterical moms suggested a simple explanation for why TV self-censorship increased in 1968: it was a necessary response to viewer complaints.

Myth, in Roland Barthes's formulation, is a second order of signification that functions to dehistoricize history. Because myths expunge ideological conflict from historical phenomena, they make history seem natural or commonsensical: "[Myth] abolishes the complexity of human acts, it gives them the simplicity of essences, it does away with all dialectics, with any going back beyond what is immediately visible, it organizes a world which is without contradictions because it is without depth, a world wide open and wallowing in the evident, it establishes a blissful clarity: things appear to mean something by themselves."[38] Robert Kennedy's death functions mythically in industrial accounts of censorship in that it serves as a simple, blissfully clear explanation: the industry dramatically increased children's television censorship in 1968 as an inevitable result of the assassination. Seeing Kennedy's death as the sole cause of public anxieties about violence erases the complex social web of political interests that formed the context of such fears.

Nineteen sixty-eight was a landmark year of violent events, violent events shown on television, and publicly expressed fears about TV representations of violence. In 1968, TV news covered the Tet Offensive. This coverage is often credited with producing a massive shift in public opinion about the war.[39] Television news coverage of the Vietnam War would increase thereafter, to the extent that some would label Vietnam "the television war." Television news also reported a spate of assassinations, not only Bobby Kennedy's but also Mahatma Gandhi's and Martin Luther King Jr.'s. TV showed the 1968 Chicago Democratic National Convention and later the violence at Kent State University and at the Rolling Stones' Altamont concert. It had also covered the 1965 Watts riots and numerous demonstrations in which police beat up student protesters and Civil Rights advocates.[40] Television coverage of these tumultuous events increased viewers' anxieties not only about violence but also about TV itself, which many people vilified as a major perpetrator of violence.

The medium of television became closely linked with the messages of violence it conveyed, and many people came to regard television itself as violent. In a book published in 1978, technophobe Jerry Mander stated that he had been "engulfed by the sixties," the decade when television had replaced "real" experience. Mander argued that "there is ideology in the technology itself. To speak of television as 'neutral' and therefore subject to change is as absurd as speaking of the reform of a technology such as guns."[41] The common industry retort to this kind of argument is that "television holds a fairly accurate mirror to our society. If you don't like what you see in the mirror, don't break the mirror."[42] Critics less fatalistic than Mander, such as Action for Children's Television, would try to reform "the mirror" throughout the sixties and seventies by putting pressure on both the FCC and network Standards departments. Congressional investigations of television's negative effects also put pressure on the FCC and Standards departments.

U.S. broadcasters regulate themselves largely out of fear of federal (FCC and congressional) intervention; historically, federal concern about television content has been variable. The threat of federal intervention was of particular concern in the late sixties, as America's "living room war" raged.[43] In 1967, one producer of children's programs stated that he felt he had relative autonomy from network Standards departments. But his relationship with the network changed dramatically by 1970, a state of affairs he attributed not to RFK's assassination but to the 1969 Senate Subcommittee on Communications investigation of television violence. As the Vietnam War raged, the subcommittee chair, Senator John Pastore, expressed his conviction that *television* perpetrated violence. According to the children's TV producer, "Senator Pastore has put the president of the network on the stand. Presidents of networks are not used to being pushed around. Now everyone is overreacting. Now the networks are telling the producers how to produce, the directors how to direct, the writers how to write."[44]

Some TV producers challenged Pastore because they sensed that political hypocrisy underpinned his position on TV violence: "Pastore and others like him should understand their own failure to improve the slums, improve educational opportunities, and get out of Vietnam, is a much greater failure to improve society than that of television. I think Pastore knows this. He's not so stupid as to think that television created Sirhan Sirhan. He's got an issue—like Joe McCarthy. It's a nice way to get reelected."[45] This producer's statement challenges the myth that RFK's assassination explains the rise of self-regulation. Here, Sirhan Sirhan is merely one of many factors, including Vietnam. Another producer mentions Vietnam as well: "Television alone isn't responsible for teaching violence. Agnew recommends violence by supporting the shooting in Cambodia. Television and motion pictures are fall guys for a sick society. It's easier to point the finger at them than look at Agnew, and Vietnam, and poverty."[46] These producers' statements illustrate that although many industry insiders posit an overly simplistic causal relationship between RFK's assassination and increased television censorship, others formulate a more complicated argument about why censorious *external* pressures (from Congress) resulted in increased *internal* (industrial) regulatory pressures.

Three-Way Mirror?: Industry, Television, and Society

In his 1977 doctoral dissertation on internal regulation at NBC, sociologist Robert Pekurny reiterates the idea that Standards departments of

1968 merely reacted to public anxiety over RFK's assassination. Trying to make sense out of the apparent inconsistencies he found, Pekurny cites one puzzling incident:

> Specific standards in terms of violence include a rule that guns are not to be pointed at or held in the vicinity of the head or neck of a character. This dictum grew out of a *gut reaction* among NBC executives. Likewise, until the summer of 1974 there was a prohibition of the use of cross-hairs, as in a gun sight. This latter rule grew out of the public outcry over the Martin Luther King and Robert F. Kennedy assassinations in 1968 which led to a review of NBC standards, and an increase in the importance of the BSD [Broadcast Standards Department] within the network, especially in relationship to the Programming Department. . . . This prohibition was quietly removed when the network realized that the opening title film on its eight-year-old series *Ironside* contained such a use of crosshairs. While the prohibition was canceled, the change was kept quiet lest there be a flood of scripts using such an effect.[47] (my emphasis)

Pekurny takes censors at their word when they tell him that many of their decisions are gut reactions, which seems to be a manly version of women's intuition. Standards personnel supposedly had a gut reaction in 1968 that led them to beef up their regulation of violence in general and children's programs in particular. This somatic explanation reduces complex industrial issues to intangible, personal, interior states. Like other cultural myths, the mythical gut response erases historical conflicts; it accounts for complex phenomena as if they were ahistorical manifestations of common sense.[48] The gut reaction concept reinforces the idea that Standards departments are above all reactive, that they merely respond to what they see happening in society. In this way, censors stand outside of the social and look in, as neutral and omniscient mirrors. They are not concerned about assassinations, merely about public responses to them.[49]

All too often, the broadcast industry imagines itself as outside of the social world. It is affected by societal changes or conflicts but is basically neutral and not involved in them; the industry simply placates hysterical mothers or antiviolence legislators like Senator Pastore. This self-image must be questioned. The TV industry is intricately bound up in a morass of (self-) regulatory policies, congressional investigations, and, importantly, as the next chapter will explain, its own internal politics. When the FCC or Congress takes a deregulatory, free market approach, the TV industry profits along with other industries. When anxieties about violence peak among viewers, FCC officials, or congressional representatives, these anxieties also peak among network censors. The industry may be part mirror, but it is also part windowpane; self-regulation is not only a reflection of industrial and social tensions but also an active participant in those social and industrial tensions.

Those who attacked TV images of violence in 1968 hoped that improving TV would improve society. During this time, like today, violent images on TV were often simply referred to as "television violence," as if television representations *were* violence in the same way that, say, a kick in the head is violence. This is wishful thinking because if TV violence were real violence, then censoring TV would actually make the world less violent. Unfortunately, excising bad images will not necessarily fix problems outside the world of television. In *Color Adjustment* (1991), Marlon Riggs's award-winning documentary about African Americans and television, Henry Louis Gates Jr. speaks of a utopian day when racism will be over and TV will picture an African American man who is prosperous, well respected, professional, and not a victim of racism. Gates is speaking of *The Cosby Show*, and his point is that the show has not brought about that utopian moment. The show is not an indicator that racism no longer exists, and it cannot single-handedly eliminate racism: "Images are part of a larger formula of social behavior, and you can't give them all of this importance, that they will free us if only we could control them. They do not have enough autonomy to liberate us." Eliminating images of guns held to people's heads did not bring Bobby Kennedy back to life. Likewise, contrary to what Focus on the Family might hope, banning *Beavis and Butthead* will not eliminate teen interest in starting fires, snot, frog torture, and other nonwholesome fare.

Violent images are not the only images the networks regulate in the name of keeping children safe. As the next chapter will demonstrate, sexist and racist images are also subject to regulation. As with the regulation of violent images, the industry sees itself as entirely reactive censors of racism and sexism. But what about the industry's own sexism and racism?

"We Call Our Company Motel"

Looking for Sexism and Racism in the

Children's Entertainment Industry

2

In his scurrilous insider's account of Hollywood's self-censoring agency, the Production Code Administration (PCA), Jack Vizzard explains that the PCA was staffed by hard-working, somewhat prurient louts who could outcuss Columbia Pictures' notoriously foulmouthed Harry Cohn. Vizzard begins with these attention-catching lines: "Being a censor is like being a whore; everyone wants to know how you got into the business."[1] In the past, institutional censorship has typically been seen as a dirty job most suitable for men. But there is a long tradition of women's involvement in censoring entertainment texts at the grass roots level (through women's clubs, for example), and women also have been heavily involved in censoring movies at the state level, beginning in the teens and continuing well into the sixties.[2] Nonetheless, within the entertainment industry, men have largely dominated as censors. Women have most frequently undertaken censorship as a volunteer activity, whereas men have been *professional* censors. Children's Standards departments, which are staffed largely by women, are the exceptions to this rule.

Vizzard's macho anecdotes are not remarkable in and of themselves. It is not at all surprising that men working during Hollywood's Golden Age were sexist. What Vizzard's anecdotes inadvertently reveal, however, is the extent to which the labor politics of censorship matter. Understanding censorship is not merely a matter of asking *what* is cut from a text (or added) but also a matter of asking *who* does the censoring and within what kind of industrial parameters. Examining the politics of censorship at not only the representational level but also the labor level adds a new dimension to our understanding of what censorship means as a political act.

By examining the gender, race, and labor politics of the cartoon production and censorship process, this chapter asks: How are children's television images judged dangerous or safe, who makes such judgments, and what kinds of hierarchies exist in the industrial power structure of children's television production and censorship? This last question is perhaps the most difficult to answer, for although animators and Standards staff are more than willing to discuss the politics of censorship or free speech, they are less forthcoming when it comes to describing the nitty-gritty politics of their own institutional configurations. Racism in cartoons and within the TV industry is perhaps the most difficult topic to discuss, as both the networks and the cartoon studios tend to agree that race is a nonissue, a problem that has already, in large part, been solved. Yet I have found that the cartoon production process is fraught with power struggles between people at different levels of racial, corporate, governmental, national, and gendered hierarchies. Examination of completed cartoons can certainly reveal a great deal about industrial politics, as chapter 4 will demonstrate, but the process of the production of those cartoons bears scrutiny as well. In formulating criticisms of media racism, sexism, violence, and commercial exploitation, we need to look behind the scenes, where racism and sexism are not images, where they are unbound by metaphor. This chapter strives to make a case for the need to discuss production politics and, implicitly, the need to reroute attention from the typical subject of TV censorship debates, the *individual* endangered child, to issues of *structural* inequities.

My analysis depends largely on a magazine article and two kinds of industrial memos. According to a 1993 *Entertainment Weekly* exposé, Standards is a civilizing force fighting against impossibly crude animators. From Standards memos, however, a more complex picture emerges wherein censors and producers negotiate two kinds of representations: representations of potentially imitable acts (such as crashing through plate glass windows) and representations of exploitatively sexualized female bodies (protruding busts and butts). These memos indicate the gendered power struggles underpinning the producer-censor relationship. A third set of documents, memos from a toy company to a cartoon producer, illustrates how Standards criteria have been internalized by producers. These memos show that Standards has become a kind of panoptical presence in children's television production. Even in preproduction, animators feel the censor's eye. The memos verify that self-censorship in the children's TV industry is extensive. In fact, much self-censorship is impossible to document because censorship's rules are so internalized. Censorship molds the way stories can be imagined by employees of the children's television industry, and in this respect, it remains an intangible object of study.

Regulating Gender and Race

Plenty of tangible documentation of censorship does exist in the form of memos exchanged between producers and censors. However, as I mentioned previously, these documents are unavailable to researchers. Nonetheless, I fortuitously acquired a number of Standards memos in the course of an interview I conducted with Hanna-Barbera cofounder Joe Barbera and a longtime Hanna-Barbera employee who regularly interacts with Standards departments. These documents—twenty-four memos produced between 4 August 1992 and 1 February 1993—reveal some of TV censors' central concerns. The memos also point to the nature of the friction between male cartoon producers and female Standards staffers.

Throughout my interview with them, both subjects stressed violence and imitable acts as Standards' single "irrational" criterion for complaint. The whole notion of "criteria" or "standards" on the part of network employees was consistently in question. The interviewees portrayed Standards staff as irrational and fickle. While the interview subjects discussed only imitable violent acts, the documents told a different story about censor concerns. The Standards memos were indeed full of concerns about imitable violent acts, but concerns about representations of female sexuality were also constant. To anyone familiar with animation history, this might not be surprising; commercial cartoons have repeatedly reinforced gender stereotypes and narrativized violence against female characters. Sybil DelGaudio aptly notes that female characters are minimal in theatrical cartoons, present only in the guise of male transvestism or as the object of pursuit:

> [T]he cartoon seems to be a favorite place for the depiction of the pursuit/capture plot structure. When female characters enter the picture, they automatically take their places in line with the pursued, while the means of pursuit is changed to seduction and the end is clearly sexual. In fact, if some male cartoons are about violence, it seems conceivable that some male-female cartoons are about rape—specifically, how

funny rape is. Metaphorically speaking, this seems implied in the idea that it is humorous to see a male chase a female who doesn't want to be chased.[3]

On one level, it appears that DelGaudio's institutional history is just that: *history.* A glance at Saturday morning programs does not find the rape scenarios so typical of theatrical cartoons. In fact, producers make at least perfunctory attempts to incorporate "positive" representations of female characters into the Saturday morning schedule. Even the hypermacho, boy-targeted *Biker Mice from Mars* (1994) includes a "positive" female character in the form of a mechanic who is much smarter than the alien mice dudes. However simplistic the idea of "positive" female characters may be, the presence of such characters illustrates a minimal concern among producers and the networks to avoid political impropriety. When asked about the self-regulation of gender in cartoons, ABC, Hanna-Barbera, and Disney executives were all prepared to explain to me which of their cartoons contained "positive" images of women.

But the Standards memos sent to Hanna-Barbera complicate the idea that sexist representations are ancient cartoon history. Throughout the memos, the female network censor expresses a concern about both sexual language and sexual imagery. For example, in response to language in a final script, the censor asks, "Since the 'hore' in the marching songs may be interpreted as 'whore,' please substitute one of the other nonsense words they used for 'four.' " In response to another final script, the censor says, "Please substitute something like 'get a date' in the Sportscaster's line '. . . Winner will *go one-on-one* with Miss Vavoom' " (original emphasis). In response to a storyboard,[4] the censor asks producers to "please delete or substitute for one of the wolves calling out 'that's some Eskimo Pie,' since we would not want any viewer to misinterpret this as sexual innuendo in a children's program" and "please delete or substitute for Ms. Vavoom's reference to Droopy as her 'doggie-*style* champion,' again to eliminate the possibility of misinterpretation" (original emphasis).

The censor is equally concerned about the sexual innuendo of images. In fact, she comments on imagery even *before* it exists, as a precautionary measure. That is to say, concern about images exists not only at the storyboard and screening stage but also at the script stage, before the costumes, settings, and actions have been drawn. In response to one final script, the censor notes, "Please exercise caution not to over-do the sexist elements when Dripple is mesmerized by the cheerleaders. Acceptability of these scenes will be determined at the storyboard stage." Censor concern about proper female costuming is recurrent. In a later response to the cheerleader cartoon, the censor writes, "It is not clear from these sketches exactly what the Cowgirls will be wearing so a reminder to please exercise caution that their costumes and movements are not too revealing. (The movements of the Dancing Girl on Page 16 are acceptable.)" The censor is cautious about the mesmerizing cheerleaders at the script stage, before image production. Later, she is cautious because the storyboard's preproduction images have not revealed the cheerleaders' costumes and movements. The censor notes not an inappropriate image but a lack of image, which she interprets as a potential site for conflict if any problems are not fixed before the cartoon goes into production.

As perhaps should not be surprising in light of the character's name, Standards is particularly concerned about the depiction of Vavoom's body. Responding to a final storyboard, the censor writes, "Please make sure that Miss Vavoom's neckline is high enough to provide adequate coverage (no cleavage please)." Another final storyboard elicits these comments: "Please make sure that the dress Vavoom is wearing is not too revealing and that she is adequately covered. The dress should not be low cut in the front or back and should not be sleeveless," and "here again, please exercise caution with the costuming of the young ladies, they should be adequately covered, no bare midriffs or low-cut blouses." Feedback on another storyboard reads, "Please show more of Dr. Vavoom's figure so that the focus is not just on her butt," and "a reminder that Dr. Vavoom should be shown wearing her complete costume which includes a shirt under her jacket so that we do not see her cleavage." It is possible that animators made this busty character a "doctor" in hopes of circumventing censorship, the rationale being that a censor might approve a "negative" image of cleavage if the cleavage belonged to a "positive" character, a female doctor. Apparently, however, the censor did not find that the character's being a doctor counteracted the obtrusive presence of her butt and chest.

The contrast I found between my conversation with Hanna-Barbera employees and what I read in the Standards memos was striking. As the memos show, what the censor objects to most often is sexist material. Yet the producers told me that the censor only makes demands having to do with violent representations that children could hurt themselves by imitating. Moreover, the censor does not merely call for image excision, as the interview subjects implied. Frequently, she tries to be helpful by making suggestions about how to fix improper elements; the animators see such suggestions as just another impingement on their creative expression. In sum, in this particular network-studio interaction, there seems to be an unbridgeable gap between censor and producer perceptions. The interview subjects apparently do not see their gender faux pas, only their imitable violent ones. If certain sexist representations are absent from the studio's final cartoon product, this is not because sexism no longer exists in the animation industry. Rather, the reduction of sexist representations is the result of extensive interaction between producers and censors. In the course of this industrial exchange, the studio repeatedly submits material objectionable to the network, and the censor repeatedly censors that material.

Censors and producers of children's programs are in agreement on one point: racial slurs are a crime of the past. Racism is so taboo that it is utterly absent (at the explicit level, at least) from producer-censor documents, and to mention racial stereotyping to children's television producers and censors is to invite long explanations of the abundant "positive" images of race evident in today's cartoons (or at least an explanation of the absence of "negative" images). A 1979 *Emmy Magazine* exchange between three women experts on children's programming illustrates uncertainty about what constitutes "positive" and "negative" representations of nonwhite cultural identities:

> Susan Futterman (ABC): . . . Speedy Gonzalez . . . is a very happy character who usually ends up on top. And, although he ends up on top, he talks with a very strong accent and is dressed as a peasant. We invited in some leaders from the Mexican-American community, and we all looked at this together. Their feeling was that, maybe, at some point in time, when we reflected many images of Mexican-Americans on children's programming, it would be appropriate to include this as one of the images. But they were very uncomfortable with it being the only image that is presented on Saturday morning. We respected that opinion and decided against the show.
>
> Faith Frenz-Heckman (CBS): That happened at CBS too.
>
> Margaret Loesch (NBC): I find that ironic, because I also consulted the

Mexican community. As a matter of fact, the broadcast-standards editor at NBC who approved that show is a Mexican-American. He speaks with a heavy accent, and he thought it was wonderful.

Frenz-Heckman (CBS): Which shows you how subjective broadcast standards are.

Like the producers described in chapter 1 who blamed Bobby Kennedy's assassination for increased regulation, these three children's television executives put themselves in a "mirror" position, whereby they do not have their own opinions about culture. Unable to determine for themselves what may be insulting, they ask "leaders from the Mexican-American community" what is offensive and then make their programming decisions reflect the token Mexican American advisers' opinions. The fact that Futterman's and Frenz-Heckman's Mexican Americans decided against the Speedy Gonzalez cartoon whereas Loesch's approved it illustrates the confusion that results from the whole process. Loesch in particular is surprised that anyone could find Speedy Gonzalez offensive since an NBC employee who has a heavy accent like Speedy Gonzalez approves of the show. Loesch is surprised because she depended on her informant, her heavily accented coworker, to help her make a decision about Speedy Gonzalez. Although children's TV programmers and producers adamantly deny that racism is represented in children's programs, shaky racial politics clearly underpin network decisions about "positive" and "negative" images of people of color. Twenty years after the *Emmy* dialogue was published, it is still not unusual for the networks to consult token ethnic authorities when unsure if a character is "positive" or "negative." The current consensus seems to be that Speedy Gonzalez is off-limits.

In this article, racism is articulated as an issue not of structural inequality but of individual immaturity. Loesch says, "We have all matured a great deal in the past 20 years, particularly in the area of being aware of racial problems. . . . I don't think, given the choice, that we would ever go back to degrading blacks or people of other races. I think we've all matured."[5] Loesch's use of "given the choice" is crucial, for it indicates that racism is not so much missing from animation studios as it is forbidden. The big-lipped mammy and black cannibal stereotypes so common in cartoons of the past are absent from newly produced cartoons, perhaps because such images are not allowed or perhaps because of socially conscious animators. Either way, as the next section will explain, the U.S. cartoon industry absolutely depends upon the exploitation of people of color. Like the microelectronics, garment, and other industries, the animation industry is supported by the very people whom Loesch says the industry is too mature to degrade in its images — "blacks or people of other races."

Gender, Labor, Power, and Industrial Politics

Both network censors and cartoon producers are more likely to prosper if material that might cause controversy can be caught in advance of broadcasting, but a shared drive for profitable programming does little to assuage the antagonism between Standards staff and animators, and it seems that gender plays a pivotal role in this antagonism. The networks do not release data on their employees' gender, but it does not take much research to realize that children's programming is an area with a particularly high proportion of women employees.[6] *Emmy Magazine*'s "Roundtable" column, in which network executives discuss their areas of expertise, generally features few women, but the panel is made up entirely of women when the topic is children's programming.[7] Although both men and women can be found in the upper ranks of children's programming, the majority of employees in children's Standards departments are women. Why this gendered division of labor? One explanation is that the networks perceive women as ideally suited to censor children's programming because women know what is best for children. Ironically, the female executives, who sometimes use token people of color to make judgments about racism, are themselves tokens. Another reason so many women are hired in children's Standards may be because the job requires so much management of sexist representations. Higher-ups may see women as native informants (real women!) and therefore ideal censors of sexism. From the animators' standpoint, however, the female censors are not useful sexism specialists but rather industrial incarnations of the hysterical angry mothers described in chapter 1.

A Standards and Practices director for ABC estimates that two-thirds of her staff are women, most of whom are concentrated in children's Standards. She explains that "women gravitate to the issue of children very easily and find themselves attracted to such positions."[8] This statement implies, rather problematically, that regulation of children's programming springs in part from a "maternal instinct" (gut reaction?) on the part of female censors. In a less essentialist and more practical vein, the Standards director further explains that she hires mostly women because she seeks out elementary school teachers, the vast majority of whom are women. She favors elementary school teachers because they "really know kids inside and out," and she says she is particularly drawn to teachers who have worked with minority children and children with "special needs." In sum, this TV industry worker argues that her hiring of women is not a "bias" but rather a result of her available applicant pool. The fact that this pool is mostly made up of women is also the result of certain cultural biases about the appropriate gender needed for certain jobs. Such biases are readily apparent in the animation industry.

As in the glory days of theatrical animation, the U.S. television animation industry continues to be a "boy's club" in which the majority of "creative" personnel are male.[9] In the thirties, Disney's production staff was "overwhelmingly male except for the 200 women in the Painting and Inking Department. . . . The hands of women, painting and transcribing the creative efforts of men, performed the tedious, repetitive, labor-intensive housework of the Disney enterprise."[10] Today, Los Angeles's Local 839 of the International Alliance of Theatrical and Stage Employees (IATSE) encompasses three main categories of animation workers. These are, in descending order of pay and skill, creative workers, rendering artists, and technical workers. Creative workers conceptualize and design animated films; rendering artists are skilled animators who execute the creative workers' specifications; and technical workers, as Allen J. Scott describes it,

> are unskilled or semiskilled workers (mainly female) who carry out routine labor tasks under intense supervision; by far the majority of these workers are engaged in so-called "ink-and-paint" operations, i.e., the detailed coloring in of the xeroxed celluloid overlays that constitute the raw material of any animated film. The ink-and-paint department of an animation studio is reminiscent of the sewing section of a typical clothing factory with its serried rows of female operatives sitting at their work tables and performing endless routine motions.[11]

The hands of women still perform the "labor-intensive housework" of animation.

Most U.S. animation production is for television, and production is in cycle with the television season. When cartoon production is done for the season, many workers find themselves temporarily laid off. According to Scott, in May 1983, the unemployment rate for U.S. creative workers was 5.0 percent; the rate for rendering artists was 33.6 percent; and the rate for technical workers was 56.8 percent.[12] The average weekly wage for that year was $764.52 for creative workers, $583.27 for rendering artists, and $448.82 for technical workers. Although the three categories of unionized animators have a long tradition of solidarity, over the course of the eighties this solidarity dissolved. Highly paid workers sought "to consolidate their more secure positions in the labor market and to align themselves more directly with management."[13]

Scott's data points toward the gender and class inequities that support the animated film industry. His data shows that in terms of industrial power (mostly) male animators are above (mostly) female inkers. But my research indicates that there is an additional twist in the industrial power structure of animation: female Standards workers are higher in the hierarchy than male animation producers. This may be difficult for animators to negotiate. Within the studios, these "creative workers" are at the top of the production hierarchy, but once their work is sent to Standards, they are suddenly disempowered. The censors send their responses to scripts, storyboards, and completed cartoons back to the production companies' creative workers, and the censors ultimately have veto power. The gendered split between animators and censors does not "naturally" produce conflict, but cultural attitudes about gender held by the two parties do exacerbate their interactions.

In one sense, the hierarchy I have described is artificial, for clearly producers (cartoonists) and distributors (the networks) are dependent on each other. The networks *need* the cartoons they get from production companies, and it would not be in the networks' best interest to make it impossible for production companies to sell them acceptable cartoons. But even if the relationship is symbiotic, the fact remains that Standards staffers have the right to tell producers that their cartoons are unacceptable. Although producers are used to this relationship and some take it in stride, Standards departments are clearly resented by many creative workers. Don Jurwich, a Hanna-Barbera creative worker who frequently interacts with Standards departments and is responsible for making sure their directives are carried out, says he has been working not "with" but "against" Standards for years. He explains that Standards employees "look at the final print, and if we haven't done something, most of the time they will not air it until we fix it. Once in a great while you can talk them out of it. The problem with all this is there's no absolute about it. And they have different people. [One Standards person], she'll do some of the shows, and another person will do some of the shows. Her bias is different from this other person's bias. It's very difficult to get a fix on anticipating what they're going to call for." [14] He adds that the process is "arbitrary" and that one Standards employee is particularly "capricious."

Adrienne Bello is another censor whom Jurwich and other beleaguered animators would probably call biased, capricious, and arbitrary. Bello represents an interesting case study in gender and power in the children's television industry. She is a former ABC Standards employee who now works for Disney as a sort of middle person between creative workers and network censors. In effect, Bello precensors Disney's TV cartoons. She explains: "At ABC I had a bit more power because I could ultimately say, 'You don't change it, it's not going on the air,' whereas at Disney it's more of a head-on fight with the producer. And they take it more as a personal attack. 'You [Bello] should be trying to create the most exciting cartoons,' and 'You're squelching our creativity.' " [15] Although Bello does not voice her power at Disney in terms of gender, her case presents an interesting example of the gendered power relations I have described. When Bello was at ABC, she was above animators in the industrial hierarchy; now she is a woman in production but with more power than most women in production, as she is not a low-level animator or inker. While a Standards employee, Bello could veto a cartoon. Now she works with (and against) producers to make cartoons that Standards will not veto, but she herself no longer has veto power. Disney's TV animators expect "capricious" external censorship, but internal regulation must seem like adding insult to injury.

A series of interviews conducted by Thomas F. Baldwin and Colby Lewis as part of the Surgeon General's 1972 Report on Television Violence illustrates one way television producers manage their relationship with Standards staff. Although Standards workers actually have power to force or negotiate script changes or changes in filmed productions, in the Baldwin and Lewis study, producers describe Standards employees as insignificant network minions, employees at the bottom of the production hierarchy. For example:

> We fight them as hard as we can in regard to their absolutely asinine decisions. You can get away from the rules by going to the top. It's useless to argue with the shop girl, so you go to the store manager. I call the boss and say, "Would you like to hear what your people are doing? Isn't that asinine?" And he's likely to agree.

> The higher up the ladder of censors, the more you're allowed to do until at a high level you reach a man who throws you back to the page-boy with whom you started.

> Network continuity acceptance [a.k.a. Standards] people here are henchmen who carry out orders from higher administrators. There may be a lack of communication in this chain. The guy at the top's instruction "Let's have less violence" can evolve into "Let's not kill anybody" without his knowing. We ought to pursue the question: "Who's really censoring American television?" [16]

The power relations reflected in this rhetoric are striking. Producers explain that at the top one finds "Mr. Big," whereas "page-boys" or "shop girls" work in the lower ranks. Here, Standards staff is not only feminized ("shop girls") but also simultaneously infantilized ("girls" and "boys"), while fully adult men only exist in the upper echelons of the network power structure. Although the producers in the Baldwin and Lewis study make live-action programs, their attitudes are representative of those I have encountered among animation producers: in describing Standards staff, producers tend to affirm an employee hierarchy that privileges "creative" workers over lowly, "unskilled" ("uncreative") workers. Yet Standards staffers *are* skilled, and they are not actually beneath the animators in the industrial hierarchy. Standards staffers are not hired because they are arbitrary and capricious women. Their educational backgrounds vary, but many are educators or have postgraduate degrees, often in child development or child psychology.[17] They are skilled professionals. Nonetheless, producers treat them as if they were beneath producers in the industrial hierarchy, denigrating them as unskilled, uncreative minions—"shop girls."

If it is difficult to find data on the gendered power struggles that under-pin the children's television industry, conducting research on the anima-tion industry's racial politics is even more frustrating. No one really wants to talk about it. But the fact is that since the mid-seventies, the major ani-mation companies have subcontracted their most tedious, labor-intensive work overseas. The studios will not divulge information on their overseas contracting, but outsiders estimate that costs can be cut by as much as one-half by sending work to Australia, Spain, Japan, Mexico, Taiwan, the Philippines, and South Korea, where unskilled laborers can be paid signifi-cantly less than U.S. workers.[18] In 1990, one animation executive estimated that over 60% of the animation work for Saturday morning cartoons was done in Asia. He also predicted that as costs rose in Japan, Korea, and Tai-wan, U.S. studios would open shops in Indonesia, Thailand, and possibly Vietnam. (Indeed, the U.S. trade embargo with Vietnam ended in 1994.) In order to keep wages even lower than international labor laws specify, some of this runaway production work is black market, particularly in countries such as Mexico and Argentina where no animation industry was estab-lished before the U.S. animation companies arrived. According to a *New York Times* article by Barbara Basler, the white managers of overseas U.S. animation operations "are reluctant to discuss specific salaries, but one animation executive says that 'a rule of thumb is that an Asian makes in a month what an American would make in a week.' In Hollywood, an ap-prentice animator earns roughly $750 a week; an experienced one makes $1,500 to $2,000."[19] These 1990 figures may be inflated, for they indicate twice the salary Scott's research uncovered in 1983. In other words, over-seas apprentice animators may earn closer to $450 for a month's work. Inkers are considered unskilled labor and earn much less than the low-salaried apprentice animator.

For Basler, overseas production is problematic but not because it is highly exploitative. Rather, as Basler explains, overseas animation opera-tions pose problems because of cultural differences: "All this foreign con-tracting must be carefully translated. But even meticulous translations can leave room for misunderstandings when the people drawing and color-ing the cartoons have minimal knowledge of American humor, culture and slang."[20] The author relates a series of "slip-ups" that were caught by "Western supervisors." For example, once a U.S. layout artist wrote on a *Transformers* battle scene, "Enemy is now out to lunch." Making an atypical creative maneuver, a Japanese artist drew the robots sitting down for a picnic. It is this pesky Asian labor force—not white managers or their corporations—that Basler implicates as the most problematic aspect of overseas production.

Ellen Seiter has suggested in reference to the toy industry that reformers who attack children's entertainment for its violence, sexism, or commercialism may have misplaced their energies. Criticisms of toy and animation companies need to focus on exposing exploitative production practices, which are of course characteristic not only of the toy and animation industries but also of other industries that manufacture products requiring monotonous, unskilled labor. Like the clothing and electronics industries,[21] the toy and animation industries depend on a largely female labor force. Officials of transnational corporations declare that women laborers are preferable to men because they are more docile and patient and less likely to unionize. One U.S. electronics industry manager of a factory based in Mexico says, "A man just won't stay in this tedious kind of work. He'd walk out in a couple of hours."[22] A personnel manager of an electronics assembly plant in Taiwan asserts that "young male workers are too restless and impatient to do monotonous work with no career value. If displeased, they sabotage the machines and even threaten the foreman. But girls? At most, they cry a little."[23] In their ground-breaking *Women in the Global Factory*, Annette Fuentes and Barbara Ehrenreich show that women may be preferable to men for reasons besides reluctance to unionize or commit sabotage; in some runaway production factories, women are sexually exploited. A Mattel worker in the Philippines says, "We call our company 'motel,' because we are often told to lay down or be laid off."[24]

Armand Mattelart explains that "even if certain forms of protest are permitted, they are still referred to traditional images of women: hysteria is somewhat less dangerous than unions, and spirit possession is the only cultural outlet for woman workers." Thus, in Malaysia, women have reported being affected by spirits during particularly difficult work periods. Sometimes these crises are collective, and whole factories are shut down for hours or even days while the problem is dealt with (by performing an exorcism, for example).[25] Seiter also notes forms of resistance that are strongly culturally coded as feminine, reporting that in a Malaysian Mattel toy plant, "young female workers engage in collective fits of screaming provoked by their long silent hours at low pay."[26]

In light of runaway labor conditions, TV reformers and Standards personnel who insist that all sexism, racism, and violence be expunged from cartoon representations seem laughable. Reformers and Standards personnel have a narrow vision of who is worthy of protection and of how protection operates. They seek to protect U.S. child viewers from *images* of racism, sexism, or violence that they consider dangerous, while the racist and sexist exploitation that supports the production of such images is left unscrutinized. Unfortunately, most of the public focuses on representational issues rather than labor issues as well.

"No Reservoir Tip": Public Discourse on Standards and Practices

The operations of broadcast Standards departments rarely enter into public discussion. Although concern about children's TV programs and viewing habits is constantly expressed in newspapers and popular periodicals such as *TV Guide*,[27] there is little public awareness of how Standards departments work or even of their existence. Reformers or moral crusaders (like James Dobson of Focus on the Family) are more likely to propose that networks do away with certain programs altogether than to propose that they tighten Standards control over programs. Children's programs are more often labeled "good" or "bad" than "redeemable"; being redeemable would mean that Standards could doctor a show to make it good for children.

I have found only one nonscholarly or nonindustrial article on the role Standards plays in children's programming. "Censor Overload" appears in *Entertainment Weekly*, a publication geared toward a general readership.[28] The article opens by asking, "How does so much violence, sex, and bad taste end up in children's programming?" The very question indicates that both Standards departments and producers consistently fail to maintain the standards of "good taste" they both claim to uphold. The article speculates that the answer to the question can be found by looking at "the offscreen battles waged between the networks and creators of the shows." "Battles" suggests that the producer-censor relationship is an essentially hostile one; the word does not connote any space for negotiation or compromise. The article prints excerpts from Fox Standards documents ("confidential memos"), which the article promises will "give an eye-opening, behind-the-scenes look at how much the makers of one children's program [*Eek the Cat*] tried to get away with and how the network compromises on some battles to win others." "Confidential" and "behind-the-scenes" address the reader as if he/she were an industrial spy snooping out the secret story on censorship. According to the article, it turns out that there is space for compromise after all. The "bad taste" that makes it on the air is the product of a compromise whereby Standards personnel, anxious to get rid of animators' most repulsive script ideas, will bargain to keep only the least offensive elements of a script. In this article, animators are the bad guys, and Standards personnel are good guys fighting impossible odds. This account is clearly at variance with industrial accounts in which both sides acknowledge that, some compromise not withstanding, Standards usually gets its way.

The anonymous *Entertainment Weekly* author has clearly picked memo directives that he/she hopes will shock readers. Yet in spite of the author's attempt to obfuscate and sensationalize the censorship process, these memo directives actually reveal quite a bit about how industrial self-regulation works. In the memo excerpt for "Eek's Long Christmas Night," the Fox censor writes, "I found the shot of Rambo blowing Santa Claus to bloody smithereens excessively violent. We would like to edit this so we don't see Santa exploding." This comment reveals as much about the Standards employee as it does about the cartoon. Although the phrase "bloody smithereens" might aptly describe the scene, it is also possible that the censor is overstating his/her case to shame the animators into submission; it is unlikely that the animators of this Saturday morning cartoon actually thought that graphically eviscerating Santa would be acceptable to the network. About the same cartoon, the censor also comments, "Even though it is Eek's fantasy, it will not do to show the child walking into the surf to commit suicide." The desired reader response to this memo excerpt is probably one of disbelief ("overload") that animators would produce a cartoon in which such a horrible thing happens. From the industrial point of view, however, the problem with the representation of suicide is that it is considered "imitable," and Fox, like the other networks, forbids cartoons from showing certain imitable acts. Disney's Adrienne Bello, for example, explains that she will not allow a representation of a character getting into a realistic small space:

I'm a *cheap insurance* policy for them because whenever I read a script or look at a storyboard or look at a rough cut, I make sure that there's nothing that a child could possibly imitate. *Everything has to be blown way out of synch.* For example, if you have a character in a cartoon jumping into a drawer or a cabinet, I want to make sure that it's not a regular-size cabinet that the character can really fit into. Because I don't want a child at home copying it, jumping into the bottom of a dresser drawer and having the whole thing topple over onto him. So what I do is make it a teeny drawer. If we have a character jump into a drawer, it's like a pencil drawer, and the character squishes into a place that they could never really get into. So I take it *out of the realm of reality.*[29] (my emphasis)

To the industry, suicide is not so much a matter of morality or ethics as it is a matter of corporate liability. (I should add that my cynicism is unfair to individual censors who are sincere about their fears of dangerous imitation.) That Bello refers to herself as a "cheap insurance policy" underlines the financial stakes and high-pressure work conditions at play in censoring cartoons containing imitable representations. According to Bello, imitation, and therefore liability, will result from too much reality in a cartoon.

Although the censor in the *Entertainment Weekly* article discourages the representation of suicide, he/she is not so careful about all imitable acts. One response seems particularly inappropriate: "Please don't show Cupid using a switchblade knife, an illegal weapon. How about an ax or a chainsaw?" The censor's suggestion privileges one corporate concern over another. The *illegal* switchblade is obviously not allowed, so the censor suggests other *legal* weapons. The censor's concern to avoid representation of an illegal act (possession of a switchblade) here overrides concern over possible imitation. Since many children might have access to common tools such as an ax or a chainsaw, the censor is not doing a very good job. Although this efficient censor wisely recommends omitting the switchblade, he/she errs by suggesting other inappropriate weapons. In the response to "Eek's International Adventure," on the other hand, the censor responds more appropriately (from the corporate perspective) to a representation of violence: "It will not be acceptable for Jed and Ned to pull out shotguns and shoot at the Sticky Bears. Perhaps they would use something not-replicable, like shooting guitars or banjos." This response is appropriate because the censor not only rejects the "imitable" gun but also suggests acceptable alternative weapons.[30]

Censors have concerns other than eliminating representations of imitable acts, of course. The notes for "Catsanova" read: "It will not be acceptable to show an irate ex-postal employee murder his coworkers. Perhaps we could see the man entering the post office with a stylized automatic weapon as Eek is leaving, so adults will be able to imagine what comes next, but young children won't be witness to the violence. Let's discuss this . . ." (ellipsis in original). This passage reveals something about Fox's public relations worries. Since children cannot really be ex-postal employees and generally do not have access to automatic weapons, the issue is not so much imitation as the possibility of complaints from the U.S. Postal Service. Like Production Code administrators, network censors attempt to avoid maligning any profession. But rather than asking animators to simply eliminate the joke altogether, the censor asks that the joke be made less crude. The joke is to be revised so that only older viewers will get it. The joke's repackaging suggests that the networks know that cartoons address an intergenerational audience. The censor assumes that this children's show has adult viewers who will appreciate a topical reference to the spate of postal-worker killings that occurred in 1993. The suggested revision implies that multiple, age-specific decoding strategies are expected and even encouraged by censors. The fact that both animators and censors assume an adult audience runs counter to the common perception of children's TV as an electronic baby-sitter that adults rarely, if ever, watch.

At several points, the Standards documents cited in "Censor Overload" illustrate what I call the "overkill tactic." Responding to "Eek vs. The Flying Saucers," the censor asks the producers to "please delete 'Marilyn Chambers' and 'edible underwear' from Eek's list of the wonderful stuff on earth." This note perhaps reveals more about the producers than it does about the censor. First of all, I suspect that the producers did not expect these two items to pass. The animators may have included these items to strengthen their bargaining position. In other words, like some thirties and forties movie producers, TV producers often include outrageous material they know will be cut so they can bargain more successfully for other controversial material. This is the overkill tactic. The fact that the "objectionable" material is merely a few words rather than a storyboarded narrative makes the scenario I have drawn all the more likely; to include porn star Marilyn Chambers in a character's dialogue does not represent a major investment of financial or creative energy that would be wasted by censor rejection. Animators' use of the overkill tactic demonstrates that, like Golden Age film producers, TV producers try to outmaneuver censors. The author of the article is not interested in teaching a film and TV history lesson to *Entertainment Weekly* readers, however. He/she cites the mention of Marilyn Chambers and edible underwear in scripts merely to illustrate animators' outrageously bad taste. "Censor Overload" offers no historical context that would enable a reader to understand *why* "violence, sex, and bad taste end up in children's programming." Rather than merely looking at outrageous "behind-the-scenes" memos for an explanation, the author might have found answers by watching classic racist, sexist, violent cartoons.[31]

In the context of U.S. cartoon history, the censor's response to "The Eeksterminator" indicates that sexual innuendo and current social commentary are tenacious cartoon conventions. The memo excerpt reads: "Please delete Zip's line 'I wear protection' and Mom's response, 'That's very nineties of you.' (Also, no *reservoir* tip on top of his suit please. [original emphasis]) The cartoon's very title, alluding to the popular Arnold Schwarzenegger *Terminator* films, indicates that this cartoon will reference popular culture outside the cartoon. References to popular culture have been a generic convention at least since the Fleischer studio's thirties cartoons, although in the public imagination, Warner Bros.'s postwar production represents the maverick cartoon exploitation of popular culture. Today's *Tiny Toons*, explicitly indebted to Warner Bros. mythology both narratively and stylistically, draws heavily on the pop culture parody convention. The *Eek* animator's reference to safer sexual practices may have seemed excessive to the censor, but the line "that's very nineties of you" is straight out of *Tiny Toons*. Not only does the condom reference fit into a tradition of pushing the boundaries of acceptable sexual innuendo in cartoons, but it is also the kind of thing that producers might have thought could pass based on the logic that kids would not get it. The memo excerpt from "Road Trip" is another example of an outrageous detail that the producers perhaps did not expect would be approved by the censor (again, the overkill tactic) or that they perhaps hoped would pass because only adults would understand: "Please substitute a teacher's name that isn't a form of cancer" and "please substitute another name for the band Quiver-

ing Schpincters [sic]" ("[sic]" in original). Like *Pee-wee's Playhouse*, *Eek* is
expected to play to two audiences.[32] Although *Pee-wee* was certainly unique
in its overtly risqué texts and subtexts, the *Eek* article and Hanna-Barbera
documents examined in this chapter suggest that intergenerational appeal
may be more the rule of "children's" cartoons than the exception.[33]

One censor comment in the *Entertainment Weekly* article is not a response
to overtly risqué humor or to representations of violence. The Standards
employee says, "Please do not stereotype the boy in home economics class
by making him 'effeminate appearing.'" It is hard to imagine why the
author cites this "effeminate appearing" boy as an example of "censor
overload." One possible explanation is that the magazine assumes that its
readers are homophobes who would be shocked by the very idea that gay-
coded imagery could exist in cartoons. (This is ironic, of course, in light
of the long history of cartoon transvestism and homosociality.)[34] Network Standards departments are sensitive to gay stereotyping in large part
because of homosexual pressure-group activism, but "Censor Overload"
readers are not provided this context and might well interpret this censor
comment as bigoted homophobia or, conversely, as appropriate antigay
sentiment on the censor's part rather than as a response to political activist
groups. Either way, the reader is directed to see elimination of effeminacy
as a battle won by censors. This censoring of gay-coded cartoon characters
is not an isolated incident. Among the Hanna-Barbera memos I discussed
earlier, there was also a note on a gay-coded character: "It will be fine to
portray the Captain as prissy or fussy but please avoid any gay stereotyping such as lisping, etc." Censors do not try to improve gay images in the
same way that they try to remove sexism from female representations.[35] A
female character (implicitly straight) can be made "positive." To children's
TV censors, there is no such thing as a positive gay character. If there is
any doubt about sexual orientation, TV producers are quick to set viewers
straight. When questioned about the sexual orientation of Tinky Winky, a
male Teletubby who carries a purse, the president of the show's U.S. production company said, "There isn't a boy on the planet who hasn't picked
up his grandma's purse and carried it around." The message, he claims, is
"It's okay to carry this bag. You're not going to grow up to be an interior
decorator."[36]

In his 1977 dissertation on NBC, Robert Pekurny also discusses Standards policy on homosexuality without explaining the historical context of gay and lesbian pressure groups.[37] Pekurny describes protests of representations of homosexuality as individual complaints. His comments are of particular interest here because the complaints he describes are not objections to "negative" stereotypes per se but rather expressions of concern regarding the health of child viewers. Pekurny writes that "several years ago two mothers individually wrote to NBC saying that the continuous telling of jokes on NBC programs in which characters named Bruce were depicted as effeminate or homosexual might be having a detrimental effect upon the psychological development of their sons who happened to be named Bruce. The logic of these two well-written letters persuaded NBC executives and a directive was issued requesting the end of such jokes."[38] Here, a homophobic response to homophobic programming results in fewer homophobic jokes, all in the name of protecting child viewers. Lesbian and gay characters are the subject of intense scrutiny, from all political camps, when they are on adult programs; their presence on children's programs is unthinkable from the networks' standpoint, although clearly not from the animators' standpoint. Any attempt to represent a gay- or lesbian-coded character on a children's television program, with or without homophobic intent, is sure to raise red flags among censors.

Self-Censorship: The Internalization of Standards

The documents from Standards to Hanna-Barbera give the impression that there is tremendous conflict between producers and censors. And the *Entertainment Weekly* article implicitly constructs such tension as the core of Standards-producer exchanges; this tension creates "censor overload." Although producer-censor relations often may be quite tense, it is also true that producers have come to avoid tense encounters by censoring themselves before submitting scripts to Standards. In other words, Standards criteria have become internalized. Although it would be impossible to fully document such internalized self-censorship, it is safe to assume that many ideas are discarded/censored before they are even written down. Several memos sent from the Tonka toy company's entertainment coordinator to the Kushner-Locke Company illustrate the existence of internalized Standards directives. Ironically, these memos are included in an Action for

Children's Television (ACT) Federal Communications Commission (FCC) brief designed to incriminate toy and TV producers for not serving children's best interests.

ACT's 1988 brief to the FCC regarding the revision of programming and commercialization policies argues that the FCC should reinstate its prohibition against program-length commercials (or product-based programs, as I prefer to call them). ACT strives to prove that toy companies actually control the production of programs based on their toys. This proof enables ACT to define such programs as "commercial speech," which is not protected by the First Amendment as extensively as noncommercial speech is. In other words, the government is constitutionally empowered to regulate commercial speech. Opponents of defining product-based programs as commercial speech say that such regulation would be censorship. In this debate, censorship and regulation are articulated as identical procedures—the potential FCC banning of product-based programs—but such a ban is defined as regulation if it is not a First Amendment violation and censorship if it is.

To prove its case, ACT submits memos from the Tonka Corporation to the Kushner-Locke Company, which apparently played a role in producing the Hanna-Barbera cartoon *The Challenge of the GoBots*. In its internal copy of the document, ACT highlighted the parts of the memos germane to its argument. For example, the reform group highlighted Tonka's question, "As bandit fires the Shark Missiler, will we be able to see it's [sic] barrel expand, as the toy does?," and Tonka's observation about a flaw in a script: "Snapper Claw 'reels the Professor in.' Snapper Claw doesn't 'reel'—just reaches out to grab and lift." ACT sees the Tonka comments as proof that the *GoBots* program is an ad for GoBot toys since Tonka is clearly asking the cartoon's producers to make cartoon representations of toys mimic actual toys as accurately as possible. However, this concern about correct cartoon representations of toys might also be explained as concern to avoid misleading advertising, concern that came about largely because of ACT's watchdog activities. ACT regularly monitored commercials, looking for toy ads it felt were deceptive. For example, it complained to the FCC when a toy car ad showed cars moving faster than they could in the course of "real-life" play and performing stunts they could not perform. In their ads, toy companies continue to push the boundaries of fantastic representation of toys, but they also respond to the demands of watchdogs and strive to avoid the kinds of representations that ACT and other pressure groups are sure to complain about.[39]

Tonka undoubtedly wanted its toys to be accurately represented on *GoBots* because it saw the program as a means of selling toys, and ACT is smart to use these documents as proof that the company itself sees the show as an ad. But it is also appropriate to read Tonka's requests to Kushner-Locke as examples of self-regulation. After all, why not make a toy look better on TV than it really is? Wouldn't this increase sales? It might increase sales, but it might also anger parents, children, and watchdog groups. Tonka's warnings to avoid certain representations simultaneously illustrate the commercial nature of the *GoBots* and Tonka's desire to accurately and nondeceptively represent its product to viewers. As evidence that the program is really an ad, these memos prove that Tonka *does not* serve children's best interests; as evidence that Tonka does not misrepresent its products, these memos prove that Tonka *does* serve children's best interests. Both of these interpretations are legitimate, but ACT and Tonka are on opposite sides of the fence, so each chooses the interpretation that best suits its needs.

Many of Tonka's directives to Kushner-Locke illustrate the internalization of Standards criteria. Tonka repeatedly points out places in the Kushner-Locke scripts where the words "destruction" or "destroy" are used in dialogue; it also consistently advises "no destroying," clearly in anticipation of Standards response. Also, Tonka notes several instances in which firearms are used in imitable, and therefore inappropriate, ways. Like Standards personnel, Tonka suggests alternative ways to handle the scenes: "Barry pulls Dirk's needler out of his boot and points it at him. Calling out this type of action could make it imitable. Let's have Barry take the needler and hold it—muzzle down—ready to raise and fire marksman style." In another instance, Tonka advises: "The Major is pointing his weapon at Max—Can't have him doing this. He can be guarding Max, but shouldn't be aiming at him." In one instance, Tonka even comments on dialogue that might be misinterpreted as risqué: "Delete or revise 'ugly puss.'" All these directives suggest that Tonka has internalized Standards criteria, criteria that came about, in no small part, as a result of ACT pressure. The documents illustrate that *GoBots*'s makers are aware of the industrial imperative to curb representations of violence in certain ways.

Censorship as Heterogeneous Process

The elaborate exchanges between censors and producers illustrate that censorship is not a repressive *act* that simply impinges on passive texts. As Michel Foucault states, "We must cease once and for all to describe the effects of power in negative terms: it 'excludes,' it 'represses,' it 'censors.' . . . In fact, power produces; it produces reality; it produces domains of objects and rituals of truth."[40] Censorship is a *process* that is not merely repressive but also productive in its effects, and censors are not the faceless, ominous threats to free speech that libertarians and laissez-faire businesspeople often paint them to be. They are industrial employees who, rather than simply mirroring cultural anxieties about violence, sexism, or racism in children's television, actively interpret and reinscribe those anxieties.

As the various voices of cartoon production and regulation demonstrate, censorship is a heterogeneous concept that is understood differently by different institutional players. How you understand broadcast Standards depends upon who you talk to, what kinds of documents you study, and how extensively you contextualize the production of those documents. If one reads such resources with and against each other, the animation industry emerges as a complexly self-regulated, global industry. Examining censorship's multiple angles in this way enables one to avoid the oppositions so commonly at play in attacks on children's entertainment. The binaries that frequently underpin adult criticism of children's media include dangerous text/endangered child, passive text/active censor, fun-loving animator/stern censor, bigoted animator/politically correct censor, concerned reformer/malicious industry, censorship/free speech, sexist/not sexist, violent/nonviolent, and racist/not racist. Disgruntled parents, teachers, and reformers often declare themselves *for* one term in the binary and *against* the other. When censorship is reified in this way, when it is perceived as a straightforward act of excision rather than a process, and when the actors of censorship are made invisible, it cannot be properly understood, interrogated, and then fought for or against. It is simply admonished.

The next chapter on the reform group Action for Children's Television elaborates on the limitations of the censorship/free speech binary, arguing that censorship is not a question of either/or but rather a matter of degree. Chapter 3 also seeks to deconstruct the concerned reformer/malicious industry binary by showing that these two ostensible enemies actually tend to play by the same (often liberal) rules. Whereas the child imagined by the industrial censor is a mimetic machine, dangerous to the networks because of the ever-present threat of lawsuits, ACT's mimetic machine-child is dangerous to itself. ACT's fantasy child was duped by corporate hawkers of sugar and toys, but ACT itself was duped by corporations who offered the reform group not Cocoa Puffs and Barbie dolls but a conception of "free debate in a free society" that was isomorphic with its own.

Action for (and against) Children's Television

3

"Militant Mothers" and the Tactics

of Television Reform

People criticize ACT for the lack of creativity today. We never asked for that. They don't remember what it was like before we were around. There was no *Sesame Street* or *Electric Company*. It was never our idea to sanitize the superheroes and reduce the art of animation to its present standards. The broadcasters are responsible for what's on the air today, not Action for Children's Television. We're trying to see that the product is improved, not worsened.[1] — Peggy Charren, ACT cofounder

Action for Children's Television (ACT) sought to make children's television better; it was often accused of making it worse. Many broadcasters and certainly cartoon producers have argued that ACT hampered free speech. Indeed, in spite of its pro-TV projects and its self-constructed image as noncensorious, some of ACT's campaigns were censorious. From 1968 to 1992, ACT worked both for and against children's television programs.

Citizen groups such as ACT challenge television by calling for broadcaster accountability. Although there are many left- and right-wing media activists, media activism is often moderate in its politics, as in the case of ACT. ACT's history demonstrates that media resistance in and of itself is not necessarily radical. It is the voices of the least radical citizen groups that both governmental regulatory agencies, such as the Federal Communications Commission (FCC) and Federal Trade Commission (FTC), and network executives are most often willing to listen to. ACT is important not only because it served as an advocate for certain kinds of children's television and as an opponent of other kinds of children's television but also because, for the media and the government, it superseded other kinds of more radical activism.

ACT's moderate politics enabled it to attack certain corporate actions in the name of middle-class children, but ACT was loath to threaten corporations economically through boycotts or stockholder pressure. This reluctance made ACT palatable to both regulatory agencies and the media. Although the FCC and FTC have only infrequently acted on ACT's complaints and suggestions, they have repeatedly *listened* to ACT. ACT used tactics common to other media reform groups—such as attending FCC meetings and citing the Communications Act of 1934—and to a certain extent, these tactics worked better for ACT than they did for anyone else. The group has not always succeeded, but it has repeatedly been heard by the media and the government, which has not been the case for activists whose politics have been considered more "dangerous" or "extremist," such as feminists, Civil Rights activists, and AIDs activists. In its seventies campaign against sugared products, however, ACT uncharacteristically, dramatically, and ultimately unsuccessfully threatened the sugar industry, a corporate octopus. ACT's most radical undertaking, this campaign has been largely forgotten, perhaps because it seemed so out of character.

The Public Move for Media Reform

The seventies witnessed a widespread media reform movement—or rather movements. Activists with wide-ranging concerns challenged corporate media production with a level of energy and determination that was unprecedented, with the exception of the reform movement against radio commercialization in the late twenties and early thirties.[2] The roots of the seventies media reform movement are intertwined with the Civil Rights and anti–Vietnam War movements; it was Civil Rights and Vietnam War activists who first learned how to use the television medium to their advantage, to the consternation of those who disagreed with their politics.

At the time ACT was formed in 1968, the public and the government were deeply concerned about how TV depicted people of color. Debates about TV's representation of people of color predate this era, though.

Throughout the fifties and sixties, racist viewers complained that the television industry was reacting to the Civil Rights movement by presenting more images of people of color, particularly African Americans.[3] Antiracist viewers also objected to the new images on TV, which consisted mainly of two kinds of representations: blacks protesting and being beaten on the news, and middle-class and (arguably) depoliticized blacks on shows like *I Spy* and *Julia*.[4] "There were now 'two black realities'—the synthetic reality of the sitcoms and the one broadcast by the news programs—which for a decade, though juxtaposed strangely, could never be reconciled."[5] Black media reform activists of the seventies addressed this juxtaposition of images and called for other kinds of images.[6]

Sixties Civil Rights activists saw TV news as an ally, to a certain extent, and even as "the chosen instrument of the revolution," as one television historian has phrased it.[7] Martin Luther King Jr. explained that public demonstrations were necessary, in part, because African Americans were not given access to other forms of expression and self-representation such as the print and broadcast media.[8] "Lacking sufficient access to television, publications and broad forums," King said, "Negroes have had to write their most persuasive essays with the blunt pen of marching ranks."[9] It was precisely those marching ranks that finally gave blacks access to television; the news showed blacks attempting to enroll in the University of Alabama, assembling in Washington, D.C., to demonstrate support for President John F. Kennedy's Civil Rights Act in 1963, and being blasted by fire hoses in Birmingham. King understood the televisual impact of these events and the importance of TV visibility of black struggles. On television, northern audiences saw violence against southern blacks for the first time, and, importantly, isolated southern blacks could feel solidarity with others involved in the struggle.[10]

Many white southerners expressed anger not just at President Kennedy and the federal government's desegregationists but also at television itself for producing and disseminating what they saw as antisouthern propaganda. The governor of Mississippi, Ross Barnett, complained about an NBC program called *The American Revolution of '63*: "Fellow Americans you are witnessing one more chapter in what has been termed the 'Television Revolution.' Information media, including the TV networks have publicized and dramatized the race issue far beyond its relative importance in today's world."[11]

Southern politicians were not the only ones to question the "Television Revolution." In 1968, the government's *Report of the National Advisory Commission on Civil Disorders* (or Kerner Commission) devoted a chapter to mass media riot coverage, which the commission found wanting. A year later, the National Commission on the Causes and Prevention of Violence published its findings, which also confronted the power of the mass media. Government reports asked whether the media correctly represented activist activities and questioned how activists themselves used the media.[12] After the violence of the 1968 Chicago Democratic National Convention, popular debate about activist media use increased, and it was widely felt that the mass media had not merely recorded but had actively participated in the Chicago confrontation between the police and peace demonstrators. The demonstrators had cheered the arrival of NBC cameras, shouting, "The whole world is watching!" and "Sieg heil!" at the police armed with nightsticks, mace, tear gas, and guns.[13] One contributor to the National Commission on the Causes and Prevention of Violence report stated that at Chicago, "what 'the whole world was watching,' after all, was not a confrontation but the picture of a confrontation, to some extent directed by a generation that has grown up with television and learned how to use it."[14] By the year of ACT's founding, those unsympathetic to Civil Rights activism and Vietnam protest would lament that activists were savvy in media manipulation and that TV allowed itself to be manipulated. Those more sympathetic would say that alternative viewpoints had finally found much-needed representation.

It was in the context of volatile governmental and public debates about the media that ACT appeared, asking the federal government to hold broadcasters accountable to the nation's child TV viewers. ACT did not initiate government concern about television's possible effects on children, but it was the first prominent activist group to focus on children's television. ACT did not steal the spotlight from Vietnam and Civil Rights activists, but it did act as a kind of regulatory safety valve: it was politically easier for the FCC to address ACT's complaints than to address the complaints of more "extremist" activist groups.

Whereas some seventies activists saw the media primarily as a technological means of broadcasting their messages to the public, groups like ACT focused their activism on the corporate media institution itself, seeking to make those using the airwaves answerable to citizens. In the early sixties, commissioner Newton Minow had popularized the idea of the FCC actively serving the public interest (which he defined in elitist terms), but this pseudopopulist stance was quickly suppressed by the Johnson and Nixon FCCs, which catered to business interests.[15] In principle, broadcasters nonetheless remained accountable to the public because, according to the Communications Act of 1934, broadcasters did not own the airwaves. Rather, they received short-term licenses from the FCC to use publicly owned airwaves, operating "in the public interest, convenience, and necessity." It was the FCC's responsibility to define what the "public interest" was and how broadcasters could best serve that interest. As far as the FCC was concerned, the public interest was served by providing access to clear, nonoverlapping signals sent by corporations. The possibility of activists using the Communications Act or its rhetoric ("the public interest, convenience, and necessity") was certainly not foreseen. In fact, the act initially signaled the end of reformist debate over whether broadcasting should be commercial. "The Communications Act of 1934 . . . had been the conscious result of keeping the public and Congress itself as far removed as possible from any debate over broadcast issues."[16]

Nonetheless, public debate about broadcasting did not disappear after the act was passed. A variety of parents' groups protested children's radio throughout the thirties, accusing it of "overstimulating" children and causing delinquent behavior, and anti-TV sentiment existed in the earliest days of television's proliferation. In the fifties, many Americans saw television as a potentially dangerous medium: citizens undertook letter-writing campaigns and boycotts to keep alleged Communist actors off television; a plethora of medical authorities questioned the biological and psychological dangers of television; and women's magazines asked if TV would bring families together or tear them apart.[17] But there had never been a readily apparent means by which citizens who were dissatisfied with broadcast practices might influence FCC policy. This changed as a result of action taken by citizens in 1964. Civil Rights petitioners, spearheaded by the United Church of Christ, protested that the Mississippi TV station WLBT should not have its FCC license renewed because it did not properly serve its community. The petitioners charged that the station had denied blacks access to facilities, had promoted segregation, and had failed to present problack perspectives on its news programs. The FCC responded that the church group could not be an active party to WLBT's license renewal proceeding; only corporate claims regarding economic injury or electrical interference would be heard by the FCC.[18] But in 1966, the Court of Appeals challenged the FCC's dismissal of the United Church of Christ, forcing the FCC to give the petitioners a hearing.

As a result of the court's WLBT decision, the petition to deny license renewal to broadcasters who did not serve the public interest, convenience, and necessity became a viable method for citizens to oppose broadcasters at the federal level. Now citizens could do more than picket, sign petitions, or write angry protest letters to advertisers and network executives; they had governmental recourse. Groups ranging from the National Association for the Advancement of Colored People (NAACP), to the Tribal Indian Lands Rights Association, to the National Organization for Women (NOW), to the Polish-American Guardian Society incorporated the petition to deny into their media activism tactics. In the wake of the United Church of Christ's FCC appeal, a plethora of reform groups focusing exclusively on the media were newly formed, including Black Efforts for Soul in Television (BEST), Terminate Unfair Broadcasting Excesses (TUBE), Students Opposing Unfair Practices (SOUP), Protesting Unfair Marketing Practices (PUMP), and ACT. ACT was unique in its focus on children, but it clearly rode the contemporary wave of media criticism and activism. ACT was not unique in its tactics (using the Communications Act to justify the right to petition to deny license renewal)[19] or in its central belief that citizens have the right to protest broadcasting policy and practices. Perhaps the most unique thing about ACT was that the media actually provided the group extensive coverage. The media's interest in ACT was largely a result of the group's moderate, motherly image. By covering ACT, the media could pay lip service to "women's issues."

ACT's Image and Media Tactics

In 1968, feminists staged a protest at the Miss America Pageant, marking the first major feminist intervention in network television. Outside the pageant, the protesters picketed and performed guerrilla theater, crowning a live sheep Miss America. Inside the pageant, protesters unfurled a "Women's Liberation" banner and shouted "Freedom for Women!" Although TV cameras inside the pageant ignored the protesters, home viewers could sense something was wrong when they heard shouting, and the 1967 Miss America began to tremble and stutter.[20] That same year, when a group of women from the Boston suburbs founded ACT, TV cameras eagerly turned to cover the group. Confrontational but less threatening than the so-called bra-burners who had disrupted the Miss America Pageant, ACT offered much that appealed to news cameras: professional sound bites that were argumentative yet relatively inoffensive since, after all, these were mainstream moms acting in their children's best interests.

ACT was an activist woman's group that garnered positive media attention, in part, because its tactics diverged dramatically from those of radical feminists. To the mainstream media, the moderate, middle-class ACT with its prochild platform seemed comfortably "normal" compared to other social movements of the day, such as Women's Liberation, Civil Rights, and Gay Liberation. Cofounder Peggy Charren states: "[A]*ll of us had young children, and all of us had worked . . . outside the home.* And I think that is the essential ingredient to the start of ACT. I think the fact that we had work experience was important. We tended to see this as a *professional effort from the moment we started. We wanted to organize in a way different from just sitting together and talking.* We were very much aware of what you do to start an organization; you name it, you incorporate, you have limited liability" (my emphasis).[21] Like members of the middle-class women's movement, ACT praised working outside of the home as inherently positive. And ACT founders wanted to go beyond "just" talking or, in the terms of Women's Liberation, "consciousness-raising," in order to take action for (and against) children's programming, which meant starting a legitimate, incorporated organization. Although some contemporary Women's Lib groups were certainly as organized and efficient as ACT, ACT fostered an *image* of organized efficiency that made these moms even more respectable in the media's eyes.

Broadcasters and FCC commissioners were willing to listen to ACT, in part, because it represented itself as a group of concerned mothers. "ACT was born of the *mothers'* indignation about the programs—and the incessant commercials—television offered *their children*" (my emphasis).[22] In 1972, when broadcasters argued there was not enough "scientific" evidence to prove that advertising affected children adversely, Charren replied, "There are millions of mothers out there who are not willing to wait for a lot of research. Generations of children are growing up."[23] Such maternal rhetoric both legitimated and hindered the group. The press and the television industry could easily label and dismiss ACT activism—intended to protect children from poor-quality TV—as "maternal instinct." Indeed, the industry and the mainstream media often disparaged ACT members as "those ladies from Boston" or "those militant mothers from Newton." In 1969, the *Boston Globe* both condescended to ACT and acknowledged its potential activist power: "[T]he hand that rocks the cradle is now doubled up into a fist. Its aim: to pound some sense into the television industry. As yet, it doesn't pack much of a punch. . . . But women aroused can be formidable foes indeed. Television had better steel itself for the assault to come."[24] The *Globe* painted ACT members oxymoronically as violent-yet-maternal adversaries of the industry, adversaries who derived their power from their status as scolding mothers.

ACT wanted to be taken seriously, not to be dismissed as a group of fisted, hysterical moms. Members thus strove to project an image of being very well informed. Charren explains, "We . . . made sure to get our facts straight, to educate ourselves on what the problem really was. One of the first things we did was subscribe to all the industry magazines, so we could see what the other side was thinking."[25] ACT found that industry and government policymakers were willing to listen to its informed arguments, yet their responses to ACT varied from polite to condescending. Senator John Pastore praised ACT cofounder Lillian Ambrosino as "a very, very alert, young girl,"[26] and FCC commissioner Dean Burch said that ACT's representatives were "very compelling [and] not a bunch of crybabies."[27] ACT members knew they were troublesome to the FCC and, it seems, delighted in their ability to make waves. In celebration of its fifteen-year anniversary, the group released a history of itself entitled *Rocking the Boat*. The cover showed a 1970 *TV Guide* cartoon picturing ACT members as soggy middle-aged women struggling to climb aboard a boat flying an FCC banner. The boat was already filled to capacity with white men in business suits (figure 1). Although ACT tended to avoid any in-depth discussion of its all-woman status, its use of this cartoon comically highlighted its awareness of a gendered divide between ACT members and government officials, an awareness that must have been constant for ACT but was rarely publicly acknowledged. And this is why the FCC was willing to listen to ACT. The group stuck to the controversial yet relatively nonthreatening political

Figure 1. Cartoon depicting ACT members rocking the boat. *Source: TV Guide*, 13 Apr. 1970, p. 18.

terrain of children's television and focused on commercialism, avoiding public discussion of thorny issues such as sexism.

A brief comparison of the FCC's initial meetings with ACT, NOW, and the National Black Media Coalition will make clear the contrast between the FCC's perceptions of ACT and its perceptions of groups it considered more radical. ACT first met with the FCC in 1970, armed with detailed, practical proposals for rules to govern children's programming. This meeting set the ball slowly rolling; eventually, the FCC formed a permanent (as opposed to ad hoc) children's unit (1971) and issued a Children's Policy Statement (1974). The commissioners found radical ACT's proposal to do away with children's advertising, but at least ACT did not attack privately owned, for-profit broadcasting across the board. ACT was not against commercial television per se but against what it saw as the exploitation of children.[28] ACT's demands were not necessarily seen as plausible by the commissioners, but its goals and motivations were understandable to them. Some even responded as empathic parents. One of the commissioners had been ill the weekend before meeting with ACT and was supposedly more receptive to ACT because he had spent Saturday morning watching cartoons with his children. But he opined that broadcasters might be trusted to regulate TV themselves since "capitalists are human beings and have children of their own."[29]

Before ACT's 1970 meeting, the FCC had rarely met with citizen's groups.[30] The next citizen's group the FCC met with was NOW in 1973. NOW arranged the meeting through Charlotte Reid's office. Reid, a conservative who had declared herself "not a woman's advocate,"[31] was the FCC's first woman commissioner since Frieda Hennock (1948–1955). No written record was made of the closed meeting with NOW, but according to FCC consultant Barry Cole, NOW president Wilma Scott Heide began by observing that the commissioners were seated on a dais: "We're equals! I don't look up to you, and I don't want to have to sit here looking up to you."[32] Cole's report of Heide's presentation gives a good sense of the commission's reaction: "Ms. Heide told the Commission she was about to read an essay that would provide an 'awareness experience.' She did not want to be interrupted while reading the essay; she would tell the commissioners when it was appropriate for them to speak. To the utter bemusement of the commissioners, Ms. Heide proceeded to read her essay. . . . Cole wished he had had a camera to record for posterity the expressions on the faces of the commissioners as they listened or tried to avoid listening to Ms. Heide's presentation."[33] To the commissioners' dismay, Heide read a lengthy treatise on the problems men have because of vagina envy. Following this presentation, Heide explained the ways in which media representations of women were inaccurate, and then, according to Cole, "several important and useful suggestions were offered by Ms. Heide's colleagues; for example, some methods by which the Commission should select stations for further examination of their compliance with equal opportunity requirements."[34] The details of these "useful suggestions" are forever lost since no official record was kept of this meeting and no action was taken on the suggestions. According to Cole, Heide had set the wrong tone, and thus NOW's practical proposals fell on deaf ears. Although the other NOW representatives were deemed courteous, "the milk was spoiled. The experience provided ammunition for those in the FCC who believed that meetings with public groups were a waste of time, a hairshirt."[35] Clearly the experience also confirmed the sentiments of FCC commissioners who believed that feminists and feminist issues were too weird for FCC consideration. NOW goals were not only threatening but also nonpractical in the eyes of the commissioners. The FCC did not see vagina envy as an appropriate subject for it to address. ACT, on the other hand, like the citizens who used the Fairness Doctrine to oppose TV cigarette ads in 1969, offered what were deemed practical and appropriate suggestions.³⁶

The FCC was more receptive to people of color, at least initially, than it was to the feminists of NOW. After the 1973 NOW meeting, a meeting with blacks, Native Americans, Asians, and Latinos was arranged by BEST, the group that previously had been instrumental in gaining the appointment of Benjamin L. Hooks, the FCC's first black commissioner. The citizens offered a balance of criticisms and practical suggestions; the meeting was fairly amicable, but no action was taken on the citizens' suggestions. Likewise, the FCC did not respond to the Latino Media Coalition's request that a task force be formed to address Latino issues. Apparently, "the decision not to form a task force was consistent with later decisions not to become involved in any type of advisory committee relationship with any minority groups." ³⁷ After this brief period when the FCC seemed willing to hear out people of color, albeit without taking any action in response to their complaints, a volatile meeting with the National Black Media Coalition in November 1973 changed the FCC's attitude. James McCuller, the group's leader, criticized the FCC for its disinterest in black issues, and when Chairman Burch suggested that he "construct a dialogue, not a diatribe," ³⁸ McCuller angrily and extensively detailed a long history of whites silencing blacks. He indicated that Burch was like a master silencing a slave. This encounter convinced the commissioners that citizen's groups were irrational and impossible to deal with. Yet the FCC continued to deal with ACT and to maintain a children's television task force. In other words, although throughout the seventies the FCC had reservations about citizen's groups across the board, it was its experience with "irrational" blacks and women that really turned the FCC off.³⁹ The FCC continued to interact with the group it perhaps found least threatening, a group of white middle-class mothers.

ACT was fairly successful largely because it was an incorporated organization that played by the rules not only of the FCC but also of big business. Even as it attacked certain products and business practices and called for the elimination of ads on children's shows, ACT confronted television *professionally*, using language and strategies comprehensible to TV and FCC executives. ACT's tactics were the kind that appealed to Nicholas Johnson, an early seventies FCC commissioner who was atypically sympathetic to citizens' protest. Johnson detailed his concerns about corporate concentration of media ownership and his high hopes for citizen-induced reform in *How to Talk Back to Your Television Set* (1970), which, amazingly, drew praise from both Tommy Smothers and William F. Buckley Jr. In his book, Johnson promoted the kind of moderate and, at the time, moderately successful approach that ACT took, which he called "the law of effective reform." He conceded that the public can try to affect broadcast policy by many means: picketing, signing petitions, and staging sit-ins. However, he believed that ultimately the most effective reform would come through appealing to official channels and making positive, legally sanctioned suggestions. In his concern for citizens' rights and corporate accountability, Johnson was an anomalous FCC commissioner. His relationship with other commissioners was fraught with difficulty; he was consistently outvoted on major policy decisions, and he wrote unexpurgated dissents. He went public with his gripes, testifying before Congress that broadcasters were "vicious" and "evil" and that the FCC was abusing the public trust.[40] Although he was rather radical for an FCC commissioner, Johnson did not condone impassioned polemics about slavery or vagina envy. To work toward practical goals, Johnson suggested that

> in order to get relief from legal institutions (Congress, courts, agencies) one must assert, first, the factual basis for the grievance and the specific parties involved; second, the legal principle that indicates relief is due (constitutional provision, statute, regulation, court or agency decision); and third, the precise remedy sought (new legislation or regulations, license revocation, fines, or an order changing practices). When this principle is not understood, which is most of the time, the most legitimate public protests from thousands of citizens fall like drops of rain upon lonely and uncharted seas. But by understanding and using the right strategy the meekest among us can roll back the ocean.[41]

ACT shared Johnson's David and Goliath philosophy and understood the principles of "the law of effective reform" very well—so well that the group was incredulous in the eighties when the same tactics no longer worked. In that deregulatory climate, it simply did not matter how much factual evidence one could gather or what legal precedents one could invoke (such as the FCC's prior decisions regarding children's television). Johnson's principles could not compete with the eighties FCC's free market mentality.

But throughout the seventies, ACT was fairly successful not only at affecting public policy but also at attracting an audience for its concerns and raising public awareness of children's TV as an important public policy issue. ACT's media-savvy tactics made the group, and cofounder Charren in particular, into *the* voice for children's television advocacy. Recall "the leaders of the Mexican-American community" and the heavily accented coworker that I discussed in chapter 2: the networks like having an expert consultant to advise them on touchy issues. As Kathryn Montgomery has explained, over the years, the networks have learned to manage advocacy groups by insisting upon the "one-voice concept." The networks prefer to listen to only one group protesting a particular issue. If forced to choose among several groups vying to represent a community or communities, the networks (and the mainstream media in general) naturally choose the most moderate group. ACT quickly became the one voice of children's television advocacy that was heard by both the networks and the mainstream media. Whenever newspapers or news shows needed a sound bite on children's television, they called ACT, and they have continued to call Charren even since ACT disbanded in 1992.

One way ACT caught the media's attention and established itself as the one voice of children's television advocacy was by staging events such as its annual symposium on children and television, at which keynote speakers included celebrities such as Fred Rogers and Bob "Captain Kangaroo" Keeshan. This event was cosponsored by prestigious organizations that legitimated both ACT and the symposium: the American Academy of Pediatrics, the Yale Child Study Center, and the John F. Kennedy Center for the Performing Arts. ACT also received media attention for giving achievement awards to individual affiliates for local programs, to the networks for national programs, and frequently to corporations that had sponsored programs, such as Exxon, General Mills, Sears Roebuck, McDonald's, and the Warner Amex Satellite Entertainment Corporation. Notwithstanding its complaints that market forces objectified children, ACT was more than willing to reward corporations that it felt served children's needs. Unlike other media activists who focused exclusively on attacking what was wrong with TV, ACT was willing to reward TV that it considered high quality.

In fact, ACT's support of "good" shows was crucial to its anticensorship stance. As Charren put it: "It was never our idea to sanitize the superheroes and reduce the art of animation to its present standards. . . . We're trying to see that the product is improved, not worsened." [42] In spite of its real desire to eliminate bad programming, ACT insisted upon its investment in promoting good programs, and this insistence was crucial to the maintenance of its anticensorship image. ACT believed in the possibility of freedom from censorship. This is crucial, for at base ACT was ideologically compatible with corporations and the FCC for two reasons: it was white, nonfeminist, and non-"extremist," and it understood free/unfree (or uncensored/censored) as binaries. Like the broadcasting industry and the FCC, ACT opposed censorship, assuming that it was antithetical to American democratic society rather than part and parcel of that society.

ACT and the Politics of Censorship and Boycott

The Coalition for Better Television (now the American Family Association) and the National Coalition on Television Violence (NCTV) were high-profile media reform groups that threatened sponsor boycotts in order to eliminate/censor certain programs. Conversely, ACT persistently and adamantly opposed boycotting as a media reform tactic. There is a striking contrast between ACT's philosophy and tactics and the philosophy and tactics of these two more radical media reform groups. In a 1981 television debate with Donald Wildmon of the ultraconservative Coalition for Better Television, Charren explained that ACT harangued broadcasters instead of advertisers because targeting advertisers

> is not the way to behave in a free society. . . . If I go to the broadcaster who's using public airwaves and say "you're not serving me," and somebody else thinks that he is being served (or she), she can go to the broadcaster and say "That woman is wrong. You are serving me." And then it's a question of broadcaster decision, majority rule, or whatever. It can even be a case at the Federal Communications Commission, and everybody can testify. That's how a free society works. If you go to an advertiser, the advertiser's very vulnerable. . . . [T]he advertiser doesn't want any controversy . . . doesn't want to be part of a hearing where both sides get the right to decide how the issues should go. [43]

Charren further wondered "what kind of a free press would we have" if advertisers could influence television and newspaper content. Charren may have erroneously implied that we now live in a "free society" in which benign advertisers do not influence television and newspaper content and press censorship does not exist less out of naïveté than as an anti-Wildmon tactic. But her liberal rhetoric does demonstrate an ongoing belief in the moderate tactics of "the law of effective reform." Wildmon, whom the media has taken as the "one voice" of right-wing extremist wackos for almost twenty years, used a means of "talking back to his television set" that largely ignored the pragmatic law of effective reform but demonstrated an equally pragmatic vision of how American government and businesses operate. Government regulation of business is slow. Antitrust cases can be drawn out over decades. Conversely, direct economic pressure, or the threat thereof, can be fast and efficient and is a perfectly legal way to bring about censorship. Wildmon's group took a shortcut, bypassing the FCC and going straight to the industry's jugular, the sponsor. The Coalition for Better Television threatened to "vote" with its collective wallet by boycotting sponsors of the shows it found objectionable.[44] Wildmon has repeatedly declared, sounding vaguely libertarian, that "the network can show what it wants, sponsors sponsor what they want, and the consumer can spend his money wherever he wants."[45] This may not be "the way to behave in a free society," but it is one widely sanctioned way to behave in a survival-of-the-fittest capitalist society.

ACT decided to pressure networks and government agencies rather than specific sponsors because it seemed like the appropriate way to promote broadcast reform in a democratic society. The studio audience of the Charren-Wildmon debate clearly agreed with Charren. Ironically, Wildmon was barely allowed to get a word in edgewise by Charren and audience members who attacked him for being against free speech. With his southern accent and uncultured grammar, Wildmon easily served as a free speech whipping boy for the studio audience of liberal, middle-class Bostonians. But Wildmon had the last laugh: he understood that speech is not free but costly, that voting with one's wallet is not only a very effective way but also practically the only way to get the TV industry's attention. Wildmon's bigoted Christian fundamentalist agenda is sexist, racist, and homophobic, but he also happens to be a savvy activist. I compare him to Charren to show that different styles of activism use the con-

cepts of "freedom" and "democracy" differently and produce different results. ACT members changed the FCC guidelines for children's television
by approaching the FCC as citizens voicing their opinion, whereas Wildmon's Coalition for Better Television made the networks increase their
self-regulation of TV sex by approaching the TV industry as a potential boy-
cotter. Wildmon's success was quicker but not longer lasting.

In spite of the Government in Sunshine Act[46] and the fact that the FCC
has issued calls for citizen letters and held public panel discussions in the
past, the commission has always been more receptive to TV industry opinion than to public opinion. Citizens may see their letters to the FCC as
votes, but the commission does not read and tally them that way. For example, in response to ACT's regulatory proposals in 1971, the FCC received
80,000 pro-ACT letters. The letters were "stacked in large boxes for later
filing in bound volumes. There was no timetable for examining the letters
and no one on the staff was considering reading them. 'What's the sense in
reading them?' [an official in the Broadcast Bureau's Rules and Standards
Division] asked. 'They all say the same thing.' "[47] These letters may have
helped legitimate ACT and its complaints, but they did not count as votes.
Receiving 800,000 letters instead of 80,000 would have meant more filing
for grunt workers at the FCC, but it would not have made ACT's case any
stronger.

The NCTV was another group that, like the Coalition for Better Television, favored sponsor boycotting as a media reform tactic. The NCTV
repeatedly wooed ACT, hoping it would lend its support to the NCTV's
project. NCTV chair Thomas Radecki told Charren that he was trying to
pull together different groups in order to make a "united national effort"
to oppose TV violence.[48] However, ACT's tactics were irreconcilable with
those of the NCTV. The NCTV monitored programming, counting acts of
violence and regularly releasing rankings of programs and lists of sponsors
whose ads appeared on high-violence shows. The NCTV encouraged letter-
writing campaigns and sponsor boycotts based on the rankings. ACT also
monitored programming, but it did so primarily to gauge deceptive advertising, which is legally censorable/regulatable by the FTC. Because ACT
defined the NCTV's monitoring as censorious (which it was), it could not
possibly lend its support to the group.

In an effort to convince Charren that the two groups' goals were not irreconcilable, Radecki argued that

in the past you have shied away from firm efforts on the TV violence issues worrying about First Amendment issues. NCTV is certainly not attempting governmental censorship but only to offset the distorting effects of commercialization on TV with which you are very familiar. Thus actions such as public exposure of TV vilence [sic] advertisers, stockholders pressure, or national product boycotts are not really censorship. Indeed, we are aware that the networks are censoring off non-violent and news programming of certain types because it doesn't fit the profit mission of commercial TV.[49]

ACT would not be swayed. Affiliation with Radecki was almost as unthinkable as collaborating with Wildmon. The Coalition for Better Television had a right-wing image, whereas the NCTV had a more left-wing image, but both groups had a procensorship image. (Interestingly, the NCTV did hope to form an alliance with the Moral Majority but soon realized, to its disappointment, that the Moral Majority only paid lip service to concerns about violence. Really, it only objected to TV sex. It condemned *The Love Boat* as one of the most objectionable programs on television, whereas the NCTV felt that *The Love Boat* was one of the least violent and therefore least objectionable programs on TV.) [50] Perhaps ACT sensed that to much of the public, TV sponsor boycott, regardless of its goals, was irredeemably linked with censorship. Although broadcasters frequently held that ACT was censorious, this was not the widely held public opinion, nor was it ACT's view of itself.[51] Association with the NCTV would have tarnished ACT's anti-censorship image. This is not to say that ACT was not sincere in its anti-censorship stance, merely that ACT's choice not to align itself with certain media reform groups, a choice that was grounded in high principles, had certain political results that were in the long run advantageous to ACT.

ACT could not have approved of Michigan housewife Terry Rakolta's 1989 campaign against *Married . . . With Children* and other "trash TV," as she put it. The campaign involved hit listing particular programs and threatening advertisers with boycott. In spite of Rakolta's obvious right-wing position on many issues, Corretta Scott King stated her support for the campaign: "At the risk of disappointing some of my fellow liberals, I tip my hat to Terry Rakolta. . . . I know that to many artists and civil libertarians, such citizen initiatives raise the specter of censorship and represent a threat to free expression. But . . . boycotts and selective patronage are not only consistent with our democratic values, they are an essential tool for encouraging corporate social responsibility." [52] One can guess that "fellow liberal" ACT would not have been thrilled by King's words. Although ACT certainly would not have been critical of fifties and sixties Civil Rights activists whose boycotting of products and services had proved a crucial tactic, it consistently held that the kind of boycotting Rakolta advocated was not democratic and not the appropriate way to encourage corporate social responsibility.

By choosing not to boycott or encourage stockholder pressure, ACT chose not to attempt to damage corporations. ACT did attack particular corporate practices, however. For example, ACT gave McDonald's awards for sponsoring PBS shows but condemned McDonald's for its Ronald McDonald Family Theater, which ACT considered a plug for McDonald's. Yet as Armand Mattelart has explained, corporations perform public ser-vices—like sponsoring PBS programs—in order to offset their negative corporate images: "At the same time as ITT was plotting against Allende, it was giving its patronage to the production of twentieth-century ballet in New York. While IBM was being hauled up before the anti-Trust commit-tee, it was sponsoring an excellent documentary on madness on the public television network. The notions of 'quality of life' and 'corporate respon-sibility' were behind these new public relations exercises." [53] Both the PBS show sponsored by McDonald's and the Ronald McDonald Family Theater were advertisements for McDonald's. Indeed, ACT's own awards were ads for McDonald's.

The proboycotting Coalition for Better Television and NCTV seemed to understand what ACT did not—that where media reform activism is con-cerned, it is not a question of whether noncensorship or censorship will win. Rather, it is a question of what I call "competing censorships." Pro-ducers and pressure groups are both censors in that they want *their* version of the TV text to be *the* version of the TV text at the expense of other ver-sions. A pressure group that protests racist images wants those images removed and replaced with "better" images, and a group that protests the very presence of images of people of color wants those images removed. My point is not that censorship is a positive social force because it may eliminate racist images but rather that it is ubiquitous and is inherently neither progressive nor conservative.

Furthermore, it is unfair to dismiss media pressure groups because they are censorious, as if without them TV programs would be censorship free. There is no such thing as a free or uncensored text, but the idea of freedom from censorship is a particularly seductive lure that sidesteps many other crucial political issues that a pressure group raises. Although it is easy to condemn right-wing groups like the Moral Majority or the Christian Coalition by labeling them censorious, it is much harder to both analyze their motivations and arguments and formulate an argument against the morals they seek to instill in others. For example, right-wing religious groups hope to save the family by eliminating adult programs like NYPD Blue. Rather than accusing such politicos of hampering free speech and telling them to shut up, leftists might rebut by offering an alternative definition of the family or questioning what it actually means to "save the family."[54] The cry of censorship is all too often used to silence, not encourage, the open debate that Charren advocated.

ACT used the "freedom from censorship" lure repeatedly and successfully. ACT argued it was noncensorious on the grounds that it acted *for* children's TV, not *against* it. Like ACT, the networks and the FCC defended their own interests by using the concept of freedom from censorship, so although the networks and the FCC were often irritated by ACT, they found the group's central anticensorship stance palatable. Early ACT member Judy Chalfen recalls that "when we first talked, we were most concerned with violence . . . but we got off that. Violence is so hard to define and really, it's just part of the whole picture of poor quality." Charren adds, "[W]e knew that if we got into violence alone, we would be treading into the area of censorship. That's not what we wanted."[55] ACT deliberately shifted its focus to commercialism as an anticensorship tactic. It also gave out awards and objected to sponsor boycotts, as described above, in the name of opposing censorship. Siding with TV producer Norman Lear and others who were under attack for their adult programming, ACT also came out strongly against the Family Viewing Hour in 1976. And in its book *TV and Teens,* ACT included an interview with Lear.[56] Lear has been attacked repeatedly by overtly procensorship media reformers, so ACT's obvious respect for his work and his opinions were proof positive that it aligned itself on the side of free speech.

ACT's campaign against indecency legislation also bears witness to the group's sincere anticensorship beliefs. After the *Pacifica* decision in 1975, in which indecency was declared regulatable/censorable by the FCC, a "safe harbor" for indecency was established; the FCC declared 12:00–6:00 A.M. to be a legal broadcasting time for so-called indecent material. ACT opposed the safe harbor idea, not because it wanted indecency banned around the clock but because it opposed any indecency regulation on First Amendment grounds. In 1988, a federal appeals court overturned the FCC's safe harbor order in *Action for Children's Television v. FCC*. At this point, Congress, spearheaded by Jesse Helms, imposed an around-the-clock prohibition on indecency, eliminating the safe harbor altogether. In *Action for Children's Television v. FCC* (1991), the court of appeals held the elimination of the safe harbor to be unconstitutional.[57] Helms and others fought this ruling, but the Supreme Court upheld it in 1992.[58] It is striking that ACT would go out on a limb to challenge indecency and safe harbor rulings, which were ostensibly motivated by the desire to protect children. ACT's challenges to the FCC and to the Helms contingency demonstrate the depth of its anticensorship convictions.

ACT's interest in media education was further evidence of the group's genuine desire to be for, not against, children's television. In a platform statement, ACT explained that its goals were "a combination of advocacy and education." ACT's advocacy activities were focused on what it opposed: advertisements. ACT's education goals focused on the positive. ACT educated "organizations and individuals by planning national conferences and publishing handbooks on various aspects of children's television, encouraging programming on the arts, science, consumer education and for the disabled child. . . . [ACT educated] adults about the critical effect television has on children, through its reference library, national speaker's bureau, and distribution of materials."[59] In its first fifteen years, ACT commissioned fifteen studies on children's programs and commercials. ACT put together a "resource list" of the titles, all of which could be purchased from ACT. The studies were wide-ranging, including *Images of Life on Children's Television: Sex Roles, Minorities, and Families*, *Pre-Christmas Advertising to Children*, *Romper Room: An Analysis*, and *Mothers' Attitudes toward Children's Television and Commercials*. Interestingly, the project on mothers' attitudes was the first study ACT commissioned, which further illustrates that it presented itself as a maternally motivated group. Importantly, while these studies were evidence of ACT's desire to educate, they were self-serving as well. ACT commissioned studies that it could use to prove its arguments. From reading trade publications, ACT knew that the point of kids' TV was to sell stuff to kids, but it realized it had to do more than just go before the FCC or broadcasters and say that. As Charren put it, "[W]e needed statistics to back us up." [60] ACT's commissioned studies served not only as educational material for others but also as a source of statistics for the group.

At ACT's Resource Library, researchers could find books, videos, pamphlets, unpublished research reports, and bibliographies on different aspects of children's television. ACT also began producing public service announcements in 1975 and 1976, and in 1977, it released a documentary film about TV marketing to children, *It's as Easy as Selling Candy to a Baby*. It seems that ACT's community outreach really took off in 1976 when Ann Landers mentioned the group in her column. ACT received 25,000 inquiries about children's television and responded by distributing a poster of parental guidelines for child TV viewing called "Treat TV with T.L.C." Apparently, "tens of thousands of 'T.L.C.' posters [were] handed out. Another ACT poster, 'Nutrition Games,' [was] designed to suggest appealing alternatives to TV-advertised snacks." [61] The nutrition poster was aimed at elementary school children and came with a teacher's guide. It was also ACT's first bilingual (Spanish and English) instructional effort. This and other outreach projects demonstrate ACT's commitment to education rather than censorship. However, ACT was not immune to censorious impulses; censorship is not an either/or choice of media reform groups but rather an inevitable component of their activism.

The Attack on Sugar

ACT never planned boycotts, but it did target specific TV ads for toys and food by filing complaints with the FTC. Over the years, ACT singled out TV ads produced by Hudson Pharmaceutical (maker of Spider-Man Vitamins), General Foods (Cocoa Pebbles), General Mills (Trix), Quaker Oats (Cap'n Crunch), and many other corporations. From 1978 to 1981, however, ACT did more than target particular ads. The FTC had always worked on a case-by-case basis, ruling on particular product ads, but in 1978 the FTC agreed to investigate ACT's contention that children's advertising as a whole unfairly exploited children. As usual, ACT went high profile with the antisugar campaign, and the TV and print media paid much attention to the FTC case. "You got it Twinkies-freaks," the *Chicago Tribune* condescendingly proclaimed, "ACT is going after TV advertisers, those Madison Avenue magicians who insist on selling children the chocolate-star-spangled illusion that life can be dandy with sugar and candy." [62]

ACT's mandate was to eliminate child-directed television ads in general, but the particular focus of its FTC complaint was sugared foods such as candy and breakfast cereal. At points in its campaign against sugared products, ACT seemed to directly contradict its "public debate in a free society" platform. In a 1975 speech to the Parent-Teacher Association, Charren boasted that "ACT representatives and other concerned individuals have joined in an attempt to persuade General Mills to stop their test marketing of a new breakfast food, 'Magic Puffs,' which has been advertised to children on television. A chemical analysis of the cereal indicated that it contained more than 53% sugar, and could therefore be more appropriately categorized as a candy than an essential ingredient in a nutritious breakfast. Based on precedents . . . the group has reason to believe that their efforts will be successful." [63] Charren added that "another nutritionally deficient cereal," a "sticky breakfast concoction" being test marketed as Mr. Wonderfull's Surprize, was permanently withdrawn from the market because of activist pressure. Consumers have every right to protest breakfast cereals, but product hit listing is exactly what ACT repeatedly rejected when TV programs were under attack. In other words, when Wildmon tried to deny *Dallas* to the world by boycotting the show's sponsors, Charren accused him of operating outside of the bounds of open debate in a free society, but ACT successfully obliterated Magic Puffs and Mr. Wonderfull's Surprize before they were released to the general public. It seems that the moral imperatives underlying the Coalition for Better Television's and ACT's campaigns were not as dichotomous as they appeared to be, in spite of the obvious political differences between the two groups. Wildmon's group objected to *Dallas* and other programs portraying sinful people, whereas Charren's group objected to the corrupting evils of sugar. Both felt they had the right to make decisions for other more vulnerable and less enlightened consumers.

In its campaign against sugared products, ACT vilified food companies, their ads, and sugar itself. ACT's stance, as summarized by a sympathetic member of the FTC, was that "sugar commercials . . . call upon the child to make very sophisticated health judgments, [but] until children are about to the age of twelve or so they lack the cognitive ability and experience to make long-range abstract decisions. . . . They don't know what a commercial is and lack the experience or maturity that adults have to treat commercials with some judgment."[64] These are dubious claims on several counts. For one thing, the speaker underestimates the intelligence of children, who voice skepticism about ads at an early age.[65] Moreover, he/she assumes that *adult* viewers make "very sophisticated health judgments" and "long-range abstract decisions" about food products they see advertised, when actually adults are just as likely as children to buy a food product because they like its image, not its nutritive value. In fact, marketers know that some health-conscious adults can be persuaded to buy nonnutritious foods such as candy and soda if they are labeled "low fat," "no fat," or "lite."

ACT's FTC actions were not simply based on the premise that commercials are inherently bad for easily duped children. ACT also specifically demonized ads for sugared products for not promoting proper ideas about how and when to consume foods. Objectionable ads did not advise children to brush their teeth immediately after eating sticky foods. ACT attacked the Mars Company for a Milky Way campaign that irresponsibly advised children to eat the candy bar "wherever you are . . . at work, rest, or play," and ACT denounced an ad showing a boy eating a Milky Way while white-water rafting. Such food was inappropriate for consumption while engaged in a wholesome sporting activity. Plus, it would have been impossible for the boy to brush immediately after consumption. ACT also attacked ads that suggested eating foods dangerously—by sucking and holding them in your mouth. In 1977, Charren complained to the American Dental Association about "ads for sticky between meal sweets that stress and emphasize that 'chewy chewy caramel' candy is 'fun on your tongue and made to last.'" She deemed these ads problematic because "it is the stickiness of sucrose and the frequency or duration of exposure that are the prime factors that determine the cariogenicity of sucrose. Yet, those are exactly the qualities that are glorified in candy commercials!"[66] ACT criticized ads that strove to appeal to the ways children take pleasure in sweets—by sucking, chewing, and slobbering. The ACT campaign *against* sucking and chewing and *for* prophylactic brushing was supposedly merely a matter of promoting good dental hygiene, but clearly this puritan dental campaign also depended on very *adult* and "proper" (and middle-class) conceptions of how children should sanitize their pleasures in the name of good health.[67] ACT sought, first, to protect children from their own naïveté, which supposedly allowed them to be seduced by dangerous advertisements, and, second, to reconstruct children as educated, mature consumers. The reform group implied that if advertisers would properly inform children about the healthful way to eat sugared foods, children would happily oblige and reform their eating habits. They would eat like adults.

ACT's campaign to eliminate deceptive and dangerous ads in order to control child desire for and consumption of food was symptomatic of the broader adult desire to control and discipline the child body. Many adults object to television on the grounds that it makes children unmanageable. Because of TV, the argument goes, children do not sleep, eat, study, or play when adults want them to. ACT took a moderate position by implying that the correct TV messages would help children use their bodies properly. More conservative TV critics argue that it is the television apparatus itself, regardless of content or message, that takes control of the child's body, addicting the child, making his/her eyes glaze over, draining him/her of creativity, and so forth. In spite of their differences, a similar moral imperative sustains both kinds of TV protest. Conservatives like Marie Winn (author of *The Plug-In Drug*) argued that *all* TV made children stupid and passive, whereas the liberal ACT argued that only *some* TV made children stupid and passive. Both conservative and liberal camps assumed that children are excessively malleable viewers, and both sought to protect and control the bodies and minds of implicitly middle-class child viewers. Winn posited that certain middle/upper-class-coded activities such as Victorian-style parlor games and visits to museums were inherently better than TV viewing, whereas ACT's abstract notion of "quality" indicated a disdain for "low-quality" or escapist television. Like Winn and many other intellectual television critics, ACT must be held up to scrutiny for "its simple advocacy of 'good' culture—as universal and self-evident—over mass culture, and its facile distinctions between the commercial and the artistic, the worthwhile and the merely sensually pleasurable."[68]

To argue that the adult desire for a controlled, rationally consuming child body has Foucauldian dimensions is not to disparage all adult control of children. My intention here is not to advocate permissive childrearing tactics. Rather, I am pointing out two things. First, ACT's antisugar campaign, apparently waged selflessly on behalf of children, was not merely an act of altruism; it was fueled by the adult desire not only for healthy, cavity-free children but also for tidy, properly bourgeois children who do not snack recklessly. Second, ACT's conceptualization of the proper middle-class child viewer was not a unique one. Rather, across the political spectrum, child TV viewers tend to be problematically figured as unsophisticated, feckless viewers desperately in need of education from inherently more sophisticated adult TV viewers. ACT represented a moderate incarnation of a typical adult attitude toward child viewers. That is, ACT did not argue that television was inherently destructive of the traditional family, as Winn did, or that TV viewing was inherently passive. Rather, the group argued that better programs (which often meant more "tasteful" programs that rated higher on ACT's cultural capital scale) and parental intervention could change TV "from a passive to a positive learning experience."[69] An educated child would view ads for sugared products with a critical eye, knowing that it was inappropriate to eat candy bars between meals (or at meals, or ever, for that matter). Whereas more conservative TV critics tend to see TV as a lost cause and "media literacy" as oxymoronic, ACT believed that through activism TV shows could be fixed and through education TV viewers could be fixed. Notwithstanding ACT's "simple advocacy of 'good' culture—as universal and self-evident—over mass culture" and however problematic ACT's view of the unenlightened child viewer may have been, ACT exhibited tenacious optimism and steadfastly stood its ground against adults who thought TV was unredeemable.

The manufacturers of Count Chocula and Lucky Charms certainly did not admire ACT's tenacious belief in the power of citizen advocacy. In response to ACT's antisugar campaign, in 1978, cereal manufacturers, advertisers, and broadcasters coordinated an attack on the FTC children's advertising rule-making proceedings, pooling together a reported $30 million for the lobbying effort. By 1980, the powerful prosugar industry lobby had won the legislative ear, and Congress voted to eliminate the FTC's authority to promulgate industrywide rules about unfair advertising. (Anticipation of the Reagan administration's deregulatory policies may have played some part in this turn of events.) Then, in 1981, the FTC staff said that "child-oriented television advertising is a legitimate cause for public concern" but recommended that the commission terminate the children's ads rule-making proceeding. The upshot was that the FTC's hands were tied. It could regulate individual ads on the basis that they were deceptive, but it could not consider whether all ads for candy and cereal—or advertising as a whole—might be unfair to children. The campaign to eliminate TV ads for sugared foods was officially dead.

Examination of three commercials from the late sixties and early seventies will clarify what ACT objected to in commercials and how ACT's campaign, although it officially failed, did influence (or censor, depending on your perspective) TV representations of sugared products while leaving unchanged some of the classic conventions of kid-targeted ads. An ad for Hostess Cupcakes opens with live-action kids spotting an animated cupcake captaining a ship. The cupcake invites them aboard, and they become animated. They go to Cupcake Island, where they are threatened by an octopus, who, it turns out, is easily placated with cupcakes. Captain Cupcake takes the kids home, and they return to their live-action form. Another animated ad, for General Mills's Frosty-O's cereal, takes place in the Wild West. A little man asks a big unshaven desperado why he's shooting holes into cakes. The answer: he's making them into "sugary doughnuts." The roughneck then commences to shoot at the little man's feet, until the man advises him that there's an easier way to make doughnuts. As the little man sings, "Shaped like little sugar-frosted doughnuts— Frosty-O's!," the cartoon ends with the two reconciled, eating Frosty-O's together, using an old saloon sign as a breakfast table. In a third commercial, a cartoon boy exclaims, "Look, a fire chief." An Ed Wynn sound-alike answers, "Not me! I'm a Twinkles sprinkler. I spray Twinkles with sugar in bright party colors." He uses a fire hose to coat the cereal with sugar, and then he and the boy happily consume Twinkles together, as the Twinkles sprinkler half sings, "Sugar-frosted Twinkles in bright party colors."

Largely because of ACT pressure, today's ads could never be like these. They portray play with guns, which is now forbidden in (censored from) children's ads; they do not state "with juice, toast, and milk, part of a complete breakfast" (an effort to make cereal seem more nutritious); and they gleefully use the word "sugar," which has now been euphemistically replaced by "honey." Although ACT's official complaint about these kinds of ads was that they promoted improper health messages, I believe that what ACT opposed was commercial narratives, which it saw as tricks used to deceive children. ACT pressure failed to eliminate such "tricks." The cupcake ad depicts the alluring fantasy of entering the world of animation; the exciting movement between cartoon and live-action worlds is still a convention in many children's ads. The Frosty-O's commercial plays on a favorite kid genre, the Western, and the Twinkles ad features a favorite kid character type, the firefighter. All three make sugared foods into sites of fun and adventure. Even if ads can no longer praise sugar as a high-energy food, sweets persist as transformative agents in the world of kid's television. Starburst candies, for example, change boring schoolrooms into tsunami-flooded fruit-fests. "Children's advertising offers an appealing vision of a world where 'kids rule.' Like most popular entertainments, commercials are utopian in some respects—portraying a childhood world more exciting, intense, and exhilarating than everyday life." [70] In protesting commercials for sugared products, ACT implicitly sought not only to eliminate bad health messages but also to remove intensity and exhilaration from children's TV commercials.

Sugar Paranoia

From today's perspective, an antisugar crusade may seem laughable or eccentric, but ACT's antisugar campaign was far from trivial. In the seventies, sugar was as demonized as fat is in the nineties. A plethora of anti-sugar books and articles enjoyed popular success. [71] Sugar was the highly contested subject of legal and governmental debate, and in 1973, doctors testified about sugar before the Senate Committee on Nutrition and Human Needs. The senators and doctors debated whether or not sugar was an "antinutrient" and whether or not it was fair to label sugar a "carbo-hydrate." Previously, the FTC had made sugar companies stop advertising sugar as a nutrient and an energy builder. [72] One reason that ACT could not continue its antisugar campaign in the eighties was undoubtedly because public anxieties about sugar had died out; the new villain was cholesterol, and the new panacea was oat bran. [73]

The U.S. health-food movement of the seventies rejected First World processed foods, embracing and romanticizing unrefined Asian foods. One health-foodist, in fact, attributes the rise of the movement to the U.S. rapprochement with China. At a time of backlash against sixties radicalism, the health-food movement was vaguely countercultural, a tepid expression of antiwar and hippy sentiments. Health-food advocates were not only perceived by conservatives as unpatriotic for rejecting hotdogs, meatloaf, and other classics of American cuisine but also as radical, or even pinko, for promulgating nutritional pacifism: to eat vegetarian was to eat without killing. Vegetarianism was also symptomatic of a widespread cynical attitude toward the government in the wake of Vietnam and Watergate. In the seventies, there was a burgeoning awareness of the dangers of pesticides in produce and hormones in meat. With this awareness came the realization that the government was not doing anything about it. As vegetarian guru Anna Thomas put it, "In these strange seventies, ominous and dramatic new reasons are compelling people to reexamine their eating habits." [74] The U.S. military continued to spray napalm and Agent Orange in Southeast Asia, while back in the States, the banning of DDT pesticide spray in 1970 represented a battle won for health-foodists.

Along with the health-food movement, sugar paranoia reached its peak in the seventies, and ACT's campaign both benefited from and contributed to this paranoia. William Dufty's antisugar polemic, *Sugar Blues*, was a 1975 best-seller. This book was a virtual bible for the health-food movement. Simultaneously left wing in its critique of the sugar industry's imperialism and capitalist opportunism and right wing in its moral tone and antidrug message, the book is hard to peg politically. Comparing sugar to opium, morphine, and heroin and calling sugar companies "pushers," Dufty blamed sugar for everything from acne to scurvy and bubonic plague. Although Dufty's critique of sugar focused on its potential for inflicting bodily harm, he also criticized sugar's potential for spiritual and moral harm. Sugar could blight body and soul. Infused with antihippie sentiment and fire-and-brimstone moral rhetoric,[75] Dufty's text easily lends support to Elizabeth Walker Mechling and Jay Mechling's argument that the pervasive antisugar sentiment of the seventies can be read as a backlash against the countercultural drug and sex "excesses" of the sixties. As Susan Willis observes, "[T]he stand against sugar [was] . . . a call for a moral return to social order." [76]

The antisugar crusade should also be considered in light of cultural anxieties about Vietnam and Vietnam veterans. Antisugar crusaders aligned sugar "addiction" with moral and physical weakness, whereas those who could defy the "diseasestablishment" (Western doctors and sugar companies) and kick the habit were strong. They were winners; sugar junkies were losers. In 1970, 96 percent pure heroin was readily available on the streets of Saigon, and around 28 percent of the U.S. troops took hard drugs. Over half a million became addicted.[77] As those troops returned to the United States, veteran drug addiction became a national concern. To those who reacted to addicted vets with moral outrage, such troops were symbolic of the entire Vietnam endeavor: we had failed because we had been literal and figurative drug addicts—losers.[78] Dufty went so far as to blame sugar for fostering a desire for other drugs in Vietnam: "Refined sucrose might have worked as a stimulant through World Wars I and II; but by the time of Korea and Viet Nam, the troops were so glutted with sugar that many turned on to hashish . . . pot . . . grass and even stronger addictive drugs" (original ellipses).[79]

Dufty praised the fortitude of the Vietcong, who had no refined sugar and ate brown rice. It was their sugar-free moral fortitude that made our Asian enemies superior to us. Dufty explained that a Japanese philosopher who had recently returned from Saigon told him, "If you really expect to conquer the North Vietnamese . . . you must drop Army PX's on them—sugar, candy, and Coca-Cola. That will destroy them faster than bombs."[80] In effect, this was the strategy the United States inadvertently deployed against its South Vietnamese allies, whom it supplied with strength-sapping Minute Rice. In 1971, a Pentagon official explained that Vietnamese rice was "useless to a soldier in the field since it would have to be cooked in the field."[81] To remedy the situation, the Pentagon had been supplying instant white rice to the South Vietnamese since 1968, at a cost of almost $1 million a month. In Dufty's argument, the rice, like Coca-Cola, made the South Vietnamese soldiers weak, dependent, and malnourished. There is, no doubt, a grain of truth in this; Dufty is right to criticize the introduction of refined sugar and Minute Rice into Vietnam as imperialistic and detrimental to the health of the Vietnamese. Where he errs is in his casting of sucrose and the U.S. "diseasestablishment" as the conspiratorial villains in his melodrama. The introduction of refined sugar and instant rice was one of a multitude of signs that the United States did not understand Vietnamese culture, that it did not understand its allies or its enemies in Southeast Asia.[82] Unwanted U.S. processed foods served as metonymic reminders of the unwanted U.S. military presence.

Certainly, the U.S. crusade against sugar in the seventies was not a direct result of veteran drug addiction, countercultural backlash, and U.S. defeat in Vietnam. It is not my intention to imply such historical causality but rather to show several possible ways of understanding why antisugar alarmism took off in the seventies. Antisugar sentiment should not be dismissed as a senseless, widespread whim; nutritional fads are meaningful cultural phenomena. Without an understanding of the antisugar movement, ACT's antisugar campaign might seem trivial or misguided, when it was not. Although ACT did not speak of sugar in Dufty's radical, pedantic terms, the group certainly profited from his high-profile attack. Judging from press coverage of the campaign and the fact that the FTC actually listened to ACT, ACT's campaign clearly tapped into already-existing cultural concerns.

The Attack on Chester Cheetah

After the antisugar campaign, ACT's nutritional concerns would resurface only tangentially in its campaign against a cartoon program designed to sell Chee-tos. The Frito-Lay Company tried to make its animated spokescat, Chester Cheetah, into a regular cartoon in 1992. By this time, the FCC had already rejected ACT's petitions against product-based programs such as *Strawberry Shortcake* and *Transformers*, which were created to promote toys. But ACT had a slightly different case with the Chester Cheetah cartoon. Chester Cheetah had been a well-established commercial logo since 1986. The character had not existed before Frito-Lay created it to sell Chee-tos, and it had not existed as a toy. It was therefore possible for ACT to argue that Chester Cheetah existed purely as an advertising character and that the cartoon would therefore serve as an ad for Chee-tos. Since commercial speech is not as extensively protected by the First Amendment as noncommercial speech, ACT saw its attack on the show as noncensorious.

Interestingly, throughout its Chester Cheetah FCC petition, ACT's rhetoric consistently condemned the show not only as a "program-length commercial" but also as unhealthy because of its lead character's passion for junk food. Although ACT did not explicitly make its good-nutrition platform part of its attack, it included nutritional analysis of Chee-tos Paws in the appendix of its FCC petition, consistently referred to Chee-tos as "cheese-flavored," and referred to Chee-tos Paws as "cheese-flavored snacks *supposedly* shaped like the paws of a cheetah" (my emphasis),[83] as if part of the problem with Chee-tos Paws was their lack of verisimilitude. Footnotes in the FCC petition labeled Chee-tos as junk food, attacked their fat content, and quoted a professor who said that " 'junk food' programming perverts the marketplace of ideas."[84] However, ACT stated that "although Chee-tos Paws may be a 'junk food,' the case does not turn on this fact,"[85] realizing that having already lost its nutrition case at the FTC, it certainly was not going to win it at the FCC.

In fact, ACT did not officially win this case; the Bush FCC simply was not going to rule against *any* broadcast content unless it could be declared "indecent," like Howard Stern's graphic radio monologues. Frito-Lay eventually withdrew its plans for the cartoon project, probably realizing that because of protest, *Yo! It's the Chester Cheetah Show* might have done more harm than good for Frito-Lay profits. Frito-Lay claimed it was just a coincidence that the project fell through at exactly the same time that ACT was attacking it, but Charren triumphantly announced, "We feel we have zapped, for the time being, the problem of logos turning into half-hour programs."[86] At the same time, apparently in response to the ACT pressure on Frito-Lay, Kraft dropped its plans to make a cartoon starring its Macaroni and Cheese promotional character, Cheesasaurus Rex.

In its FCC petition, ACT avoided describing Chester Cheetah as a "real" character in order to maintain that he was merely a commercial logo. Of his character, the ACT petition notes only that he is "crazy about Chee-tos and often appears wearing sunglasses. He also likes rap music." ACT said nothing about the politics of Chester's ethnicity, barring the connotations of "rap music." Chester Cheetah was a jive-talking cool cat whose rhyming speech was unmistakably coded as black. (Frito-Lay was an old hand at appropriating the ethnic order; in the seventies, the company created the Mexican-stereotyped Frito Bandito, which Latino protesters forced off the air.)[87] In his more recent incarnations, Chester Cheetah's voice is noticeably less black coded. In its own newsletters, ACT had been outspoken about racial stereotyping in cartoons, and the group surely realized that Chester was an African American stereotype. In fact, one of the cosupporters of ACT's FCC petition against Chester Cheetah was Black Citizens for a Fair Media. But this group's complaints against Chester Cheetah were not explicitly stated anywhere in the press coverage of the Chester Cheetah protest. Perhaps as a tactical maneuver, the politics of Chester's ethnicity took a backseat to ACT's prochild politics. On a practical level, Chester's black stereotyping could not have been the focus of the petition; ACT knew it would lose if this had been its grounds of critique. Regardless of what ACT members or Black Citizens for a Fair Media might have believed about the show's racial politics, in order to censor it, they had to prove that it was exploitative commercial speech.

Action for/against Censorship?

Some of ACT's activities were censorious in effect. ACT influenced cereal commercial conventions, played a major role in keeping *Yo! It's the Chester Cheetah Show* off the air, protested deceptive advertising, and was in part responsible for network self-regulation of representations of sexism, racism, and violence. On the other hand, ACT actively worked against censorship by opposing TV sponsor boycotting, the Family Viewing Hour, and anti-indecency legislation and by promoting viewer "education" and appreciation of "quality" programs.

To argue that ACT censored is not to condemn ACT but to complicate the notion of what it means to censor. Prior to the attack on *Yo! It's the Chester Cheetah Show*, ACT had attacked specific ads but not specific shows. Even when asking the FCC to ban all product-based programs, which ACT maintained were really commercials, ACT avoided publicly hit listing particular shows. (Conversely, the files in the ACT archive indicate that internally "Strawberry Shortcake" may have functioned as a code word for the anti-product-based programs campaign.) Yet ACT did hit list and induce the censorship of *Yo! It's the Chester Cheetah Show*, and its attack on ads, coterminous with a widespread social movement against sugar, resulted in dramatic changes in how sugared cereal could be marketed. It is true that commercial speech does not enjoy the same First Amendment protection that noncommercial speech does, but that does not mean that attacking and eliminating commercial speech is not an act of censorship.

It would be misguided to lump ACT together with more overtly censorious media activist groups. Clearly organizations such as the Moral Majority and the Coalition for Better Television did actively labor, and laboriously pray, for the broad-based censorship of television they found to be immoral or anti-Christian. These groups exhibited a greater power and will to censor than ACT ever did. If ACT had a moral agenda, it was mild mannered and innocuous compared to the holier-than-thou sexist, racist, and homophobic fundamentalist Christian agenda. But as different as the liberal ACT was from conservative activists, the Moral Majority and ACT do not merely represent procensorship and anticensorship contingents. Rather, they represent different or competing censorship contingents.

The concepts of censorship and free speech are often waved like banners in the United States, as if their meanings were immanent. But the various meanings of censorship and free speech are created and re-created only through their social enactment. Ultimately, whether or not censorship is "bad" does not inhere in censorship itself as a concept but in how censorship is culturally executed. For example, many of us would agree that the Fairness Doctrine was an example of "good" censorship. Eliminated by the Reagan FCC, the Fairness Doctrine directed broadcast license holders "to devote a reasonable amount of time to the coverage of controversial issues of public importance and to do so fairly by affording a reasonable opportunity for contrasting viewpoints to be voiced on these issues." The mandate to provide "balanced presentation of . . . opposing viewpoints" meant that if a broadcaster expressed a controversial or slanderous opinion on the air, someone on the other side of the issue (only two sides were assumed for any issue) would get a chance to rebut, free of charge.[88] The Fairness Doctrine regulated broadcasters' speech so that others might have access to speech. However, in the early sixties, the Democratic National Committee orchestrated a covert campaign to use the Fairness Doctrine to eliminate the far right's right to free speech: "Our massive strategy was to use the Fairness Doctrine to challenge and harass right-wing [radio] broadcasters and hope that the challenges would be so costly to them that they would be inhibited and decide it was too expensive to continue."[89] The committee used the Fairness Doctrine to get free airtime devoted to the support of New Frontier policies. This is a good example of how, in the course of its social execution, "free speech" is not inherently liberatory. The committee used access to literal and figurative free speech to curtail someone else's speech. Most journalists saw the Fairness Doctrine as censorious, whereas most activists saw it as an anchor for free speech, but it could actually be both.

Censorship and free speech are competing, heterogeneous, nonbinary cultural constants. Even the adamantly anticensorship American Civil Liberties Union must acknowledge cases in which there are "competing civil rights," in which value judgments must be made and someone must be censored. It is crucial to argue for a notion of competing censorships in the United States, where censorship is so frequently denied discursive existence at the national level. It is precisely because the United States does not have official state censorship and is not overtly fascistic that censorship can thrive here. Censorship can never be challenged within a system where it is insufficiently acknowledged. Admitting censorship's prevalence does not have to make one into a despairing cynic. Rather, acknowledging the pervasiveness of censorious impulses—from the left, right, center, and every other direction—enables critical thought, discussion, and activism. It enables one to go beyond the all-too-common, politically narrow position of being merely for or against censorship.

Any number of media reform groups could be taken as case studies illustrating censorship's inevitability. ACT was not the most censorious or worst media reform group but rather one of the best—the best at simultaneously resisting and advocating censorship; the best at gaining access to the FCC because of its moderate self-presentation; and the best at getting press coverage because of its savvy media tactics and its maternal image. But ACT was not unique in other ways. The group's concerns about child consumption of both sugar and TV were problematic in the same ways that many adult campaigns for children are. Campaigns for children's rights frequently evince class bias and blindness to cultural differences linked to gender, race, and ethnicity; presume the authorization to speak for all children; myopically focus on the local at the expense of broader, global contexts; and depend on simply drawn moral lines.[90]

ACT admirably tried to force broadcasters to serve children, not advertisers. Anyone who feels that broadcasting should not be subservient to commercialism owes a debt to ACT for raising public awareness of how the FCC and the TV industry operate and for attempting to force programming changes through means other than casting a Nielsen family vote. Certainly, ACT should not be demonized for its well-meaning reform efforts. But it is important to examine why ACT's activism was palatable to the press, the government, and much of the public. In the seventies, ACT was tolerated and managed by the FCC. In the eighties, Reagan's FCC, particularly Chairman Mark Fowler, dismissed ACT as a group of censorious, meddlesome kooks. The very foundations of liberal media activism were SNAFU: situation normal all fowler-ed up.

Toys, TV, and Toaster Pictures

Children's Entertainment and

the Free Market Mentality

The product-based cartoons of the eighties incurred the wrath of many adults because of their commercial intent: they were explicitly designed to sell toys and other kid merchandise. Never before had an entire genre of television programming been subject to such vociferous attack by censorious adults. The protesters (ACT, among others) did have valid grounds for complaint: the shows were a product of the conservative politics of deregulation, a politics that defined democracy as the capitalist right to profit. Yet there was more to these programs than their commercial intent. Many critics assume that product-based programs were a homogeneous mass, but I take these media texts as focal points for reading both eighties deregulatory politics and the race and gender politics of children's entertainment.

In the first major article written on product-based cartoons, Tom Engelhardt argues that in "program-length commercials,"

> [p]lots repeat each other from one show to another, no matter who produces them. Whether aimed at little girls and syrupy sweet, or at little boys and filled with "action" sequences in which the forces of Good triumph, however provisionally, over the forces of Evil, they involve an obsession with theft, capture, and kidnapping (emphasis on the "kid"), with escape, chase, and recapture, with deception and mechanical transformation from one shape or state of being to another— all strung together to make each show a series of predictable permutations. Lame homilies (what the industry calls "prosocial messages") are then tagged on and the shows are set in motion with crude animation techniques.[1]

Although Engelhardt's obvious disdain for the shows indicates little effort to understand what might have made them so appealing to child viewers, his essay does succinctly describe some of product-based cartoons' central qualities: those intended for boys have more "action-packed" fight scenes than those for girls have; plots center around conflicts between good and evil; theft, capture, and recapture are often the focus of the action; in some boys' cartoons, mechanical transformation is a central factor; prosocial messages, about the value of cooperation or friendship, for example, are commonly (and often awkwardly) worked into the plots; and many product-based cartoons are cheaply made and not very smoothly animated. Interestingly, Engelhardt opens with the girl/boy ("syrupy sweet"/"action") binary only to elide that binary and argue that the cartoons are basically identical regardless of their gender coding.

Like many critics of eighties children's programming, Engelhardt bases his evaluations on adult notions of aesthetic and narrative quality. He gives the reader little understanding of *what* millions of children viewed and, presumably, for innumerable reasons took pleasure in. Like Engelhardt, many concerned legislators, parents, and pressure groups assume that children's pleasures in commercial, noneducational toys and TV are false, even dangerous pleasures. They argue that toy companies use toys and their television tie-ins to brainwash children: first, the TV program encourages children to coerce their parents to buy them toys, and second, the show "programs" children to play in certain ways with these new toys. Protesters assume, in other words, that TV toys endanger children's creativity because the kids merely plug the toys into the TV narratives with which they are already familiar. Such a conspiracy theory even seems to be confirmed at the level of authorial intention; toy producers explicitly state that TV toys succeed precisely because they "have play built into them."

Most opponents of the product-based genre have refrained from discussing what the genre actually is, preferring to attack its coercive commercialism.[2] Critics say that identifying the "program-length commercial" is a matter of common sense, whereas defenders of the genre within the industry claim that the "program-length commercial" does not hold water as a legal category to be targeted for government regulation. Television producers and executives argue that product-based programming cannot be singled out for censorhip because all TV is commercially motivated, and you cannot attempt to curtail such obviously product-based shows as *Transformers* without also attacking more "wholesome" merchandise-promoting programs such as *Sesame Street*. I believe that in order to really understand what was going on with these controversial cartoons and what was at stake politically and culturally in the controversy, it is crucial to discuss the genre in a way that can account for market interests without discounting narrative issues. It is easy to dismiss product-based programming as merely "bad" or, from the industry's standpoint, as merely profitable, but such evaluations do not help us understand what the shows actually are or why children might enjoy them. Rather than just being for or against these shows, I propose to investigate the multiple politically charged meanings they offer to viewers.

Product-based programs are not, in fact, identical, although they appear that way to many grown-up viewers. There are basically three kinds of protagonists in product-based programs: muscled superheroes, mechanical transformers, and nurturing caretakers.[3] Muscled-superhero cartoons are boy-targeted action cartoons featuring characters with superhuman capabilities. They have tremendous physical strength, and they use their special powers to fight evil forces. Many of these characters have secret or double identities, and their transformations from one form to the other often constitute the shows' most climactic moments. The muscled-superhero cartoons are often set in a vague future or past, and the characters often have mystical powers.[4] Popular muscled-superhero cartoons include *He-Man and the Masters of the Universe*, *Thundercats*, and *Teenage Mutant Ninja Turtles*.

Mechanical-transformer cartoons are another extremely popular kind of action show directed at boys. Mechanical transformers can change from one kind of machine (or occasionally animal) to another. Transformer cartoons emphasize technology and tend to contain fewer supernatural elements than the muscled-superhero cartoons do. For instance, in each episode of the muscled-superhero cartoon *Thundercats*, to activate the magical Eye of Thundera housed in the hilt of the Sword of Omens, Lion-o bellows, "Thunder, thunder, thunder, Thundercats," followed by a climactic "HO!" Conversely, the culminating moment of the mechanical-transformer show *Voltron* comes when the spaceship group leader says, "Activate interlock. . . . Dynatherms connected. . . . Infracells up. . . . Megathrusters are go. . . . Let's go Voltron!," and all the ships merge to form Voltron, a gigantic space robot. Although some mechanical-transformer shows, such as *Voltron*, do have magical elements in them and the muscled superheroes do use technical devices, the most special climactic moment is technological and mechanical in the former and magical and fantastic in the latter.[5] Mechanical-transformer shows include *Transformers*, *Challenge of the GoBots*, *Voltron*, and *The Mighty Orbots*. As Stephen Kline has remarked, citing Gina Marchetti, these boys' cartoons are like adult action-adventure narratives of the Arnold Schwarzenegger ilk in that the visual display of violence at times displaces characterization and plot development.[6]

There are some transforming girls' toys—dolls that "grow" older or younger, lockets that turn into combs, and pregnant dolls with pop-open bellies, but cartoon characters intended for girls are very rarely transformers. Characters for girls may have strength of resolve, but they do not have muscles and rarely change form.[7] Rather, as static caretakers, they help bring about change in others. The protagonists of nurturing-caretaker cartoons do not exist within an explicit mother-father-child family triad and do not directly assume the culturally sanctioned female subject position of daughter or mother. Nonetheless, the characters are maternal in the most traditional sense; they are loving problem solvers who nurture not only each other but also natural phenomena such as fruit growth (*Strawberry Shortcake*), flower growth (*Rose Petal Place*), and rainbow coloring (*Rainbow Brite*). Although the characters in them are less dynamic, these cartoons are similar to the adult woman's film in terms of their emphasis on interpersonal relationships and female bonding.

Fostering Collectability

If boys' and girls' cartoons and toys seem as diametrically opposed as *Rambo* and *Pretty Woman*, they do have at least one trait in common: their success depends on the enthusiasm of youthful toy collectors. Intertextuality, which fosters toy collectability, is central to Marsha Kinder's explanation of the "supersystem." She describes a supersystem as

> a network of intertextuality constructed around a figure or group of figures from pop culture who are either fictional (like TMNT [Teenage Mutant Ninja Turtles], the characters from *Star Wars*, the Super Mario Brothers, the Simpsons, the Muppets, Batman, and Dick Tracy) or "real" (like Pee-Wee Herman, Elvis Presley, Marilyn Monroe, Madonna, Michael Jackson, the Beatles, and, most recently, the New Kids on the Block). In order to be a supersystem, the network must cut across several modes of image production; must appeal to diverse generations,

classes, and ethnic subcultures, who in turn are marketed with diverse strategies; must foster "collectability" through a proliferation of related products; and must undergo a sudden increase in commodification, the success of which reflexively becomes a "media event" that dramatically accelerates the growth curve of the system's commercial success.[8]

In sum, the supersystem is a megahit entertainment concept around which toys, films, television shows, and video games revolve. Obviously, any corporate producer of children's entertainment wants to make a product with supersystem potential, and each Saturday morning program or syndicated afternoon program might be seen as a bid for supersystem status. Any children's program designed to promote an extensive toy line has built-in supersystem potential.[9] The existence of multiple texts that consumers read in relation to each other ("intertextuality") is central to the potential supersystem and the product-based program; a program's success depends on recognizability incurred from consuming other products.

To foster collectability, toy companies must create numerous distinct characters. The more characters and accessories there are, such as vehicles and weapons, the more toys can be created. Often a toy company will suggest or, more often, require that TV producers add new characters or accessories that the toy company has developed. A *TV Guide* writer explains that "[t]oy company research-and-development staffers sometimes have a hand in adding new characters to kids' shows that may be introduced as toys. Mattel routinely showed new *He-Man* and *She-Ra: Princess of Power* products with character potential to Filmation executives, who sometimes incorporated them and sometimes didn't. That's how Enchanta the Swan, a *She-Ra* vehicle, was added to the show."[10] Other authors more candidly acknowledge that animators do exactly what the toy companies who contract them tell them to do. Emily Sacher's research indicates that licensees can have tremendous influence over how their properties are displayed: "They can specify how their characters must look, what they can and cannot say, and what environments they must live in. They can tell a lunchbox maker, for instance, that the characters' clothing is not appropriate and must be changed. When [television] programming is involved, they can demand to see—and edit—story lines."[11]

Producing numerous appealing and differentiated characters benefits toy companies by fostering collecting among young consumers. That's why the muscled-superhero, mechanical-transformer, and nurturing-caretaker cartoons have enormous casts of characters, and that's why producers attempt to give each character some kind of unique, identifiable quality. On *G.I. Joe*, a macho-techno show somewhere between the muscled superheroes and mechanical transformers, the Bazooka character is coded as unique by his name, and his name is reinforced by the fact that he carries the team's bazooka and chews bubble gum; on *Thundercats*, each character has a special trait like speed or intelligence.[12] The nurturing caretakers are also individually coded: the Care Bears each have a different character-indicating mark on their bellies (a cupcake, sun, or moon, for example), the *Strawberry Shortcake* characters are linked to different fruits or fruit desserts, the *Rainbow Brite* characters are aligned with different colors, and so on. To increase sales to young collectors, all three types of programming introduce new characters as often as possible. The Care Bears were quickly joined by the Care Bear Cousins, and Strawberry Shortcake made many new friends when she took a trip around the world and when she went to Big Apple City for a bake-off. Indeed, one might postulate that the reason friendship is so important in nurturing-caretaker cartoons is that new friends must constantly be made so that new characters (and thus new toys and the possibility for more profits) can be introduced. Likewise, in the superhero and mechanical-transformer shows, conflicts cannot be on a small scale; characters must be at war because it generates more potential for character proliferation than small-scale battle or one-on-one conflict would. In other words, armies of characters mean armies of toys. Toymakers' and licensees' desire to make profits of potentially supersystemic proportions thus influences both the characterization and the conflicts in programs based on toys. The large number of characters in all three types of programs is dizzying to most adult viewers, but proficient child viewers manage to keep the characters straight.

In fact, one study of *Transformers* found that adult viewers of the show were confused, had trouble following the basic story lines, and were amazed at how complex the technical language was ("astroid of organic nature," "disturb my cerebral circuitry"). One adult said, "[T]here are times when the show seemed over my head." The study's author, Joan E. Aitken, used three different indexes to determine the reading grade level of *Transformers* dialogue. Aitken found that the show's reading level fluctuated between tenth, eleventh, and twelfth grade.[13] Although it may be

methodologically questionable to rate cartoon dialogue using scales designed to evaluate written texts, it is nonetheless rather interesting that a
show designed primarily for elementary school children would use such
complex language. The fact that adults do not get *Transformers* and that the
language and plots are fairly complex may be exactly what appeals to child
viewers.

Many adult critics do not see the child's ability to keep track of a multitude of characters and plot lines as evidence that the stories are complicated or that child viewers are skilled. Rather, they see such viewers as
dupes; if they remember all the characters and they care about them, it
is because they are brainwashed or do not realize that the shows are not
"real life." This seemingly pitiful child viewer is not unlike the stereotypical adult female soap opera viewer. Many critics imagine that, like
the infantilized female fan of film and TV melodrama, the child viewer
"overidentifies" with the image. Whereas boy viewers will outgrow their
supposed predicament of overidentification, girls are more likely to be accused of such pathology for the rest of their lives. What was novel about the
product-based program controversy, however, was that boys were generally seen as more susceptible to overidentification than girls were. Like the
demonized *Power Rangers* of the nineties, eighties shows were particularly
feared as instigators of violent imitation among excessively identifying boy
viewers who supposedly did not understand the difference between cartoon violence and real-life violence.

In the "viewing-equals-violence" equation, "boy viewers" are unprob-
lematically homogeneous entities: cartoon violence simply makes all boys
violent. As far as the industry is concerned, however, all boys are not the
same; there are differences among viewers. This is what the industry refers
to as "demographics."

Animality and Questionable Invisibility

Toy and cartoon designers know that ethnic diversity is profitable: nonwhite characters will tap into wider consumer audiences or what the industry might simply call "diverse demographic groups." With their darker
coloring and occasionally nonwhite-coded voices, the nonwhite characters in product-based cartoons are explicitly designed differently from the
white characters. Nonwhite dolls often look like white dolls dipped in dark

paint, but nonwhite cartoon characters are crafted more carefully. These characters may mark an aesthetic improvement over nonwhite dolls, but that is about as far as the improvement goes. What is crude about so much product-based programming, I would argue, is not its minimal animation, as many disdainful adults claim, but the fact that in these cartoons, nonwhite characters are drained of otherness by narratives that rarely explicitly acknowledge cultural or ethnic differences.

Examining the industry's stance on cartoon tokenism reveals some of the contradictions embedded in "nondifference." An executive at one production company explains the company's concern with "minority issues" this way: "We make an affirmative effort to try to include minorities, the elderly, and the handicapped in a positive way. . . . We do change the shading. . . . We do try to stay away from having negative characters who are minorities. So usually the minorities end up being included in the extras. But where possible, we do try to include them in the main characters." [14] There are several ambivalent messages here. The company wants to include "positive" minority characters; it defines a positive minority character as one that is not negative. Minorities are extras, not central characters, because they could only be negative characters if they were central. Why? And why is it not possible to include them as regular characters? I would guess that according to industry logic, it is rarely possible to include nonwhite characters as leads because production companies do not want to risk low ratings or potential controversy by doing an "ethnic" show rather than a "normal" show.[15] Adding a few characters who are not white may make the show appeal to more viewers, but this is as far as the industry will go since it assumes that an all Asian or all African American show would appeal only to Asians or African Americans. In any case, the executive reassured me, the question of minority characters is moot because most of the characters her company animates are animals.

What does it mean to say that an animated anthropomorphic animal does not have an ethnicity? First, such an assertion erases an animation history rife with examples of ethnically stereotyped animals. Historically, cartoon animalization has been a strategy used to mask overt (and therefore potentially controversial or censorable) ethnic stereotyping. Apes or monkeys were often coded as black in classic theatrical cartoons. Bosco, a black Van Beuren Studio character from the twenties, was not quite human but not quite animal either. Animalization can occlude whiteness too. As Ariel Dorfman and Armand Mattelart argue in their classic exposé of Disney cultural imperialism, Donald Duck is not "just a duck," as the Disney company might assert; rather, he is a white, male, and above all American capitalist "duck." Second, the industry's claim that animal characters have no ethnicity implies that there are representational sites where ethnicity can be successfully elided and images can be stripped of social inscriptions.[16] Censors cannot prove that a cartoon dog or frog with black-coded speech or mannerisms actually "is" black. And cartoonists can always accuse censors of being racist for saying that certain vocabulary and speech patterns are inherently black.

Puppet ethnicity is equally fraught with difficulty. Clifford, the host of the 1996 show *Muppets Tonight*, had red dreadlocks and a voice clearly coded as African American. His previous appearances were in black venues such as the *Arsenio Hall Show*, and the African American voice artist who performed Clifford says he considered using Jamaican or Rastafarian intonations for the character before settling on a nonforeign (but implicitly black) accent. But both the voice artist and Jim Henson Productions declined to officially declare the character's race.[17] Even when a character is patently coded as black, producers will often not say so, perhaps out of a desire to avoid controversy at all costs. Ultimately, animality and puppetness function as trump cards that enable producers to tell censorious activists, "Don't be ridiculous! Frogs can't be black," or "Ernie and Bert can't be gay, they're puppets!" *Sesame Street* is good at having its cake and eating it too. In the seventies, it proudly declared that Roosevelt Franklin was a black puppet. If it is possible for one puppet to "really" be black, how is it impossible for other puppets to "really" be gay? It's not really a question of puppet ontology. Puppets, like animated characters, can be gay or black, just as they can be male or female. If producers deny that gay puppets or cartoon characters are possible, it is because they do not think gayness is a desirable quality.

The eighties superhero show *Thundercats* attempted to erase ethnicity altogether by seemingly making all of its characters nonethnic animal creatures. Aside from the two cute little housecatlike Thundercats, probably thrown in to offer some "girl appeal," the Thundercats are half cat, half human bipeds with humanoid muscles and feline heads. They are the only survivors of the defunct planet Thundera, which was blown up, like Superman's Krypton. Lion-o, Tigra, and Cheetarah have lion, tiger, and

Figure 2. Panthro, the African American Thundercat.

cheetah markings, manelike hair, and human mouths. Although real feline noses are wide and flat, these characters' noses are narrow. Verisimilitude is sacrificed in order to code the characters as Anglo. Panthro, conversely, has wide lips, a flattened nose, and speech audibly coded as African American (figure 2). He is the smartest Thundercat when it comes to technical matters such as vehicle repair and electronics ingenuity. He is also visually the most frightening Thundercat. Although they are all highly muscled and have scary catlike eyes, Panthro is hypermuscled, and spikes protrude from his costume. Panthro's spikes code his body as a site of pain; this visual impression may make him seem like the coolest character, or it may negate his characteristic intelligence, othering him. While Panthro's intelligence is positive, in industry terms, his visual image evokes violence, which is considered a negative quality.

Nurturing-caretaker cartoons also tend to include one or two African American characters who, at the narrative level, are just like all the other characters. The token African American on *Strawberry Shortcake* is named Orange Blossom. Her name is significant: whereas most other characters on the program are named after desserts, this character is inedible, a fruit-to-be that it would be inappropriate to consume. In its promotional book, the American Greetings Corporation explains that "Orange Blossom is possibly the prettiest little girl in Strawberryland. Despite her good looks, Orange Blossom is a shy little person who tends to downplay her own appearance and accomplishments." [18] Orange Blossom is actually not particularly pretty. Her features are virtually identical to the other characters' except that she is rendered darker. Producers "do change the shading," as the executive said, in order to maximize potential for product differentiation and appeal.

By changing the shading without changing the story, animators may simply want to avoid controversy. But do such cartoons imply that racism no longer exists in cartoons or that, in general, racism is no longer a problem? This is a very difficult question, and one that has been asked of a number of TV shows that picture people of color without explicitly addressing racial issues, such as *Julia*, *I Spy*, and *The Cosby Show*. Sut Jhally and Justin Lewis argue that by eliminating race as an issue, *Cosby* "helps to cultivate an impression, particularly among white people, that racism is no longer a problem in the United States. Our audience study revealed that the overwhelming majority of white TV viewers [of *Cosby*] felt racism was a sin of the past." [19] Cartoon tokenism—the casual inclusion of a character of color in a fantasy world where conflict is constant but racial discrimination is nonexistent—may cultivate a similar "postracism" impression.

In 1982, Michael R. Winston argued that television had shifted from representing African Americans stereotypically to erasing them almost completely. Winston noted that in the sixties and seventies, some of the worst televisual racial stereotyping disappeared. However, more "realistic" images of African Americans did not fill the representational void. Programs such as *The Beulah Show* and *Amos 'n' Andy*, which Winston considers "obviously hostile forms of racial programming," vanished, but the issue of television's inadequate representation of blacks was not resolved. Winston states that "the most significant distortion has not been the misportrayal [that is, stereotyping] of Negroes, but their exclusion from programs depicting developments in which they played important roles. *'Simple exclusion' may be the most insidious form of distortion, because it reinforces the false, but widely believed ideas that blacks have contributed little to the United States, and are significant only as 'a problem'* " (my emphasis). [20] Here, Winston speaks primarily of "nonfiction" news representations of African Americans. He illustrates his point with the example of television specials about wars that ignore roles played by blacks in those wars; blacks are only included in documentaries focusing on "racial problems." Winston concludes that although much explicit stereotyping has been eliminated from television, blacks are not better represented on TV now but rather *not* represented, a situation that seems to have improved since Winston wrote in 1982. Taking Winston's perspective, one might argue for the value of showing African American characters in cartoons without addressing issues of racial difference. In this way, blacks would be represented without being "problems."

The racial politics of product-based cartoons must be located within the larger context of the history of television cartoons' representation of people/animals of color. In the fifties, TV showed the cartoon "toms, coons, mulattos, mammies, and bucks" that had been produced for movie screens in the thirties and forties.[21] But in the sixties, largely in response to the Civil Rights movement, such stereotypes were considered unacceptable for television exhibition. There was a knee-jerk reaction in the TV industry, and blacks were virtually eliminated from television cartoons. Mexicans, Asians, and Native Americans were suddenly the archvillains in action shows like *Jonny Quest* or the bungling buffoons in comedy shows like *Gumby* or *Go-Go Gophers*, but blacks were virtually invisible in sixties cartoons. Bosco was out of the question, but Speedy Gonzalez and the Frito Bandito took his place. (Pressure from Latino activists eventually drove the latter off the air, as I mentioned in chapter 3.) In the seventies, blacks began to be represented again, often as tokens. *Josie and the Pussycats* (CBS, 1970–1972) introduced the first regular African American female character in a TV cartoon;[22] in the same year, the first all-black cartoon, *The Harlem Globetrotters* (CBS, 1970–1973), premiered; and as chapter 7 explains, the seventies saw *Fat Albert and the Cosby Kids* (CBS, 1972–1981), the longest-running TV cartoon with an all–African American cast.

In eighties product-based shows, nonwhite characters are included in cartoons "where possible," as the executive quoted earlier said. In the nineties it has become increasingly common to see Asian characters on children's cartoons, but in eighties shows "nonwhite" almost always meant black. Blacks are most often token extras, which means they are narratively negligible and included only for their to-be-looked-at-ness. If a black character is a lead, his/her ethnicity is ignored. So cartoon token blacks are both visible and invisible.[23] They are visibly black because of their darkened shading, audibly black because of their voice coding, or, occasionally, as with Panthro, both visibly and audibly coded black. But since the stories take place in the "postracist" eighties world, their ethnicity is invisible, and they "just happen" to be black. Winston argues that " 'simple exclusion' may be the most insidious form of distortion," but clearly tokenism—the "simple inclusion" of a black—can also be distorting.

Eighties robot cartoons *seem* to erase racial difference because the characters are machines. Nonetheless, the mechanical transformers do have their token Orange Blossoms and Panthros. Ostensibly, these transforming robots of the postapocalyptic distant past or distant future cannot be white, black, or any other color since they are made of metal. But there are fissures in this patina of ethnic invisibility. Jazz, a *Transformers* robot, speaks in a black-coded voice (Scatman Crothers's voice, to be precise). Blaster (short for "ghetto-blaster") transforms into a boom box. Not surprisingly, his voice is also black-coded. These black-coded voices force the realization that one cannot identify any of the robot characters as "nonethnic." That Jazz and Blaster speak in black-coded voices helps confirm that the others speak in white-coded voices. All the robots have ethnicity.[24] The inflections of black-coded English are uncanny in this mostly white robot world, and viewers may immediately wonder if they really heard them. Such doubt occurs because mechanical-transformer cartoons closet blackness. They offer no visual denotation of blackness. Instead, they locate blackness at the level of connotation, and unlike denotation, "connotation will always manifest a certain semiotic insufficiency."[25] In the Reaganite "postracist" eighties, the dominant order tolerated blackness "only on condition that it be kept out of sight."[26] When I claim that, like queerness, blackness can be closeted, I do not mean to imply that identity differences such as ethnicity and sexual orientation are simply equivalent (or mutually exclusive). In the live-action real world, it is usually easier, practically speaking, to closet queerness than it is to closet skin color. But in a cartoon world of humanoid animals and machines, ethnicity slips much more easily from the clarity of denotation into the penumbra of connotation.

Deregulation, the FCC, and the Toy-TV Industry

Clearly there is much more to product-based programs than the protoy messages that ACT and other adult critics feared. But adults wanted these shows banned from the airwaves, and since only advertisements can be regulated by the government, it made sense for censorious critics to ignore everything about the shows except their commercial messages. FCC commissioners might have agreed that the shows were ads; they simply did not agree that this was cause for concern.

For ACT, the eighties era was pandemonium; for the children's toy and TV industries, it was a lucrative renaissance. To understand this split, one must examine the history of FCC regulation of children's programming. In December 1969, the FCC issued an opinion stating that *Hot Wheels* (ABC, 1969–1971) was an unacceptable program-length commercial. ABC discontinued the program, but not until September 1971, presumably so as not to lose money by breaking contracts early. Encouraged by the regulatory climate, the National Association of Broadcasters (NAB) revised its advertising guidelines, cutting advertising time during children's programming from sixteen minutes per hour to nine and a half minutes on weekends and twelve minutes on weekdays. In 1972, the FCC banned host-selling, and the Federal Trade Commission (FTC) strongly "encouraged" vitamin companies not to advertise during children's programming. Also, as explained in the previous chapter, the FTC approved a yearlong study on the effects of sugar-product advertising to children and considered possibly outlawing advertising to children altogether. Five-second bumpers, meant to indicate a separation between programming and commercials, were made mandatory, and FCC policy statements in the seventies aggressively called for improvements in children's programming, explicitly stating that children should be treated as "special members of the viewing audience." [27] These important regulations and policy statements were due in no small part to ACT's pressure tactics.

Policy statements are largely symbolic if they have no specific directives or means of enforcement, and regulatory agencies may sometimes see such statements as sops thrown to pesky citizen's groups. But the *Hot Wheels* opinion and the children's television policy statements of the seventies are important symbols of regulatory temperament, indicating that serving the needs of child viewers was of concern to the FCC and that citizen activism directed at the FCC, although not wholly revolutionary in its effects, was not equivalent to spitting into the wind. The Reagan FCC considered the broadcast regulation and policy statements of the seventies to be in violation of broadcasters' and advertisers' First Amendment rights and argued that the "free market" (child viewers) could adequately regulate the quality of children's programs. However, the FCC did not address *how* the child audience could influence programmers and did not consider it important that, historically, children have not been advertisers' most highly valued audience. Indeed, children's programming was originally aired on Saturday mornings as a last resort; advertisers would not pay highly for this unattractive slot, and it is telling that the industry trade journal *Broadcasting and Cable* does not even include Saturday morning ratings in its regular ratings reports. The Reagan FCC thought the ratings should be the only means of regulating children's TV, but Nielsen reports on children's viewing are notoriously unreliable because children are not interested in operating people meters or filling in log books. Some adult TV viewers can be convinced they are performing a public service by allowing themselves to be properly measured, but young children are much more likely to play around with people meters and generally not to take their "responsibilities" to the A. C. Nielsen Company seriously. For these reasons, there is recurrent concern in the broadcasting industry that children's ratings are grossly inaccurate. Given all of these market factors, the Reagan FCC's idea that the child audience would be capable of influencing children's programming—and that this was a "democratic" solution to programming concerns—was patently absurd.

Yet absurdity reigned. The Reagan FCC no longer supported the NAB advertising-restriction policy, so it disappeared, and Reagan vetoed the Children's Television Act, which proposed to reinstate advertising-time restrictions. Removing the time-limit policy told toy and television executives that the earlier opinion against *Hot Wheels* was ancient history; programming based on preexisting toys would no longer be considered a violation of FCC policy or of "the public interest, convenience, and necessity." Under the policy method of regulation, or the "raised-eyebrow" approach, the FCC, the NAB, and occasionally the FTC had "encouraged" broadcasters to behave in certain ways. Although policy violators do not often have their licenses revoked, broadcasters know that such punishment is conceivable if raised eyebrows are consistently ignored. Reagan's

FCC chairman Mark Fowler opposed raised-eyebrow regulation, preferring what communications scholar Dale Kunkel disparagingly labels the
"turned-back" approach. Fowler declared: "[T]he FCC has no business trying to influence by raised eyebrow or by raised voice for that matter. I
confess that there was a romance bordering on chivalry when a Chairman
might declare television to be a wasteland. Those kinds of pronounce-
ments, as I see my job, are not mine to make. You are not my flock, and I
am not your shepherd." [28] Fowler was disdainful of past proregulation FCC
chairs and, with his wasteland barb, vented his spleen at Newton Minow in
particular. Taking an authoritarian tone, Fowler paternalistically rejected
paternalistic regulation.

In his how-to book on children's television, advertising executive and
Nickelodeon pioneer Cy Schneider shies away from discussing specific
FCC policies, largely writing off the proregulation pressure groups that
had successfully influenced the seventies FCC as "do-gooders, politicos,
pedagogues, and assorted other ax grinders." Although Schneider is only
one voice of the television and toy industry, his staunchly practical and
unabashedly capitalist sentiments are in many ways representative. As
he describes it, "consumer agitation" made the seventies (ACT's heyday)
a troubled time for children's television broadcasters and advertisers.[29]
The eighties, on the other hand, were boom years, mainly because of
"the licensed character—today's hottest salesman." At the height of the
licensed-character craze in the mid-eighties, cartoons had become virtually indispensable marketing tools within the toy industry.

Even though FCC deregulation gave television producers and ad execs
like Schneider a constitutionally backed guarantee that they could make
money without government interference, one might naively assume that
producers would respond to the accusation that product-based programs
were "just commercials" by denying it or at least feigning embarrassment.
This is not the case. Michael Hirsch of Nelvana, the animation studio that
produced the Care Bears movies and television shows, argues that the
licensed-character programs are no more commercial than any other kind
of entertainment. He sees the question of marketing tie-ins as "a red her-
ring": "The reality of our world—for adults or children—is that everything
like this gets marketed and promoted with tie-ins. Over the last few years,
animation hasn't performed well at the box office. What makes the live-
action movies work is the presence of stars. In animation, people haven't

utilized stars since the days of theatrical shorts. Well, who are stars for kids today? We realized that using pre-sold characters such as the Care Bears is just like getting Clint Eastwood or Barbra Streisand for our movie." [30] ACT's Peggy Charren responds: "That's so creepy. . . . Movie stars are not products like automobiles or detergents." [31] Charren's counterargument is weak because, in a sense, movie stars *are* products like automobiles or detergents, as any agent will admit. [32] Hirsch merely implies that animated entertainment is subject to the same marketing and creepy star system that governs live-action entertainment. Following this logic, *The Care Bears* cartoons *are* program-length commercials, but so is every other entertainment text containing actors or characters recognizable to viewers from other venues. Hirsch's rejoinder to critics represents a common industry view that licensed-character programming is not a new pariah, merely a clever marketing ploy.

Unlike Hirsch, Schneider does acknowledge that a unique marketing strategy is at work where the licensed character is concerned. He writes: "The theory behind these new shows is that young viewers have already been attracted to the characters in toy form, and will therefore be attracted to the programs. Conversely, the programs help boost retail sales of the existing and new products in these brand categories. A switch in the traditional order of progression has occurred. The product or concept has entered the framework of children's culture before becoming a movie or television program. In essence, programs become half-hour commercials for an existing brand." [33] Although the traditional order of marketing has been reversed, Schneider does not see this new development as particularly earth shattering. In fact, he likens such clever marketing to Disney's strategies for selling products in conjunction with *The Mickey Mouse Club* television program (also the show that made Mattel's Burp Gun infamous via an ad campaign engineered by Schneider). [34] Schneider marks the success of *Star Wars* merchandise in 1978 as a turning point when the industry realized the extraordinary potential of licensed-character products. He estimates that in 1976 20 percent of all toy sales were of licensed products; by 1977 the figure rose to 33 percent, and by 1987 the figure was almost 80 percent. [35] Schneider notes that ACT filed an unheeded complaint about programming based on licensed characters with the FCC, and he flippantly adds that "given the current climate at the FCC," ACT's complaints "will probably all blow over after a suitable period of apathy." [36] In fact, the FCC did dismiss ACT's complaint in 1985. However, in 1987, ACT won a suit against the FCC in the Washington, D.C., court of appeals, which helped it get the ball rolling on what would eventually become the Children's Television Act of 1990.

The History of Toy-TV Tie-ins

Table 2 indicates the changes in toy sales from 1959 to 1992 and the dramatic takeover by licensed products in the eighties. The table illustrates not only the preponderance of licensed characters in product-based cartoons but also, beginning in the seventies, a general tendency for successful toys to be based on television programming. This is not to say that before the seventies toy tie-ins with television programs were not successful. They certainly were, as the popularity of *Mickey Mouse Club* merchandise reveals. Howdy Doody merchandise grossed $25 million, and Davy Crockett products grossed over $100 million.[37] In addition, hosts of fifties and sixties children's shows promoted sponsors' products until host-selling was declared objectionable by the FCC. Although few children's shows with hosts per se still exist, this phrase is still used to refer to the practice of airing commercials for products during the broadcast of a show based on those products. In spite of the Reagan-Bush deregulatory drive, the host-selling constraint has never been lifted; ads for G.I. Joe toys cannot be aired during the G.I. Joe program.[38] In any case, the success of toys such as *Six Million Dollar Man* and *Star Trek* figures, after a hiatus in which products based on television programs were not the biggest money-makers, might be seen as a continuation of an earlier trend. The table illustrates that cartoons based on products are not a new commercial abomination but rather part of a continuing history of toy, television, and movie tie-ins.[39]

Table 2 also reveals an important shift in the types of licensed characters used for toys. In the seventies, quite a few dolls were based on "real-life" stars such as Michael Jackson, Brooke Shields, Evel Knievel, Farrah Fawcett, and Cher. The shift to using cartoon stars, which began with the massive success of Strawberry Shortcake products in the early eighties, marked the end of the popularity of toys based on live-action stars. This shift may be attributable to market oversaturation. In other words, there were too many of the same kind of toys, and consumers grew tired of them. From the industry's point of view, one advantage that the animated

Table 2. Best-Selling Toys, 1959–1992

Year	Toy
1959	Barbie fashion doll (still a best-selling girls' toy)
1960	Trolls; Etch-A-Sketch
1961	Ken fashion doll
1963	Chatty Cathy (first talking doll)
1964	G.I. Joe action figures
1965	Thingmakers Creepy Crawlers (bug-shaped-snack maker)
1967	Little Kiddles (small dolls)
1968	Hot Wheels[a]
1970	Nerf Ball
1973	Evel Knievel action figures; Baby Alive doll
1974	*Planet of the Apes* action figures[b][c]
1975	*Star Trek* action figures;[b] *Six Million Dollar Man* and *Bionic Woman* action figures[b]
1976	Stretch Armstrong, monster man
1977	Donnie and Marie Osmond fashion dolls[b]
1978	*Star Wars* action figures;[c] *Battlestar Gallactica* action figures;[b][c] Slime
1979	*Mork and Mindy* fashion dolls[b]
1981	Rubiks Cube;[a] Strawberry Shortcake doll[a]
1982	He-Man and the Masters of the Universe;[a] Smurf dolls;[a] E.T. doll[c]
1983	Cabbage Patch Kids dolls; Trivial Pursuit board game; My Little Pony dolls;[a] Care Bears[a][c]
1984	GoBots;[a] Transformers;[a] Rainbow Brite dolls;[a] Thundercats action figures[a][c]
1985	Teddy Ruxpin; Pound Puppies;[a] She-Ra doll[a]
1986	Lazer Tag; Baby Talk doll; Garbage Pail Kids
1987	*The Real Ghostbusters* action figures;[a][c] Pictionary board game; Pogo Ball
1988	*Teenage Mutant Ninja Turtles* action figures;[a][c] Li'l Miss Makeup
1989	*Batman* action figures;[c] Oopsie Daisy doll
1990	Magic Nursery dolls; New Kids on the Block fashion dolls
1991	Super Soaker water pistol; Disney's *Little Mermaid*[a][c] merchandise
1992	*Incredible Crash Dummies* action figures; Disney's *Beauty and the Beast*[c] merchandise

Source: Advertising Age 8 Feb. 1993: 52+.

[a] Indicates product on which a television cartoon was based.

[b] Indicates product referencing a live-action, prime-time television program.

[c] Indicates product referencing a theatrical film.

star has over the live-action star is that the animated star's image (though not the public reception of it) is easier to control than the live-action star's image. D. C. Denison notes, for example, that "Ideal Toys suffered . . . losses in the mid-1970's when it invested millions in an Evel Knievel toy line. A couple of years later, after Knievel was convicted of assaulting a television executive with a baseball bat, the line cooled off considerably." [40] Toy executives prefer toys like Transformers and GoBots because they have total control over the construction of the animated stars' images. The Care Bears can be counted on not to commit assault and battery, and they will never demand a raise.

As I mentioned earlier, children's toy producers also like licensed characters because they believe they have play "built into them." They come with preexisting narratives that children have encountered in other mediums such as comic books and cartoons. In other words, people in the toy industry think that intertextuality—a synergistic combination of products built around a structuring concept—yields increased play potential. Less often acknowledged is that live-action-star toys also come with preexisting, intertextual narratives; a child who plays with New Kids on the Block dolls would also know the characters through records, music videos, and fan magazines.

Dolls versus Action Figures

New Kids on the Block "fashion dolls" were best-sellers in 1990. The term "fashion doll" indicates that these toys were intended primarily for girls. Barbie "dolls" are also for girls, whereas G.I. Joe "action figures" are for boys. To be sure, children often ignore such institutional categories, placing a G.I. Joe action figure in a baby carriage or putting Barbie behind a machine gun, but the industry adamantly opposes *representing* or suggesting such play in television advertisements, packaging, print ads, and cartoons. According to toy industry historians Sydney Ladensohn Stern and Ted Schoenhaus, not showing girls in commercials for boys' toys or vice versa is one of the industry's central "generally accepted principles." [41]

Although the industry has been very reluctant to discuss the racial politics of toys and TV, many children's entertainment producers are quite willing to articulate sexism as a "problem" or at least an issue that concerns parents. For the producers of children's entertainment, reassuring gender polarities eclipses the potentially divisive issue of race. Producers tend to avoid discussing racial issues and see racism as an outdated concern. Stern and Schoenhaus flippantly admit that "without doubt, the large toy companies cater to little girls' desire to be sex objects and little boys' interest in killing everyone," [42] but they assure us that racial issues are passé: "[T]oday there are several companies, run by black entrepreneurs, devoted to promoting role models with which black children can identify, not simply black versions of white dolls." [43] By eliding differences that are not gender based, the children's toy and TV industries imply that gender constitutes the only salient difference between consumers.

However, the category of "doll" is not just about gender. It is politically charged in other ways: "Hasbro has spent the last few years trying to convince the U.S. Customs Service, and then the U.S. Court of Appeals, that G.I. Joe is a toy soldier, not a doll. Hasbro was not worried about Joe's manly pride. As toys, toy soldiers can enter the country at 6.8 percent duty (Joe is made in Hong Kong); the tariff on dolls is 12 percent. In 1989, however, the U.S. government, in the person of a Washington, D.C., judge, declared Joe undeniably a doll." [44] Produced by cheap foreign labor, G.I. Joe, it seems, is technically not a "real American hero," in spite of what the commercials say. Unfortunately, Stern and Schoenhaus reduce G.I. Joe's industrial circumstances to an amusing anecdote. Although they claim that Joe's "manly pride" is not at issue, the crux of the "joke" is Joe's emasculation at the hands of U.S. Customs and the U.S. government. The notation that Joe is made in Hong Kong is only parenthetical in this account. Since so much toy and animation labor is farmed out to poor workers (most often women) in other countries, tariffs are no laughing matter. But for the industry, flip expressions of gender inequity ("Boys are concerned about power and strength. . . . Girls are concerned with looks and cuteness") [45] function as handy rhetorical devices for avoiding consideration of the other inequities that underpin the manufacture of children's entertainment.

If toy-TV tie-ins were not new to the children's entertainment industry in the eighties, neither was the rigid conception of what makes a girl's toy a "doll" and a boy's toy an "action figure." The idea that toy soldiers are for boys and baby dolls are for girls certainly predates the eighties. But given the political temper of the times (antifeminist backlash), it should not be surprising that sales of hyperfeminine and hypermasculine toys skyrocketed in the eighties or that the product-based program thrived. Reagan-Bush politics made the product-based cartoon viable not only legally but also ideologically.

"The Calories Don't Count If You Don't Think about Them"

The hyperfeminine Strawberry Shortcake was the first character to be used in eighties product-based programming (figure 3). Strawberry Short-cake was a toy-TV tie-in that, in its first year, grossed $100 million, thereby grossing out all the "do-gooders, politicos, pedagogues, and assorted other ax grinders" who had fought so hard for the short-lived regulatory gains of the seventies. As ACT and other activists argued, the *Strawberry Shortcake* TV specials were indeed disturbing but, I would add, not merely because of the deregulation that engendered them. Close analysis of *Strawberry Shortcake* cannot tell us exactly what child viewers may have gotten from the show, but it does illustrate that product-based shows are not simply inducements to buy toys, and it also helps clarify what may be at stake in the femininity for sale on girls' television.

The *Strawberry Shortcake* TV specials are ridden with conflicts centering around puberty, motherhood, and food consumption. The show narrativizes eating disorders by showing characters who enjoy the appearance and smell of food without actually eating it. *Shortcake* reifies to a dizzying extreme the oral anxieties characteristically attributed to female subjects in our culture. It is not an overstatement to say that the *Shortcake* characters have eating disorders. Although they do not binge and purge or take laxatives, they live in a strange confectionery world where only villains and pets eat. (Actually, one of the good characters does eat; her defining characteristic is that she is always on a diet but says, "The calories don't count if you don't think about them!") Strawberry Shortcake and her pals live in Strawberryland, and in the first few shows, the characters' homes are desserts. The characters have fruit names such as Strawberry Shortcake, Lemon Meringue, Banana Twirl, and Huckleberry Pie, and virtually all of these fruity characters are female. They are all gentle and loving; they nurture each other, their fruit gardens, their pets, and the baby characters that occasionally appear on the show. The girls are grown-up compared to the babies, and they live in their own houses like adults, but they are only a few inches tall and are shaped like toddlers. Strawberryland residents spend

Figure 3. The pungently fruit-scented
Strawberry Shortcake doll.

their time planning and attending parties and celebrations.[46] They also
grow eponymous fruits that, in "Berry Talk," smell "berry nice." The girls
protect rather than eat the fruit, and narrative conflicts often center around
threats to the fruit. Since each girl is named after the fruit she grows and
wears clothes evocative of that fruit, the act of eating might actually be
construed as cannibalistic.

In "Strawberry Shortcake Meets the Berrykins," perhaps the most per-
verse of the *Shortcake* episodes, the Strawberry Kids pick the most perfect
and beautiful fruit they can find. Then, instead of eating it, they display it at
the annual berry festival. In an uncanny moment, the collected fruits split
open to reveal themselves not as fruits at all but rather as "Berrykins," little
fruitlike cherubs who give the fruits of Strawberryland their scents. The
"birth" scene frightens the girls at first, but they are ultimately entranced
by the cuddly little creatures; each girl cradles her namesake (fruitsake)
like a baby. Banana Twirl holds the banana Berrykin, for example. The
scene is disturbing not only because the girls so easily embrace the mater-

nal role but also because this role is constructed as so very "natural," and the feminine is so easily paired with the natural in an inescapable mise-en-abîme: babies come from fruits, mothers are fruit desserts, and fruits turn into babies.

In this episode, Strawberry Shortcake's skinny nemesis, the Peculiar Purple Pieman of Porcupine Peak, and his curvaceous female sidekick Sour Grapes want to become rich and famous by inventing a perfume. To this end, they combine foods in a giant perfume machine. The smoky perfume by-products form a cloud that rains on the fruits of Strawberryland. Resembling embarrassed women in douche or deodorant commercials, the girls are appalled when their fruits emanate "improper" scents.[47] One fruit smells like pizza, and another smells like chocolate. The odors are doubly offensive because they not only do not match the fruits but also are all manufactured junk foods like pizza rather than natural foods like fruits. These nonfruit, nondessert scents are alien to the Strawberry Shortcake world; Tina Taco and Pizza Patsy are unthinkable characters. Catnip scent is the only nonfruit odor, and Strawberry Shortcake's cat gets high from sniffing an improperly scented lemon. The girls are as repulsed by the deviant odors as they are normally thrilled by the proper fruit odors. Luckily, the Berrykins save the day by restoring the proper scents. By the end of the show, the polluted clouds are destroyed, and the villains are left defeated in a vat of their own foul concoction, one villain smelling of lobster cupcakes and the other of lasagna pudding. Strawberry Shortcake is magically granted her secret wish to have lovely long hair, a desire that inspired her earlier musical number, "I Want to Be Like Who I Want to Be When I Grow Up," in which she disco danced and tried on different grown-up fashion looks.

The Berrykins episode explores rites of passage such as birth and puberty. The show depicts dressing up, parties, disco dancing, and raising babies (Berrykins) as the fun parts of growing up. The nitty-gritty, more biological side of puberty—changing odors and hormones, represented by the fruits, and even menstruation, represented by the eerie instant hair growth (a change of appearance evocative of the earlier fantasy disco scene in which Shortcake plays at being a woman)—is toyed with but ultimately rejected. Rites of passage are evoked in the show, but as Constance Penley has argued, within this genre of girls' TV, characters seem to be trapped in a prejuvenile state. Penley contrasts girls' product-based programs with

Pee-wee's Playhouse, which "forgoes the easy channeling of children's sexual identification into either mastery for the boys (*He-Man and the Masters of the Universe*) or permanent regression for the girls (*Kissyfur, The Wuzzles*). Instead, the program suggests that the question of sexual difference is highly problematic and possibly never settled."[48] *Shortcake* seems to fit easily into the *Kissyfur* and *Wuzzles* genre of "permanent regression." But this regression is hardly unproblematic and certainly never quite settled. Rather, as the Berrykins episode illustrates, *Shortcake* narratives endlessly flirt with growth, transformation, sexual development, and maturity.

In counterdistinction to *Pee-wee's Playhouse*, which allows "children to explore their feelings about themselves and their world precisely because it transgresses adult standards of taste and decorum and upholds child meanings over those of their parents," *Shortcake* teaches adultlike control and good taste.[49] Although the good taste of food is denied to the girls, good taste in housing and clothing abounds. The narratives forbid food consumption but strongly encourage consumption of nonfoods such as bicycles, toys, and even houses. In this way, although Strawberryland residents may remain children physically, they play at being tasteful adult consumers. In "Housewarming Surprise," Strawberry Shortcake's friends help her move many boxes of goods out of her old, small, Shortcakelike house and into a new strawberry-theme mansion, complete with berry-shaped toilet seat. Miss Shortcake notes maturely that "you sure don't know how much stuff you've collected until you have to move." This program not only publicizes the new Strawberry house offered simultaneously in toy stores but also introduces Strawberry Shortcake's new friends (new dolls) from around the world. In the "Big Apple City" episode, Strawberry Shortcake goes to the city to win a new gazebo (also available in toy form) in a bake-off; she makes new friends along the way in "Spinach Village" and "Times Pear." Indeed, virtually every show introduces new friends, vehicles, or houses, all of which were available for purchase in toy form.

Commodities function as symbols of love and sharing in *Shortcake* narratives. Strawberry Shortcake, the Strawberry Kids' symbolic mother, fulfills her own needs only through acquiring new goods—a house, a gazebo, a swimming pool. Her pleasure in her new items generally centers around contemplation of how much her friends will enjoy them. In other words, she seems to receive most of her pleasure vicariously, through the act of sharing with her friends. Although it could be argued that this is a positive expression of community, it is also emblematic of the structuring of motherhood that Nancy Chodorow describes in *The Reproduction of Mothering*. Nurturing caretakers are obsessively selfless, nurturing *others*, whether they be friends, flora, or fauna.

Playing at adult consumption via *Shortcake* narratives may conceivably help child viewers work through anxieties about their own maturation process, and although *Shortcake*'s rigid view of sexual difference and unabashed promotion of toy consumption are disturbing, it would be perfunctory to assume that the show is altogether "bad" for all children. Ellen Seiter has argued that product-based girls' shows are valuable precisely because they are for girls, unlike the bulk of cartoons that are made for boys by producers who operate under the assumption that girls can make do with boys' fare: "Something was gained and lost when marketers and video producers began exploiting little girls as a separate market. Little girls found themselves in a ghettoized culture that no self-respecting boy would take an interest in; but for once girls were not required to cross over, to take on an ambiguous identification with a group of male characters." [50] Seiter also argues that the tremendously popular show *My Little Pony* appeals to girls because it "plays its childlike and female orientation totally straight; no attempt is made to appeal to a broader audience — and this . . . is the reason for its success." [51] *My Little Pony* may engage girls because it takes seriously characters' feelings of inadequacy and depression (not to mention anxiety about hair care!). Like *My Little Pony*, *Strawberry Shortcake* addresses anxieties that are relevant to little girls' lives, anxieties about friendship, dieting, and growing up. *Shortcake*'s discourse on dieting may be reprehensible, but girls encounter pressure to diet everywhere. Girls who do not learn about dieting from a cartoon will learn about it from an adult talk show, from an Ultra-Slimfast ad, or from observing their own mother, older sisters, or friends. One might argue that dieting and eating disorders have no place in cartoons and that cartoons should be a "safe" space, but it is unclear whether adult concerns could ever be purged from cartoons or even whether a cartoon could ever be totally safe, given the numerous competing adult definitions of what makes cartoons safe or unsafe.

One cannot be certain how effective *Shortcake*'s abstemious food messages are. That is, girls may not all *get Shortcake*'s dieting discourse. Henry Jenkins's Pee-wee study includes a child's drawing of a flying "Punk Rocker Pee-wee" modeled after Strawberry Shortcake, complete with bonnet, shoulder-length hair, freckles, and Pee-wee's bow tie, illustrating that all *Shortcake* viewers do not read the program in the same way and do not simply take away its tasteful messages about commodities and controlled eating. Notwithstanding their rigid conceptions of "built-in play" and gender binarism, children's entertainment producers might not be totally surprised by this image, but they would never themselves represent such a merging of a girl's character with the man-child Pee-wee.

Gender Binarism and the Toy Industry

The toy industry's stance on gender binarism is disturbingly cut and dried:

> Once the market is defined, even if a product itself could be enjoyed by children of both sexes (and it is difficult to imagine one that could not be) the manufacturer tends to design the specific product to be as appealing as possible to that target. Girls get pink, purple, lavender, blue, ruffles, frills, horses, flowers, hearts. *Their products have been known to induce gagging in adults*, but when Mattel designed She-Ra, Princess of Power [twin sister of He-Man], the action figure was not well received by little girls until Mattel "pinked it up." Boys get their toys black or silver, fast, scary, macho, gross, violent.[52] (my emphasis)

The acknowledgment that adults find girls' merchandise gag inducing is intriguing. Although most makers of children's entertainment pay some lip service to the need for toys that offer "positive" role models for children, they also argue that girl consumers are staunchly resistant to stronger, less traditionally feminine characters. Stern and Schoenhaus recount, for example, that the Bionic Woman doll was a disaster in prerelease test play until her beauty parlor was introduced. They also argue that there is parental resistance to sex-role stereotyping and that this resistance explains why "gender-neutral" preschool toys are available on the market. The authors explain, however, that as soon as toddlers become capable of making their own toy choices, they quickly reject the gender-neutral toys and demand strongly gender-coded playthings.

Toymakers contend that their toys and cartoons merely respond to the market. If even some parents are repulsed by traditional gender roles, and if they are presumably key players in shaping their children's gendered identities, then the only "logical" understanding of sexual difference, from the industry's perspective, is that girls are inherently weak, pink, and fluffy and boys are inherently strong, silver, and hard. Toy designers might accept that some adults are disgusted by hyperfemininity (the gag reaction to frills, flowers, and hearts), but their only concern is how such adult disgust might affect the marketplace.[53] Eliding the negative response many adults have to boys' toy guns and other macho playthings, Stern and Schoenhaus cannot imagine masculine toys inducing gagging in adults. Indeed, their book on the toy industry focuses on products targeted to boy consumers, apparently because they find masculine toys more appealing than their "cute," viscerally repulsive (gag-inducing), feminine counterparts.

Here, for example, is how Stern and Schoenhaus describe corporate discomfort with the popular seventies doll Baby Alive:

> When someone held a spoon or bottle up to her mouth, she masticated. Then, after a suitable interval, she defecated. The [toy] executives were horrified, yet fascinated. Once Loomis [the demonstrator, later a maverick in Strawberry Shortcake marketing] forgot to put a disposable diaper on the doll before feeding it, and it extruded poo-poo gel all over his arm. "Who in the world would ever want such a messy thing?" asked his disgusted boss. As it turned out, there were vast hordes of children eager to own a defecating dolly. Baby Alive was the number-one-selling doll in 1973, and [the manufacturer] went on to sell three million of them. Extra "cherry, banana, and lime" food packets were available for extra feedings (and to answer the obvious question, yes, what went in red, yellow, or green came out red, yellow, or green).[54]

Although grown-up men *designed* this scatologically intriguing doll, this passage implicates *consumers* (implicitly the girls to whom Baby Alive was marketed) as weirdos. Pathology-free executives merely created the "defecating dolly," whereas "vast hordes" of weird children (girls) wanted the doll. Conversely, toy designers consider it perfectly normal that boys enjoy weird toys like Incredible Edibles, a boy-targeted toy that molded a chocolaty, plasticlike substance into bug and worm shapes.

Even if in daily use children's toys frequently defy gender binarism, advertising directed at children seems to be able to speak only in terms of opposites. In toy-advertising campaigns, girls rarely behave in disgusting, improper, or "boyish" ways. Interestingly, while the (mostly) men who run the toy industry are repulsed by girls' toys, toy and TV protesters (primarily women's groups such as ACT and the Parent-Teacher Association) are most offended by boys' toys and TV shows, mainly because of their presumed violent effects on boys. As Ellen Seiter has remarked in her ethnographic research in preschools, a reverse sexism is definitely at play in the ways adults regulate children's media use, with boys being censored more often by female teachers than girls are.[55]

In any case, toymakers' marketplace explanatory logic—that the industry merely responds to essential masculine and feminine desires—must be held up to critique. Toymakers clearly do more than merely respond to a market; they also actively *create* that market. If girls like ultrafeminine products, their desire for such products should be seen as bound up in toymakers' views on "gag-inducing" female pleasures. The point is not that little girls are deluded by the industry or that they simply suffer from a false consciousness that could be fixed if all the sexist toy producers would just go away or if all toys were made "gender neutral." I have talked to enough feminist moms with inexplicably pink, frilly little girls to realize that carefully controlled environments will not produce "gender-neutral" kids. Furthermore, pink, frilly femininity has its pleasures, and I am not convinced it needs to be totally eliminated.

The point is that toy design and marketing are only small parts of a larger system of gender differences and inequities. As with other kinds of gendered objects, toys may provide clues about the psyches of their child owners (and their parents), but they do not simply translate into belief systems. I personally went straight from a Barbie obsession to being the only girl in the seventh grade with a *Ms.* magazine book bag. The two objects were deeply meaningful to me (at the time, I read the first object as pure pleasure, the second object as symbolic of political commitment: I was making a statement, dammit), but my fixation on the first object did not signify I was an antifeminist any more than my gravitation to the second object meant I had successfully turned into a feminist. Neither object in and of itself could function as an adequate litmus test of my subjectivity. Likewise, boys fascinated with Transformer action figures and girls obsessed with Strawberry Shortcake dolls are not necessarily doomed to a life of traditional gender roles. So I am not arguing that gendered objects inevitably yield negative effects. Rather, I would like to suggest that the "free market" that toymakers incessantly allude to is not a mechanism that benevolently responds to natural needs. Toymakers are not the only source of binaristic notions of gender, but they do have *agency* and make certain choices. They do not simply respond to consumer needs and desires. The market for toys is historically created and historically fluctuating. As Susan Willis has asserted: "The recuperation of sex roles in the eighties is a stunning reversal of the Women's Movement in the late sixties and early seventies, which called into question children's sex role modeling practices. Dress codes were condemned, co-ed sports flourished, fairy tales were rewritten, and toys were liberated. . . . [W]e like to think that the cultural turmoil of the sixties changed everything. The fact is, in mass culture today there is an ever more rigidly defined separation of the sexes based on narrow notions of masculinity and femininity." [56] Strongly gender-coded toys, such as Strawberry Shortcake, were successful in the eighties, in part, because of Reagan-era backlash against seventies feminism, which questioned traditional toys and sex roles. Strawberry Shortcake dolls and TV shows are both symptoms of and contributors to this backlash.

Toymakers' narrow notions of femininity—indeed, their revulsion toward little girls—are exemplified by one particular toy: L'il Miss Makeup, a childlike dummy head designed for girls to put makeup on. This toy was the hit of the industry's 1988 preview show, the Toyfair, where excited manufacturers expecting big sales referred to L'il Miss Makeup as "L'il Baby Hooker." Many adults fear child precociousness and corruption as the most dangerous effects of bad toys and television, and the figure of the Baby Hooker functions as an outrageous metaphor for such anxieties. Given that the producers of children's entertainment make such flamboyantly offensive remarks, it is no wonder that so many reformers blame their children's undesirable actions on an imagined antichild conspiracy operating within the children's toy and TV industries.

Cy Schneider aptly summarizes the industrial stance toward gender when he unabashedly proclaims that "[b]oys are concerned about power and strength. . . . Girls are concerned with looks and cuteness." [57] Girl consumers are considered more troublesome to create new products for than boys because their desires are so "elusive," according to the trade journal *Advertising Age.*[58] Yet despite the typical girl versus boy (or Barbie versus G.I. Joe) binarism, producers and advertisers expect one-way crossover identification to occur at least some of the time. Schneider advises toy commercial producers, "Don't show an eight-year-old boy playing with an eight-year-old girl. For boys, that's an unreal situation. Girls will emulate boys, but boys will not emulate girls. When in doubt, use boys." [59] Advertisers assume female-to-male cross identification not only in marketing toys and television programs but also when promoting fast foods, one of the key markets that target children. In a 1993 *Advertising Age* article on fast food promos targeting children, marketing directors from Pizza Hut, McDonald's, and Burger King all admitted that they tend to gear their advertising more to boys than to girls and that girls will accept advertising meant to appeal to boys' tastes.[60] Industry attitudes toward the girl consumer are highly evocative of film theorist Laura Mulvey's suggestion that "as desire is given cultural materiality in a text, for women (from childhood onwards) trans-sex identification is a *habit* that very easily becomes *second Nature*. However," she adds, problematizing such transsex identification in a way that ad executives would never dare, "this Nature does not sit easily and shifts restlessly in its borrowed transvestite clothes." [61]

If one considers *Shortcake* in the context of other child-targeted products such as fast food, it is clear not only that children's products are pervasively gendered but also, and perhaps more importantly, that manufacturers work very hard to construct the market situation to which they claim they merely respond. In the sense that it is merely one female-targeted product among many, *Strawberry Shortcake* is not unique. Like so many shows, *Shortcake* is the kind of program boys are not supposed to enjoy. Although at first glance *Shortcake* may seem atypical of Saturday morning programming since, unlike other girls' programs such as *My Little Pony* and *She-Ra Princess of Power,* it so explicitly problematizes food consumption, the show does not seem anomalous when examined in the context of commercials for candy and fast foods, which encourage boys to consume more than girls, thereby coding eating as a masculine activity.

Shortcake is symptomatic of broader cultural discourses that link femininity and sweetness. Some people who have never seen the show, and conceivably some who have seen it, mistakenly believe that the title character is actually made of strawberry shortcake. Indeed, the *Shortcake* characters do seem literally to be made of "sugar and spice and everything nice." In her exploration of the cultural association of women and food, Rosalind Coward has argued that sweets are linked to women in terms of endearment like "sweetie, sweetiepie, sugar, honeybunch, [and] lollipop." She notes a "measure of sadism lurking beneath the surface" of this "language of devouring, gobbling up, feasting with the eyes, a language which suggests the desire not only to eat but perhaps to destroy the loved object." [62] Television industry lingo itself suggests that the TV female is an object to be consumed; industry slang for women is not only "T & A" and "jiggle" but also "eye candy." *Shortcake* characters do not offer the typical "T & A" since, like anorexic girls, they never grow tits and asses, but the pungently fruit-scented Strawberry Shortcake dolls *are* "eye candy" in the sense that they are sweets for little girls to look at and smell rather than eat. In fact, you might say that the *Strawberry Shortcake* series and all the products it helps to sell instruct girls to "eye candy" rather than consume it.

Shortcake is an early narrative stop plotted on a continuum of texts that encourage female subjects to have illicit feelings about (and even identify with) food. Analyzing a text that most girls will encounter later, the woman's magazine, Coward notes that food photography in such magazines "generate[s] guilt about oral pleasures. Look at the way advertising presents food, drawing a direct equation between what women eat and what shape they will be. Tab['s] advertising campaign shows a glass . . . in the shape of a woman's body! Beside the glass are the statistics 35" 22" 35". . . . Heinz promotes its 'Slimway Mayonnaise' with a picture of a very lurid lobster and the caption 'Mayonnaise without guilt.' . . . [C]reamy foods are offered as wicked but worth it." [63] The extremes of the idealized toddler in *Strawberry Shortcake* and the idealized sexpot in *Vogue* can be achieved only with guilt and without calorie consumption. The *Vogue* reader and the Saturday morning viewer are encouraged to be relentless consuming machines of everything but food. Portraying an edible world where no one eats, *Strawberry Shortcake* is not unlike woman's magazines, which offer weight-loss articles next to high-calorie recipes for ornamental cookery accompanied by glossy photos. Coward aptly calls these photos "food pornography."

A page from the 13 July 1981 *Advertising Age* illustrates the pervasiveness of the *Shortcake/Vogue* continuum of gendered consumption. At the top of the page, there is an article on General Mills's new Strawberry Shortcake "fad" cereal, touted as " 'a little money maker' for retailers." What appears to be an ad for a drug rehabilitation program dominates the rest of the page. A woman turns away from the viewer and from framed photos of her children, her face hidden by her hair and one of her hands. The text reads, "This woman is an addict, and her children know it. . . . At one time in her life, she might have denied it, but not any more. This woman is hooked on a unique American addiction: The soap opera. Frankly, she can't get enough of it." This is an ad to entice advertisers to buy space in *Soap Opera Digest*. To convince potential clients of the consuming habits of *Digest* readers, the ad documents the number of women who are "heavy users" of air fresheners and room deodorizers, wieners, furniture polish, packaged and prepared dishes and dinner mixes, baked beans, and baby powder. With its emphasis on foods, scents, and infant care, this reads like a shopping list for a grown-up Strawberry Shortcake. Plotting *Shortcake* on the continuum of female consumption helps explain why the program has never been attacked for its representation of food and abstinence. Narratives that simultaneously encourage rampant consumption and justify consumption phobias are so common that Shortcake's perversely food-centered narratives are invisible.

ACT and Reaganomics Butt Heads

Although it bypassed actual narrative analysis, ACT did declare product-based shows to be sexist, racist dreck. But its official line, in terms of the regulatory gains it was seeking, was that product-based shows were objectionable because their only message was, as Peggy Charren put it, "buy me, buy me, buy me." Charren argued that the programs took advantage of child consumers in ways that would never be attempted with adults: "Can you imagine a TV series about Kleenex for adults?"[64] Defining laissez-faire capitalism as a First Amendment right, the Fowler FCC would not object to a program promoting Kleenex any more than it objected to shows meant to sell toys. After all, deregulation made legally viable not only product-based cartoons but also infomercials.[65] There was no need for the commission to even acknowledge the product-based program. Only the marketplace—the middle- and upper-middle-class viewers who most appealed to advertisers—had the right to remark upon program content, and unless they were Nielsen families, their opinions could be expressed in only three ways: by changing the channel, by turning off the set, or by boycotting sponsors.

So it was Reagan's deregulatory policy that made room for *Strawberry Shortcake* on television. Fowler and the FCC chairs who followed him cut the few regulatory knots that had been tied in the seventies. Fowler believed "it was time to move away from thinking about broadcasters as trustees. It was time to treat them the way almost everyone else in society does—that is, as businesses." He also said, infamously, "[T]elevision is just another appliance. It's a toaster with pictures."[66] In 1983, the FCC lifted its children's policy guidelines, and in 1984, it ruled that stations could air as many commercial minutes in a given time period as they desired. ACT unsuccessfully contested this ruling in 1985, referring back to the FCC's 1969 ruling against Hot Wheels. In rejecting ACT's complaint, the Reagan FCC seemed to reaffirm that it saw television as just a household appliance and that it was not interested in restraining the industry by regulating television content in any way. The FCC uses this argument when it suits its needs, but clearly the commission does make some value judgments about television content. In punishing bad boy extraordinaire Howard Stern for his use of "indecent" language, in questioning whether or not a televised image of an aborted fetus is "indecent," and in judging the propriety of broadcasting condom ads, the FCC feels justified in discussing broadcast content in moral and ethical terms. This is done, ostensibly, for the sake of children since indecency legislation is supposedly designed to protect them alone. The FCC judges depictions of excretory activities or excretory/sexual organs, the essence of indecency, as dangerous to children, while tacitly endorsing other, more "decent" toaster pictures. Unlike ACT and other children's activists, the Reagan and Bush FCCs found the crass commercial intent of product-based programs to be patently decent.

Nonetheless, when the American Greetings Company and General Mills created the Strawberry Shortcake doll in 1980 and produced a TV special based on the character shortly thereafter, the three major U.S. broadcast networks rejected the show, apparently fearing FCC reprimand because of the Hot Wheels decision. Consequently, the program was initially shown on non-network stations.[67] The networks' caution was unwarranted, of course. Soon afterward Fowler began to implement his "toaster" philosophy. In 1984, with the removal of advertising time limits, product-based TV specials like Strawberry Shortcake and regular series like He-Man could be safely shown by the three national networks. He-Man became the first product-based regular series to skyrocket to success.[68]

Given ACT's history of nutritional activism, one might imagine the group would object to Shortcake not only as a program-length commercial but also as a show with some disturbing messages about consumption. But ACT, like the FCC, rejected close analysis of content. ACT publicly complained about gender-specific toys and sexist children's programming but never focused an attack on specific program narratives for two reasons. Philosophically, such an action would have been impossible for ACT because it was censorious. Also, ACT could not target specific cartoon narratives because it saw the shows as little more than commercial garbage. ACT's attitude was not atypical, of course. Although arguments about the harmful effects of cartoon violence almost always find a receptive audience, arguments about specific cartoon narratives rarely get a fair hearing. Mainstream newspapers and popular magazines such as *TV Guide* find discussion of cartoon narratives laughable, as was obvious when they reported on broadcasters' responses to the Children's Television Act of 1990.

The act requires broadcasters to report how their programs address children's educational and informational needs. The act is intended to encourage new programs, but in their 1992 and 1995 reports, broadcasters merely submitted newly formulated readings of old programs. The reports offer an interesting opportunity to see how broadcasters read cartoon meanings and how congressional representatives, public pressure groups, social scientists, and journalists react to those readings. The *New York Times*'s Janet Maslin mocks broadcasters for daring to claim that "*Super Mario Brothers* builds confidence" and that "*The Jetsons* may foster interest in new technology and provide budding scientists with inspiration." Although there are certainly more complex ways to read these programs, and although Maslin correctly argues that the networks are not responding in good faith to the act's requirements, her article's primary thrust is that the networks' readings (which I find vaguely tenable) are self-evidently absurd. The cartoon illustrating her article concisely summarizes her stance toward cartoon meaning or lack thereof: a professor in gown and mortarboard lectures in front of a huge TV showing an angry rabbit clobbering a man with a sledgehammer. The illustration pokes fun at both programmers' sneaky reports and, more generally, any attempt to take cartoons seriously.[69]

Dale Kunkel, a communications scholar who released 1992 and 1995 reports evaluating broadcasters' responses to the act, offers a different interpretation of broadcasters' readings of cartoons. He simply contends that broadcasters are not being held accountable to the act. The act dictates that they must broadcast programs "specifically designed" to serve children in certain ways. Instead, broadcasters have reread programs that clearly were not specifically designed to serve children's educational and informational needs. It is a question of authorial intention. Because no one initially *meant* for *Yogi Bear* to perform an educational function like the Children's Television Workshop's *Sesame Street*, reporting to the FCC that *Yogi Bear* is educational is *breaking the law*. CTW productions are backed by research teams, and many files of data prove their educational intentions. Network cartoon producers may occasionally hire social scientist advisers, as chapter 7 explains, but since the cartoon producers have neither the CTW's prestige nor its research teams, they can only assert, not prove, educational intention. Kunkel does not argue that the broadcasters' readings of cartoons are foolish, merely that they are lies used to break the law.[70] The pragmatic Kunkel bypasses close readings of cartoons because they would not help his argument, not because he is disdainful of cartoons.

ACT likewise avoided close analysis of cartoons. The few times ACT did release content-based research, public reaction was tepid at best. In 1983, *TV Guide* gave one of its annual J. Fred Muggs awards for making a fool of oneself to ACT's Kim Hayes. The headline reads: "Face it, Kim: They're just a bunch of male chauvinist Smurfs!" The story notes that ACT found that "females make up only 16 percent of the major dramatic characters on kids' shows. The situation is so bad that according to ACT spokesperson Kim Hayes 'There is only one Smurfette amid a host of Smurfs. Is this really the view of life we want to give our children?' " *TV Guide* finds this question so obviously stupid that no further comment is given. In light of the reception of the Smurfette study, it is unlikely that any ACT commentary on *Shortcake*'s food-centered narratives would have been taken very seriously. Although ACT abhorred cartoon violence, and in spite of its apprehensions about Smurfette and other isolated examples of sexism (such as the fact that the Six Million Dollar Man doll came with a "flashy repair station" whereas the Bionic Woman came with a beauty parlor),[71] the arguments supporting ACT's legal lobbying centered around the notions of unfair commercialism and the necessity of "serving the public interest." The only content-based arguments it would incorporate into its legislative lobbying was the commonsensical assertion that shows like *Transformers* and *Rainbow Brite* were obviously really advertisements. The Reagan and Bush FCCs were deaf to this assertion.

Ironically, while ACT focused its lobbying on commercialism in order to avoid being censorious, the FCC also derailed censorship by focusing on the marketplace, but the commission defined commercialism, consumerism, and censorship in radically different ways than ACT did. The commission touted the free market as the citizen's only hope for influencing broadcasting decisions. In fact, Chairman Fowler actually advised ACT to model its tactics on those of right-wing protest groups. As *Advertising Age* explained, Fowler told ACT, "If you want more children's programming, take a lesson from the success of the Moral Majority and let the advertising and TV industries know you are prepared to organize boycotts."[72] To the commission, the *only* democratic way to regulate content was to threaten boycott.

While ACT was attacking product-based shows, other public pressure groups in the early eighties were making headlines and forcing the television industry and the FCC to take notice. Whereas the bulk of sixties and seventies media protest had been of a liberal or leftist bent, many of the high-profile protest groups of the eighties were decidedly right wing. The explicitly procensorship group Morality in Media attacked R-rated and X-rated cable programming, and as chapter 3 explains, the Coalition for Better Television, in alliance with the Moral Majority, undertook a nationwide campaign against TV sex and violence and threatened a massive boycott of products advertised during objectionable programming. In this climate, with public and governmental eyes focused on the censorship of prime-time sex and violence, the persistently anticensorship ACT did not stand a chance with its comparatively mild argument that programs based on toys exploited children.

Indeed, the argument that cartoons were worse for children if they were based on preexisting products came across as naive. ACT asserted that cashing in on an already popular TV character by marketing toys was ethically better than creating a character in order to make popular licensed products. In a world of conglomerates, such an argument quickly hatches into a chicken-egg debate. Corporate synergy makes transmedia intertextuality virtually inevitable because one megacorporation owns the means to produce, distribute, and sell a wide variety of products. Toys, TV shows, video games, and comic books orbit around each other in a sort of Möbius strip; criticizing the ensemble is crucial, but noting which product came first is probably of little value as a cornerstone of a legal argument, and, in any case, ACT's chicken-egg arguments were of no interest to the FCC.

Formed at the end of the activist sixties, ACT was ill-suited to compete with eighties right-wing activism, activism that the Reagan and Bush administrations and their FCCs were clearly sympathetic to. This is not to say that ACT had no success in the eighties: in 1987, the courts ordered the FCC to investigate the product-based program phenomenon, and the Children's Television Act was finally passed in 1990. But the Reagan and Bush FCCs turned a deaf ear to ACT, while right-wing groups like the Moral Majority occupied the limelight. The Moral Majority was concerned about rich bitch Joan Collins on *Dynasty*, not cute little Strawberry Shortcake, failing to see that these icons of white womanhood were two sides of one profitable coin.

Conclusion

In her 1984 account of how girls and boys play differently, Vivian Gussin Paley records the following exchange:

Andrew: All the little girls love Strawberry Shortcake now.
Teacher: I wonder why that is.
Andrew: They think she has a nice smell.
Teacher: Do you like that smell?
Andrew: Boys don't like smells.
Teacher: Don't like smells?
Andrew: I mean boys like bad smells. I mean dangerous smells. Like volcano smells.
Jonathan: Vampire smells.
Teacher: Well, Strawberry Shortcake doesn't have to worry about volcanoes or vampires. The girls never put those things in their stories [that they make up about Shortcake].
Teddy: Because vampires aren't pretty. We like stuff that isn't pretty, but not girls. They like only pretty things.[73]

Although the idea of vampire and volcano smells is intriguing, it is difficult to draw much hope for nontraditional gender roles from these comments. Like vampires and volcanoes, many product-based programs stink, not just because of their racial tokenism and sexism but also because they were made viable by deregulation. Ultimately, perhaps what stinks most about *Strawberry Shortcake* is that it symbolizes the Reagan and Bush "free market" mentality, which meant that the FCC would no longer listen to consumer complaints. Its retort was consistently, "If you don't like it, don't buy it." Like other reformers, ACT was left out in the cold because it did not buy the FCC's new philosophy. The price of the free market was citizen disempowerment.

But in spite of the setbacks of the eighties, the Children's Television Act was finally passed, which ACT saw as a milestone achievement. It represented an important victory because it meant that broadcasters could be held accountable for something besides the ratings. The act states that broadcasters must serve children's informational and educational needs, and it reinstates advertising time limits. It does not outlaw product-based programs, although it does prohibit host-selling. In other words, the act does not eliminate the programming that was the impetus for it in the first place. There are fewer product-based programs now than there were in the mid-eighties, but this is mainly because the market was overglutted with licensed characters and finally bottomed out. It was low ratings and toy sales, not high ethical standards, that brought about the lowered profile of *Strawberry Shortcake, The Care Bears, He-Man,* and other product-based programs. Nonetheless, these cartoons continue to garner high video rentals and remain in video stores, even if they have lost some of their former broadcasting visibility.

Whereas the eighties saw the adult vilification of the entire genre of product-based programs, in the early nineties, the *Mighty Morphin' Power Rangers* show became the kidvid scapegoat. Although adults objected to the licensed *Power Rangers* merchandise their children demanded, they attacked this show more for its presumed violent effects than for its commercialism. Thumbing their noses at the law once again, in their 1995 reports to the FCC, some broadcasters disingenuously claimed that *Power Rangers* satisfied the Children's Television Act's requirement that broadcasters present educational programming. The Children's Television Act clearly did not solve all the problems its advocates had hoped it would solve.[74] However, in September 1997 the act's enforcement was increased. Broadcasters are now forced to provide three hours per week of educational children's programs; they can no longer get away with sticking educational labels on old noneducational shows. In any case, it seems that children continue to like all the shows that adults hate and could not care less about whether or not the act is ultimately successful. Unfortunately, this assertion is difficult to prove because children's feelings about the act are difficult to gauge. Their attitudes about the act are conspicuously absent from public debate.

Ultimately, the only thing contemporary researchers may be able to use to construct a reception history of product-based programs is adult discourse. Charren's and Fowler's opinions were widely published, and congressional records show debates over the Children's Television Act. We have comparatively few resources to gain entry into *children's* perceptions of eighties cartoons.[75] With a few major exceptions,[76] social scientific studies (especially quantitative analyses) of children's attitudes toward product-based programs and other TV shows tend to be structured by researchers' agendas in such a way that children's voices rarely shine through. The adult voices of the eighties, conversely, rise up in a tumultuous din. It is not that contemporary media researchers could ever simply find the pure voices of past audiences; we are always working with fragments, traces, clues. But the clues we have from children are scarce, whereas adult traces abound in the magazine articles, scientific studies, TV interviews, and newspaper stories of the eighties. In all these sources, it is virtually impossible to find a quotation from a child venturing an opinion on *He-Man* or *My Little Pony*.

One can, however, find grown-ups eager to reminisce about their love for such programs. Teaching my students about the attack on product-based programs is interesting because they were children at the height of the licensed-character craze. The shows that ACT, social scientists, legislators, and other disgruntled adults dismissed as unmitigated garbage were their favorite shows. Now adults themselves, they have a lot to say about the stories and characters on shows that adults in the eighties claimed had no meaningful stories or characters. On the other hand, they are quick to criticize *contemporary* programming as being overly commercial! There seems to be a discernible pattern in adult attacks on children's culture. Adults of *any* generation will argue that the products of their own youth were good, whereas today's stuff is bad.[77]

For almost a decade, ACT and others argued that product-based programs were the ultimate pariah, but they could not censor them off the air. In the nineties, *Power Rangers* represented The Enemy, and adult censorship continued both on playgrounds and on the floors of Congress, where the v-chip and program ratings were touted as panaceas in 1996 and 1997. To the contemporary observer, it may seem that *Sesame Street* is the only show to escape the fickle ebb and flow of censorious adult opinion. As macho boys' shows and glitzy girls' shows come and go, the only mainstay of children's television seems to be the nonviolent and "gender-neutral" *Sesame Street*, a show apparently immune to the forces of censorship. But looks can be deceiving.

Turned-on Toddlers and Space Age TV

5

Debating *Sesame Street*

Many journalists, parents, teachers, congressional representatives, and academics have held up the educational public television program *Sesame Street* (1969–) as the epitome of "good" television. Many parents like the show because of its educational goals, its nonviolence, its multicultural cast, and its high production values. In 1993, the program won kudos from liberals for nodding to feminism and adding an extroverted female muppet. (This did not happen sooner because the show's muppet maker, the late Jim Henson, was resistant to developing strong female characters.)[1] The program is widely considered to be high quality and in "good taste." Notwithstanding its squeaky clean image, this program, which seems so obviously "good" at first glance, so obviously uncensorable, has been the focus of numerous adult debates over what is good and what is bad for children. Criticism of *Sesame Street* appeared immediately after its 1969 premiere and continued into the seventies.

Close examination of adult criticism of *Sesame Street* is crucial to this book for two reasons. First, I have claimed that adults are a large audience for children's programs. Adults shape the programs, decide whether or not they are successful, and discern what effects programs may have on children. *Sesame Street* continues to be one of the most well funded and successful programs on television; no children's program has been more widely discussed and studied by adults. It thus represents an ideal case study of how both academic and nonacademic adults create and read children's programs. The second reason I take up *Sesame Street* in this chapter is to expand my discussion of children's programs beyond those that are most frequently targeted by pressure groups as "bad"—cheap cartoons. It is necessary to study a good program because good programs define themselves in relation to bad ones and vice versa. Good and bad programs draw on each other for style and content. "Bad" shows incorporate educational elements and public service messages into their stories in order to combat their critics, and "good" programs use fast pacing, popular licensed characters, and popular formats (such as the game show format of *Where in the World Is Carmen San Diego?*) in order to increase their audience popularity. In asserting its own high quality, *Sesame Street* has even gone so far as to parody *Mighty Morphin' Power Rangers* in a "Super Morphin' Mega Monsters" skit about cooperation being better than violent problem solving. With the Mega Monsters skit, *Sesame Street* defines itself as good precisely by virtue of its not being the bad *Power Rangers*. The skit reassures parents that even though TV can be dangerous, they have done the right thing by allowing their children to watch *Sesame Street*. The "Super Morphin' Mega Monsters" skit illustrates that good (uncensorable) and bad (censorable) programs are not binaries but rather mutually defining. To understand adult debates over which images endanger children, we need to ask not only why some images are contested but also why other images are praised.

Bridging the Gap?

When *Sesame Street* first appeared on the air on 10 November 1969, it was unique in several ways. *Sesame Street*'s initial budget was $8,191,100,[2] the largest amount of money ever put into a U.S. educational television series. The program stressed cognitive development, whereas other programs stressed creative play (*Romper Room*) or affective (emotional) development (*Mister Rogers' Neighborhood*). In other words, *Sesame Street* strove to teach mental skills, while other programs sought to teach socialization and to help children cope with common childhood fears. Shows such as *Mister Rogers*, *Captain Kangaroo*, and *Romper Room* reflected the traditional view of the preschool years as a time when children's education should focus on teaching social skills, not cognitive ones. *Sesame Street*, on the other hand, more closely reflected the Montessori view of early education, in which preschool is a radical pedagogical experience. Maria Montessori was an Italian educator whose theories initially peaked in popularity in the teens and twenties. Educators renewed their interest in Montessori methods in the sixties, perhaps because such theories seemed compatible with postwar permissive childrearing practices.[3] Montessori's ideas were so popular that the 1964 English edition of her book *The Montessori Method*, originally published in 1912, went through nineteen reprints. Although Montessori stressed sensory and motor development through hands-on activities that the television screen could not directly provide, the *Sesame Street* philosophy had elements in common with the basic tenet of Montessori philosophy— that enriching the child's preschool experience can help counteract the negative effects of an impoverished home environment. In keeping with the Montessori method, the Children's Television Workshop (CTW), *Sesame Street*'s creator, embraced the idea that intelligence is not predetermined at birth but rather can be fostered by early education. This idea ran counter to the dominant prewar Darwinist educational philosophies that insisted on predetermined, biologically based intelligence.[4] And like Montessori, the CTW was strongly committed to teaching poor children in particular.[5]

Sesame Street rode the wave of the sixties "cognitive revolution" in psychology. Cognitive psychologists researching TV's possible effects seemed to turn away from earlier behaviorist models of subjectivity. In theory, this meant that many psychologists reconceptualized subjects as active participants in their environment rather than as passive slaves to stimuli. Cognitive researchers theorized that people used mental "scripts" to make meaning, and many developmentalists used Jean Piaget's theories to explain the child's cognitive maturation process.[6] Yet, as David Buckingham has argued, cognitive psychologists did not abandon many of behaviorism's methodological assumptions. Buckingham explains that when cognitive psychologists study media viewers and media texts,

> [c]ognitive processing is widely defined as a "mediating variable"—in other words, as something that intervenes between stimulus and response [the crux of behaviorism]. Despite the emphasis on children as active constructors of meaning, meaning is still largely seen as something contained within the text, which can be "objectively" identified and quantified. Thus, the text itself is typically defined as a "stimulus": "formal features" such as camera movements or editing techniques are seen to have fixed meaning, and their "effects" are studied in isolation from the contexts in which they occur.[7]

The CTW exemplified the cognitive revolution that Buckingham describes: the CTW rejected the old stimulus-response passive-viewer model, preferring a cognitive conception of child subjects, while nonetheless clinging to the idea of a text as a stimulus that can be fine-tuned to produce certain specific, radical cognitive responses.

The CTW did, however, try to go beyond textual determinism in conceptualizing *Sesame Street*'s child audience. Initially, *Sesame Street*'s focus was on "bridging the gap" between "advantaged" and "disadvantaged" U.S. children. *Sesame Street* would do this by aiding the cognitive development of the poor, who, the CTW reasoned, could not afford preschool. Soon after *Sesame Street*'s release, the idea of bridging the gap was deemphasized because it was found to be in poor rhetorical judgment. *Sesame Street*'s producers realized that in order to truly bridge the gap, the disadvantaged would have to learn more from *Sesame Street* than the advantaged, or the advantaged would have to be prevented from watching *Sesame Street*. So the initial goal was revised: *Sesame Street* would help *all* preschool children get a cognitive head start by teaching them letter and number recognition and helping them master other simple cognitive tasks. *Sesame Street* was a stimulus that the CTW hoped would produce a particular response: improved cognition, which would lead to greater success in school and eventually to improved socioeconomic status.

Another reason the idea of bridging the gap was finally deemphasized by the CTW was that it evoked the "deficit model" of education, which the CTW had rejected while still in its planning stages. CTW staff member Gerald Lesser explains that educators subscribing to the deficit learning model felt that compensatory education programs could improve the lot of the poor by giving them certain middle-class "advantages," such as the ability to speak standard white English.[8] Some schools might strive to give poor children a particularly structured environment to compensate for the presumed chaos of the poor child's home life, or nurturing teachers might try to compensate for a presumed lack of tenderness and love at home. Lesser argues that "correcting" the poor would not make them into middle-class children and that compensatory programs problematically seek to make disadvantaged children "like everyone else."[9] He contends that the goal of *Sesame Street*'s planners was not to make the poor into the cognitive equals of the middle class but rather "to give disadvantaged children what they need in order to cope with their environments and improve their lives."[10] This vague contention was as specific as the CTW would get about its goals for impoverished viewers.

Debating Education in the Sixties

Sesame Street's philosophy of childhood learning and cognition was clearly indebted not only to Montessori but also to Project Head Start, a component of President Lyndon Johnson's War on Poverty. Both Head Start and *Sesame Street* depended on the premise that human development occurred very rapidly in the first few years of life and that improving the disadvantaged child's early environment was imperative if one wanted "not only to relieve the symptoms of poverty but to cure it; and, above all, to prevent it." [11] Like Head Start, *Sesame Street* received government funding and drew inspiration from social scientific research that showed how environment affected early child development. At this time, two highly influential books on intelligence and early environment were J. McVicker Hunt's 1961 *Intelligence and Experience* and Benjamin Bloom's 1964 *Stability and Change in Human Characteristics.*

Hunt's and Bloom's research, Project Head Start, and *Sesame Street* should be understood in the context of late-sixties educational politics. In 1969, the year *Sesame Street* premiered, the Westingham Learning Corporation released a negative evaluation of Head Start that questioned whether its benefits were lasting, and the Nixon administration consequently reduced its support of the program. That same year, Arthur R. Jensen published his controversial article, "How Much Can We Boost I.Q. and Scholastic Achievement?" This *Bell Curve* predecessor attacked environmental psychologists for ignoring the role played by genetics in determining I.Q. Drawing on data showing that "Negroes" consistently tested lower than "Caucasians" across all socioeconomic status levels, Jensen argued that blacks had lower I.Q.'s than whites because of genetic predisposition. [12] Never questioning the objectivity or value of intelligence tests, Jensen cited data showing that 42.9 percent of the poorest blacks had an I.Q. below 75, which indicated that they were "mentally retarded," whereas only 7.8 percent of the poorest whites could be labeled "mentally retarded." [13] Jensen's views were attacked, but he had many supporters as well. [14] His data was, like so many facts, "correct and nevertheless without truth," as radical pedagogical theorists Paulo Freire and Donaldo Macedo put it. [15] Many African Americans *do* score lower on I.Q. tests than whites, but numerical test scores provide no understanding of the power relations underpinning test-score disparity. Furthermore, as anthropologist Stephen Jay Gould and others have convincingly argued, the very idea that intelligence is truly a measurable quality is disputable.

In the wake of the 1969 Jensen controversy, the nature/nurture debate was at the forefront of school-reform debates at both the local and the national level. In 1972, another controversial text appeared, Christopher Jencks's *Inequality*, which argued that school reform was not likely to lead to a changed distribution of wealth because research had shown that highly educated blacks did not reap more financial and professional rewards than did less-educated whites. Jencks nonetheless favored putting money into the school system. He felt that even though educational reform would be utterly ineffective at changing socioeconomic status, schools should be made as comfortable as possible since children have to spend all day there.[16] The children have no bread? Let them eat cake!

Sesame Street turned to the government for funding at a time when the status of U.S. education and the need for government-sponsored reform were being hotly debated. Although the government in no way controlled *Sesame Street*'s form or content, 48.8 percent of its initial budget came from the Department of Health, Education, and Welfare.[17] In her original funding proposal, CTW founder Joan Ganz Cooney argued that *Sesame Street* could be financed for as little as a penny per child per day. Although the CTW never argued against school reform, clearly *Sesame Street* had potential as a comparatively cheap alternative to structural school reform. Hoping to affect the socioeconomic disparity between blacks and whites, *Sesame Street* shared Project Head Start's goals, but it operated at a fraction of the cost. In addition, unlike Head Start, *Sesame Street* turned out to be an exportable, reusable product. *Sesame Street* proved to be a good investment. When the project was initially pitched, however, the Department of Health, Education, and Welfare was shortsighted. In explaining *Sesame Street*'s early history, Cooney is emphatic that one of the highest hurdles was convincing the department that educational TV could reach an inner-city and/or lower-class audience.[18] Perhaps the department assumed that this audience would ignore TV that was not pure entertainment. There was also reasonable concern that *Sesame Street*'s audience would be limited because so many areas of the country, particularly rural areas, had fuzzy UHF reception. PBS tended to be ghettoized at the UHF end of the spectrum, and many sets did not even have the capability to receive UHF signals. The FCC had not made UHF reception mandatory for television sets until 1962.

Cognition as a Leveler of Social Differences

Social scientific research on children and television often articulates cognitive development as a bridge across class and race differences. Indeed, such differences are often ignored or factored out of research subjects. Given the CTW's cognitive agenda, then, it is not surprising that when it was criticized for not bridging the advantaged/disadvantaged gap, it fell back on the universalizing concept of cognition as a safety net. In other words, it could offer up the defense that it was merely operating on the premise that *every* child's cognitive skills could be developed by viewing *Sesame Street*. *Sesame Street* showed an integrated neighborhood of Anglos, Latinas, Latinos, and African Americans and taught viewers how to count in Spanish. In this way, the show highlighted cultural differences and diversity. But at the same time, *Sesame Street* worked on the assumption that cognition could be the great universalizer, the leveler of cultural heterogeneity. Cognition was a kind of deep structure shared by all. The idea that our brains make us all biologically and therefore *potentially* socially, culturally, and economically the same is preferable to the Jensen (and later *Bell Curve*) approach, which holds that it is the differences in our brains that produce the differences in our lives. But the idea that cognition can be an equalizer can blind researchers to real structural inequalities (such as institutional racism) that preschool TV has never challenged.

Whatever the limitations of a deep-structure conception of cognition and however much such a conception may ignore important cultural factors, it is important to bear in mind that many sixties and seventies educators conceived of the brain as the great equalizer in order to combat racist scholars like Jensen. One study of Mexican American children illustrates the contrast between racist and comparatively liberal views of child development at the time, but the study also illustrates the troubling ways that cognitive studies cannot adequately address research subjects' cultural and material existence. Unlike Jensen, Edward A. De Avila, Barbara Havassy, and Juan Pascual-Leone deplored the disproportionate number of minorities placed in classes for the "mentally retarded" based on I.Q. scores. Their belief in deep-structural developmental similarities across racial and ethnic groups enabled them to question the cultural biases of Jensen's data.[19] De Avila et al. had no doubt that all brains are equal and that one could prove such equality by showing that children of all social backgrounds scored identically on certain tests. The researchers found that Mexican American children performed as well as Anglo children on Piagetian developmental tests. However, they also reported "aberrant" and "inconclusive" test results when they tested a group with a large number of recent Mexican immigrants and migrant workers. The researchers had not successfully accomplished their stated goal of removing all "external environmental variables" in order to examine internal developmental variables in their pure state. Their failure to accomplish such cultural evacuation did not lead them to question their methodology. These developmentalists were liberals fighting racism, and their goals sharply contrasted with the racist goals Jensen demonstrated in his I.Q. studies. But their developmental approach was akin to Jensen's sociobiological approach in that neither could account for the cultural identity of their research subjects. Both Jensen and De Avila et al. erased the cultural identities of their experimental subjects, the former in order to demonstrate the inferiority of people of color to whites and the latter in order to show that people of color were not inferior to whites. Like *Sesame Street*'s producers, De Avila et al. believed cognitivism could have emancipatory results.

Fast Pacing and the Developmentalist Debates

Upon *Sesame Street*'s initial release, many media critics and educators harshly critiqued the program for its fast-paced teaching style. Cooney's background was in commercial television, and she rejected the low-budget, slow-paced educational programming that had preceded *Sesame Street* on narrowcast ITV (instructional television). Educational programming, much of it extremely low budget and locally produced, had generally featured a teacher at a blackboard explaining concepts. Cooney criticized locally produced programming for its "slow and monotonous pace and lack of professionalism."[20] Cooney envisioned an educational program that could compete with network television. She said, "Children are conditioned to expect pow! wham! fast-action thrillers from television [as well as] . . . highly visual, slickly and expensively produced material."[21] *Sesame Street* would exploit such conditioning by being fast paced, modeling itself on Rowan and Martin's *Laugh-In* by using quick vignettes.[22]

[T]he spellbinding attraction of *Sesame Street* was its staccato style, popularized by the prime-time series, Rowan and Martin's *Laugh-In* (NBC, 1968–1973). Featuring a razzle-dazzle of zooms, quick cuts, and speeded-up action that captured viewer attention, each show comprised thirty to fifty separate segments, rarely longer than three minutes each, occasionally as short as twelve seconds. While the pacing was slowed in the late seventies, with fewer and longer segments, the tempo still contrasted markedly with the more leisurely style of such widely approved preschool series as *Mister Rogers' Neighborhood* and *Captain Kangaroo*.[23]

Animated segments on particular letters of the alphabet were conceived as ads that would interrupt the program just like real ads on commercial television. The show's adlike look was troubling to critics, who felt that it helped children develop a taste for advertisements.

Sesame Street's style may well have fostered a taste for advertising, but it is just as likely that it appealed to child viewers because they already liked the pacing, sounds, and images of commercials. The critique of *Sesame Street*'s style often assumed that the show acclimated children to advertising for the first time, an assumption that mistakenly supposed that there is an easily discernible before and after to children's introduction to consumer culture. Child exposure to consumer culture is constant. For example, it is not unusual for hospitals to outfit newborn babies in diapers emblazoned with licensed characters such as Mickey Mouse. It is perfectly reasonable for parents to attempt to shelter their children from all that such diapers symbolize, but the fact is that adults who fear that their babies and toddlers may be contaminated by TV or billboards are probably too late. Television is an important symbolic player in the uphill battle against commercialism, and many parents see public television, theoretically ad-free, as a safety zone where children will not be exposed to commercialism, in spite of the fact that corporate sponsorship is the norm on public television.[24] Parents who objected to *Sesame Street*'s commercial style may have felt that their trust in PBS had been violated.

Sesame Street's government funders worried whether the masses would watch a program on PBS, generally a site of high-culture adult programming such as symphonies and filmed stage productions. But I would posit that some of the initial resistance to *Sesame Street* came not from the masses, who were uninterested in PBS pretension, but rather from the elite, who feared public television would be corrupted by unsuitable, fast-paced programming. Some parents and critics reacted strongly against *Sesame Street's* commercial style because PBS was supposed to be above commercialism. In other words, *Sesame Street* violated their expectations about public broadcasting's "good taste."

Whereas critics feared the show would instill a taste for ads in children, the CTW saw its style choice as purely pragmatic: to compete with commercial TV for children's attention, *Sesame Street* had to look like commercial TV. Unlike the locally produced ITV that preceded *Sesame Street*, the CTW proposed not merely to teach facts but to "succeed in touching the child's imagination, his life, and his dreams."[25] Although the CTW assumed that most people would appreciate an educational program that permeated children's dreams, it is easy to see why some anti–*Sesame Street* adults might focus on the dystopian dimensions of such an invasion of the child's life. Like the CTW, these critics could see that *Sesame Street* tapped into exactly the kinds of visual and aural cues that appealed to young children: lively music, sound effects, pans, peculiar voices, and audio changes. Indeed, in a 1987 study, Dafna Lemish found that infant viewers were consistently drawn to two kinds of programming: advertisements and *Sesame Street*.[26]

So this was one camp of *Sesame Street* detractors: parents and journalists who expressed their criticisms of *Sesame Street's* fast-paced adlike style in newspaper cartoons, magazine articles, and letters to the editor. Another camp of detractors also focused on *Sesame Street's* quick pace: professional educators and developmental psychologists. Since *Sesame Street's* creators believed that children's brains are naturally curious and can be conditioned through early priming to be thirsty for knowledge, they reasoned that a preschool child who had been regularly exposed to *Sesame Street* would come to school better prepared to learn than one who had not. Having mastered cognitive tasks such as letter, number, and shape recognition and the ability to categorize, the *Sesame Street* viewer would have a higher level of cognitive development than the non–*Sesame Street* viewer. However, some developmental psychologists worried that *Sesame Street* would be harmful to what they defined as the child's "natural" maturation, and they argued that *Sesame Street* would rush a child through his/her natural progressive developmental stages. To rush a child into learning, particularly with a rapidly paced program like *Sesame Street*, would do more harm than good. A Project Head Start education specialist even feared *Sesame Street* could encourage neurotic mothering: "[T]he introduction of letters and sounds [would be] tantamount to teaching young children to read and this would lead to overanxious middle-class mothers forcing their children to watch the program."[27]

In "Turned-on Toddlers," clinical psychologist Werner I. Halpern claimed that "fast-paced TV bombardment" can "overwhelm the child's defenses against sensory overload."[28] As his essay's title indicates, Halpern implied that TV could affect children in a way analogous to drugs.[29] The TV-drug analogy is one that is still made today, but it was more common in the late sixties and early seventies when "turned-on and tuned-out" hippies were abundant and many middle-class adults were anxious about LSD use. In a 1969 *Boston Globe* article, one typical critic of drugs and TV said, "[T]he kinship of the LSD and other drug experiences with television is glaringly obvious: both depend upon turning on and passively waiting for something beautiful to happen."[30] A Piagetian, Halpern believed that the "rate of development cannot accelerate indefinitely without jeopardizing cognitive and educational growth."[31] Halpern criticized educators and parents who overzealously push children to achieve cognitive development levels beyond what he considered to be their innate developmental capability, and he cited *Sesame Street* as one of the many tools such as educational films, filmstrips, and videotapes that can be used to prod and overwhelm children. Drawing on his own clinical experience, Halpern recounted his observations of toddlers brought to the child guidance clinic of Rochester, New York's, Mental Health Center. These toddlers exhibited "behavior symptoms" that were "directly traceable" to *Sesame Street*. Some children "compulsively recited serial numbers and letters learned from *Sesame Street*. Usually these recitations occurred in the absence of any apparent cues. While they delivered themselves of these speech fragments, the children often inspected their inanimate surroundings like restless, wound-up robots."[32] Halpern argued that "sensory assault" requiring rapid perceptual shifts through the use of quick dissolves and zooms, coupled with the lack of pauses between *Sesame Street* segments, was harmful to "organismic balance."[33] If a child's nervous system was overtaxed by *Sesame Street* and other fast-paced programs, Halpern reasoned, his/her development could be irreparably damaged. This kind of argument harkens back to behaviorist criticisms of radio and film in the thirties; both me-diums were considered dangerous to children because they were "over-stimulating." The "normal" child was the least-stimulated child.

After *Sesame Street*'s release, a split emerged between psychologists who favored *Sesame Street* and those who favored *Mister Rogers' Neighborhood*.[34] The pro–*Mister Rogers* school of thought was that a young child needed to feel loved and nurtured more than he/she needed to know how to recognize let-ters and numbers. Perhaps the most outspoken pro-*Rogers* developmental-ists were Jerome Singer and Dorothy Singer. The Singers' research showed that children benefited from the kind of imaginative play encouraged on *Mister Rogers*: "They can wait quietly or delay gratification, can concentrate better, and seem to be more emphatic and less aggressive, thanks to their use of private fantasy."[35] The Singers' approach to TV was similar to that of ACT: they both promoted "high-quality" TV rather than simply con-demning TV across the board. In fact, in the early eighties, the Singers had a column in *TV Guide*, in which they advised parents how to manage their children's TV habits. They never argued that the "plug-in drug" should be eliminated altogether. Although the Singers were not outspoken anti-TV crusaders, they did argue that the general pacing of television led to short-ened attention spans in children. (Some grammar school teachers shared this concern, fearing that they could not successfully compete with *Sesame Street* for children's attention and respect. They worried that the show would make children reject school as comparatively boring, as in a 1970 cartoon that showed two boys leaving a classroom and remarking, "*Sesame Street* it's not" [figure 4]. Again, this echoes concern among teachers in the thirties and forties that they could not compete with the stimulation that radio and films offered avid child viewers.) The Singers argued that "[n]o sane parent would present a child with a fire engine, snatch it away in 30 seconds, replace it with a set of blocks, snatch that away 30 seconds later, replace the blocks with clay, and then replace the clay with a toy car. Yet, in effect, a young child receives that kind of experience when he or she watches American television."[36] Although *Sesame Street* was on noncom-mercial TV, it offered no break from the pacing of regular TV. The Singers argued that because of its emphasis on emotional development rather than cognitive skills and its slow, careful pacing, *Mister Rogers* was more psycho-logically healthy for children. Interestingly, the Singers pointed out that many adults dislike the program: "His sugary style irritates many parents.

Figure 4. Cartoon illustrating that teachers fear they cannot compete with *Sesame Street* for children's attention. © 1970 by Janice and Stanley Berenstein. *Source:* Gerald Lesser, *Children and Television: Lessons from Sesame Street* (New York: Random House, 1974).

They feel his pace is too slow and that he is perhaps not sufficiently mas-culine in his manner. *But Mister Rogers is not talking to parents. He is talking to three- and four-year-old children*" (original emphasis).[37] The authors correctly observe that popular criticisms of *Mister Rogers* spring from adult rather than child concerns, such as the desire for "sufficiently masculine" role models. The Singers reason that *adult* criticisms of *Mister Rogers* are ir-relevant because the program serves children well. One could, of course, similarly rebut adult *Sesame Street* critics. Just as *Mister Rogers* is too slow only for adult tastes, perhaps *Sesame Street* is too fast only for adult tastes.

Targeting *Sesame Street* to Adults

The developmentalists notwithstanding, *Sesame Street* did suit the tastes of many adults. One 1972 *New Yorker* cartoon poked fun at the show's adult appeal by showing a respectable society matron reminding her husband it was time to watch the show. Watching *Sesame Street* with your child was seen as a healthful alternative to using TV as an "electronic baby-sitter."[38] Another *New Yorker* cartoon, from 1970, even went so far as to construct *Sesame Street* not as a baby-sitter but as a maternal obligation. A police officer confronts a woman in a park, asking why her child is there instead of at home watching the show.

To draw adult viewers, *Sesame Street* featured guest stars recognizable primarily to adults, and celebrities who appeal to adults still commonly appear on the program. Early in the show's history, stars such as Carol Burnett, Burt Lancaster, and James Earl Jones appeared on *Sesame Street*. The show's producers earnestly claimed that such celebrities were on the show to encourage parents and older children to watch with younger viewers, the assumption being that children would benefit more from the program if they discussed it afterward with older viewers.[39] Although this is no doubt a sincere explanation of why stars and political figures such as Hillary Rodham Clinton have appeared on the program, the presence of such stars not only drew adults to watching with children but also helped them to enjoy and therefore support the program. Entertaining adults was crucial if *Sesame Street* was to succeed.[40] Whereas *Mister Rogers* was relatively cheap and was backed by the Sears Roebuck Foundation, *Sesame Street* initially cost over $8 million and received almost half of its funding from the government. The stakes were high: both taxpayers and the Department of Health, Education, and Welfare had to be convinced that *Sesame Street* was a good show.

Sesame Street's producers avoided discussing the program in overtly politically charged terms. Such caution was probably tactical. Since *Sesame Street* was funded by the Department of Health, Education, and Welfare to teach cognitive skills, it could not risk losing its funding by admitting to any implicit political goals. But whether the CTW talked about it or not, the show's style and its picture of racial integration were certainly overtly controversial. The CTW said that guest celebrities were featured simply to encourage adult viewers to join their children in front of the TV, but *Sesame Street* guests included celebrities who had long been on Hollywood's blacklist. The inclusion of blacklisted performers was an explicitly political choice and one that reveals the strong liberal convictions of *Sesame Street*'s creators. If they had cared only about their show succeeding and keeping its funding, they certainly would not have risked alienating adult viewers who would object to the inclusion of blacklisted actors such as Zero Mostel and Pete Seeger.[41]

Pat Paulsen was another potentially risky guest. Some adult viewers saw *Sesame Street*'s modern style as psychedelic and feared its potential "addictiveness." They worried that *Sesame Street* was too much like an acid trip and therefore might predispose children to dropping acid.[42] Those who disapproved of *Sesame Street*'s style as hippie or psychedelic would have found their worst fears confirmed with the appearance of Paulsen, a *Smothers Brothers Comedy Hour* regular. Even if he was only reciting the alphabet in his trademark deadpan style, Paulsen's presence connoted the *Smothers Brothers*, which had been branded countercultural and was well known for its critical stance toward U.S. involvement in Vietnam, as well as for its liberal attitude toward integration and interracial relationships. In retrospect, both *Sesame Street* and *The Smothers Brothers* seem relatively tame, and it is hard to understand why both were so controversial in the late sixties and early seventies. Both programs relied on stylistic elements—sets, costumes, zoom shots, and editing techniques such as fast cuts, shot superimpositions, lap dissolves—that strongly evoked the youth counterculture, and both portrayed an integrated world that was a relative rarity on television. Although *Sesame Street* strove to appeal to children by using a modern, youth-coded style, it risked losing some of its parent audience (the conservative Middle Americans whom President Richard Nixon referred to in 1971 as "the silent majority") because of that style.

Sesame Street needed wide adult approval to maintain its funding, but it was guided by liberal principles that meant it could not succeed with all adults. *Sesame Street*'s liberalism appealed to those who appreciated a variety of hip guest stars, some of them enemies of the right, whereas more conservative adults (not unlike the liberals who feared the show's style would indoctrinate children in commercial values) were turned off by the show's "happening" style, which might indoctrinate "turned-on toddlers" in the hippie mentality. Ostensibly a children's show, *Sesame Street* could not have been more thoroughly enmeshed in the politics of the adult world.

Communism, Integration, and Space Age TV

Sesame Street played a dual role in the drama of sixties and seventies Cold War anxiety. On the one hand, *Sesame Street* was attacked by right-wingers for its "pinko," liberal beliefs. The far right saw the show as un-American. On the other hand, the program was a manifestation of the post-Sputnik Cold War drive to ensure that U.S. children were better educated than Communist children, and in this way, *Sesame Street* could not have been more American. Panicked by the fact that the Soviet Union reached outer space before the United States did, the U.S. government was determined never to be scooped again. U.S. children would be the most up-to-date in the world; these modern children would be educated for the space age.

A key part of *Sesame Street*'s early success was its modern image, which was underpinned by a technologically deterministic faith in TV.[43] The show depended on the most advanced research in education, and it used testing to produce a body of scientific data proving its worth. As Michèle Mattelart has noted, one of *Sesame Street*'s major funders, the Carnegie Foundation,

> had taken a close interest in the psychologists, educationalists and child-specialists of the cognitive school who had been dubbed "modern" by comparison with the "traditionalists." To attain their goals, they suggested—amongst other pedagogic strategies—the technique of "verbal bombardment," on which they had experimented with children from underprivileged milieux. In their book *Teaching Disadvantaged Children*, Carl Bereiter and Siegfried Engelman draw up a list of the basic skills of which a child should be capable before entering the first year of school. These items became a programming guide for *Sesame Street*. . . . [I]t is this codified *scientific framework*, already organised in the form of a sequential programme, which revealed itself to be the most useful, tailor-made for the serialised format of *Sesame Street*.[44] (my emphasis)

Sesame Street was scientifically modern not only in its pedagogical strategies but also in its appearance. The program used computer animation, chroma keying, pixillation, word matting, abstract animation, and other techniques that gave it a technologically modern look. By using such techniques, it displayed its high budget and distinguished itself from "cheap" and "nonprofessional" narrowcast educational programs. *Sesame Street* saw itself as "space age" TV, as Loretta Moore Long made explicit in her 1973 dissertation, *"Sesame Street": A Space Age Approach to Education for Space Age Children*.

Long was a *Sesame Street* cast member with an insider's understanding of the show's goals. She explained that children need all the cognitive help they can get in order to be prepared for life in a technologically dynamic society. For her (and the CTW), technological progress unequivocally meant progress toward a greater good: "There is no reason why the same technology that puts men on the moon cannot be utilized to teach Johnny to read." [45] Long argued that education for preschool children is imperative because we need to "equip these citizens of the twenty-first century for their future, which may well include space travel, developing totally new lifestyles, and working in occupations that we have not even envisioned." [46] She concluded her dissertation with the lyrics of a *Sesame Street* song about a future when people live on the moon. As fantastic as moon habitation may sound, it does appear that *Sesame Street*'s producers saw the program as providing the cognitive training necessary for the astronauts of tomorrow.[47]

In his book on *Sesame Street*, CTW staffer Gerald Lesser excerpts an anti–*Sesame Street* article that demonstrates that some people watching the show saw not little astronauts but red-diaper babies. Lesser labels the article "an extreme instance of biased perception" that completely distorts the premises of *Sesame Street*.[48] The article is worth citing at length here in order to indicate the buttons *Sesame Street* pushed with its liberal, integrationist stance and to illustrate that some viewers read *Sesame Street* as a highly politically charged program that definitely taught children much more than cognitive skills or a protechnology space age attitude.

The young mother who sits her child in front of the TV to watch *Sesame Street* might be better off hiring Fidel Castro as a baby sitter! . . . Here are a few random facts for Moms (and Pops) to ponder:

(1) While parents study the horrors of "communism," *Sesame Street* introduces their tots to real live Reds, and sugarcoats those Reds to make them look like good guys. An excellent example is Pete Seeger, who shows up at nearly every major communist gathering and procommunist gathering in the world to strum his guitar and warble the praises of Red Revolution. Pete is a *Sesame Street* "lovable."

(2) At a time when small children should be learning the faith of their fathers and love of country, *Sesame Street* indoctrinates them into an anti-Christian, anti-national, faceless, raceless, one-worldism.

(3) *Sesame Street* purposely tries to indoctrinate children into complete disregard of racial distinctions and racial pride. Every greatest civiliza-

tion in history which dropped racial pride and tribal pride crumbled into oblivion. . . . [ellipsis in original]

. . . *Sesame Street*'s directors admit that they knocked out the house-wife-mother image to appease Women's Lib. In early programs a character known as Susan was a housewife, but this seems to offend the gruff-voiced he-gal types who preach that Mother's place is not in the home. . . . If Lib becomes strong, isn't it possible that *Sesame Street* will become even more perverted?

Sesame Street is already promoting biracial relationships. Could it not under pressure from the gruff-voice gals gradually "glorify" girl-girl relationships? Is there any real progress in doing away with Robert Louis Stevenson's Treasure Island, and replacing it with the Isle of Lesbos?[49]

The article conflates miscegenation, feminism, and lesbianism, issues that *Sesame Street* certainly made no intentional attempt to address. The quips about Fidel Castro, "Reds," and Pete Seeger illustrate that the presence of blacklisted celebrities on *Sesame Street* did more than merely encourage parents to view with their children. Clearly, some viewers were enraged by *Sesame Street*'s "Commie" cast. This article also illustrates that *Sesame Street*'s integrated world was not as subtle as Lesser implies. Lesser believed *Sesame Street* could help blacks by teaching them certain cognitive skills, but he felt the program could best address racial concerns *tangentially*. In the seminars held during *Sesame Street*'s preproduction research phase, Lesser argued that it was best "to teach about issues and emotions, not through content, but in context and through the life styles of the people on the program. An integrated cast, for example, can be a teaching device in itself. Through this *indirect* route, the program might also address itself to supplying some of the elements usually missing on television: real fathers, Negro men and women who love one another" (my emphasis).[50] Notwithstanding Lesser's claims for subtlety, the defensively racist response cited above bolsters Long's claim that *Sesame Street*'s integration was not merely a subtle detail but rather a *central component* of what Long called the program's "hidden curriculum" of racial tolerance and integration.

Unlike most research on *Sesame Street*—which includes several books and over a thousand scholarly articles and dissertations—Long's dissertation addressed the show's racial concerns directly. Long was intimately acquainted with *Sesame Street*'s goals through her own involvement with the program. She was cast as Susan, the show's African American house-wife who, as the disgruntled lesbophobe cited above correctly surmised, became a nurse in response to liberal protest. According to Long, and in counterdistinction to the majority of self-proclaimed liberal *Sesame Street* researchers, the program saw eradicating racism as absolutely *central* to its mission.[51] Citing the show's "conscious devices—an inner-city neighbor-hood, an integrated cast, an equal role for all children in solving prob-lems"—Long claims that *Sesame Street* has a "hidden curriculum that seeks to bolster the black and minority child's self-respect and to portray the multi-ethnic, multi-cultural world into which both majority and minority children are growing."[52] Interestingly, because affective learning was con-sidered untestable, Long provided proof of the hidden curriculum's suc-cess not by administering a barrage of tests but by creating a reception history. Long drew on viewer mail sent to her and the CTW to prove that the show effectively addressed racial issues.

According to Long, *Sesame Street* offered black children black charac-ters to admire and identify with to bolster their self-esteem and racial pride. Long recounts that African American children's feelings about their appearance were positively influenced by seeing *Sesame Street*'s black char-acters, Susan and Gordon. One mother wrote that her son asked her to stop straightening his hair so he could have an Afro like Susan's. Another mother wrote that after seeing a close-up of Susan's face, her child asked her, " '[D]o I have any of that stuff in my skin that Susan has?' When the mother replied 'yes, a little,' the child breathed a sigh of relief and said '*Thank Goodness!* ' "(original emphasis).[53] Another black child watching a black child on the show exclaimed, "Look! He looks like me and he knows the answers!"[54] A white mother recounted to Long that her daughter told her, " 'Susan and Gordon are bad people. They're different from us. Their hair and skin are all funny.' Some days later the child reported, 'Mommy, Susan and Gordon aren't really funny or bad. Now I know them, and every day they make me feel happy inside.' "[55]

Long explained that the decision to locate *Sesame Street* in an inner-city neighborhood crowded with garbage cans and old brownstones was cru-cial to the program's commitment to promoting racial understanding and tolerance. From today's perspective, it is hard to perceive *Sesame Street*'s antiseptic, inner-city soundstage as radical. Indeed, some people at the time criticized this set—and the rest of *Sesame Street*'s harmonious world—

as too sanitized. In 1971, the ever-cynical *MAD* magazine parodied the show as "Reality Street"; at the end of the parody, Reality Street is demolished to make way for a munitions plant. The Vietnam War or demolition crews would never disrupt the real, goody-goody Sesame Street. But the choice to represent an inner-city locale was nonetheless quite radical if one considers the sets of other children's educational programs — ITV classrooms, Mister Rogers's middle-class neighborhood, Captain Kangaroo's fantasy home, the *Kukla, Fran, and Ollie* puppet stage. Although the *Sesame Street* set was hardly an excursion into neorealist grittiness, compared to other children's educational programs, it represented a genuine attempt to show "real life" and to speak to children of color in America's inner cities. Long told a story to illustrate the effectiveness of the set:

> Many suburban children are sheltered from this type of neighborhood by their parents, and the setting of the show provides a window to the world for Whites, while helping the inner city child to relate more to us [the cast] as his neighbors. The almost magic effects of the show were related to me. . . . [S]ome children from a country day school in the suburbs of San Francisco were brought into the inner city for a trip to the museum. Going into the inner city caused much fear and trepidation on the part of school officials and parents. When they hit the ghetto neighborhood that surrounded the museum, the children on the bus became so excited that no one on the bus understood what they were saying. They were jumping up and down, saying, "Thank you! Thank you! Thank you!" Finally the teacher asked them, "Thank you for what?" and they all answered, "For bringing us to Sesame Street!" [56]

This anecdote offers an interesting contrast between adult and child perceptions. The parents feared the inner-city neighborhood their children would have to pass through on their way to the museum, a traditional site of high-class privilege. The children, because of *Sesame Street*, saw the inner city as a site of adventure rather than as a site of racism, poverty, or violence. They confused representation (*Sesame Street*'s fictional inner city) with what their parents perceived as reality (the dangerous ghetto).

Sesame Street's representation of inner city life included brownstones and trash cans. As early seventies TV critics noted, this was a completely sanitized inner city: a museum display of the inner city. Long called *Sesame Street* a "window" onto the inner city, but *Sesame Street* featured a set where sidewalks were perfect, streets were well paved, and the only thing that smelled bad was a grouchy puppet.

The Perils of Imitation and Reality Confusion

Both scientists and laypeople posit that TV can be dangerous and unhealthy for children because of their assumed inability to distinguish between television and reality. Yet Long heartily approved of the children who thought Sesame Street was a real place. Long evaluated this misunderstanding positively because it illustrates that Sesame Street can help suburban children not to fear the inner city. Long praised children who confused Sesame Street with real life in another anecdote, this one meant to illustrate how Sesame Street helps to ease the tensions of integration. A white woman recounted to Long a story about a black family who moved to her neighborhood. She knew that the other white neighbors were not pleased about the new family. She wanted to welcome the family but was hesitant about approaching them because she did not want to come off as "the block 'liberal.' " However,

> her young son solved the whole problem for her. As soon as he saw the Black couple going toward the house, he rushed over to them. Before she could catch up to him, she overheard him saying, "Hi! Do you know Susan and Gordon? Is this where Sesame Street begins?" Black people to him meant something very positive. This same Black couple had a daughter about David's age, and they struck up an instant friendship, soon going off to look in all the trashcans for Oscar [the Grouch, a character on the show].[57]

Like the museum-going white children, David seemed to believe that Sesame Street and its characters were real. He accepted blacks in his neighborhood because he associated them with Gordon and Susan (and perhaps because his mother actually was the block liberal). Although one could hardly argue that it is not "positive" for this white boy to make friends easily with a black girl, in different, less positive contexts, children's media researchers would undoubtedly object to a child mixing up television programs and reality. In other words, many scientists contend that children confuse TV with reality and that this is highly problematic when, for example, they imitate superheroes and try to defy gravity. But clearly children can also use *Sesame Street* and other programs in their everyday lives in ways that many adults approve of, as in Long's account, in which *Sesame Street* offers an integrationist fantasy that proves helpful to a child coping with a real-life integration situation. Why was it positive for the boy to think (by the mother's account, at least) that Susan and Gordon were not TV characters but real people? If you approve of his actions, he was "using" *Sesame Street* for imaginative play; if you do not approve, he was "confusing" *Sesame Street* with reality.

Children's media researchers often conceptualize child viewers as confused. Confused child viewers imitate what they see, but they become "better" viewers as they grow older: "[T]he child progressively *overcomes its inadequacies* and enters the social world of adulthood" (my emphasis).[58] As I argued in reference to the Meese Commission's attitude toward pornography consumers in the introduction, adult investigators often see the imitative research subject as immature or deficient compared to the mature, nonimitative subject (the investigator). Rather than seeing children and adults as *different* kinds of readers, they often see adult reading/viewing practices as simply *better*, as the norm toward which the child reader/viewer should strive.

What I find particularly interesting is that in studies that make value judgments about positive or negative TV imitation, one never finds that children imitate both the "positive" and "negative" aspects of a program. Researchers who favor a program, like Long, will often find that children imitate the "positive" aspects of that program, whereas those who oppose a program, like Halpern, will often find that children imitate the "negative" aspects of that program. This suggests the extent to which adult researchers' desires determine the outcomes of studies of children's media. Adult desires determine what is tested for, what is imitated, what is not imitated, how development is impaired or encouraged, and, indeed, what "development" is.

Adults will inevitably speak through child research subjects. However, better research methods can improve results so that they not only allow children more of a voice but also do not make parents (most often, mothers) feel guilty for letting their kids watch TV. Most research on children's television habits—certainly the research that gets the most press coverage—is performed by researchers who go into the studies perceiving TV as a force to be opposed. Anti-TV research is so common that it is difficult for researchers who take a different approach to convince their adult subjects of their intentions. When social scientist Paul Messaris studied how mothers discuss the relationship between TV and reality with their children, he found that "in several instances the mothers who were being interviewed required some reassurance that it would not be 'held against them' to show an interest in television. . . . [C]onsiderable tact was required on the part of the interviewers to make it clear that this was *not* a study based on a negative view of the medium. The lesson here may be that the most publicized research findings concerning television have indeed conditioned the public to expect all academic researchers to disapprove of people's use of the medium."[59] Messaris's research appears along with essays by Dafna Lemish, Ellen Wartella, Michelle A. Wolfe, and others in a book specifically designed to challenge the deeply entrenched dominance of quantitative analysis in communications studies. Their research, as well as Patricia Palmer's book *The Lively Audience* and more recent work by David Buckingham and others, makes it clear that social scientific work on children and TV need not focus exclusively on "negative" effects and the perils of imitation and confusion.[60] These researchers have shown how children and parents use TV rather than simply being used by it.

Comparing Long and Halpern reveals much about the kinds of assumptions researchers tend to make about how children use or are used by television. Long's field was education, and her goals were to advance *Sesame Street*'s integrationist, space age cause and fight educational racism. Halpern was a clinical psychiatrist trying to cure children of hyperactivity. Both assumed *Sesame Street* could alter child viewers' conceptions of reality, but they interpreted and evaluated *Sesame Street*'s effects completely differently. Halpern's view of *Sesame Street*'s effects was as dystopian as Long's was utopian. Long concluded that a black girl and a white boy can be friends because of *Sesame Street*, whereas Halpern assumed that the same program could turn them into hyperactive robots. Both believed that *Sesame Street* was a causal agent, and both assumed that viewers will imitate what they see. In Long's account, when hidden curriculum themes were absorbed, the child's imitation was healthy; in Halpern's account, when *Sesame Street*'s frenetic style was copied, such imitation was insalubrious.

I would like to suggest that although many educators, media effects researchers, and developmental psychologists find television to be problematic for young viewers because, they argue, children confuse representation with reality, such researchers only disapprove of viewer confusion when what is being represented is something of which they disapprove. In other words, some researchers disapprove of "improper" representations more than they disapprove of a child's understanding of representations as real. Many of the researchers who study media effects study the media they disdain and whose effects they therefore disdain. "Research shows," as the well-worn phrase goes, many things about children and television, but research does not simply unearth facts. It creates them. Some of these facts are valuable, but in evaluating them, one must always investigate how they are the products of a set of research conditions. The next chapter pursues this line of argument by looking critically at *Sesame Street*'s child-testing practices.

Sesame Street Technologies

The Quest for Cultural and Scientific Neutrality

6

People are usually surprised when I tell them I researched *Sesame Street* for a book on children's television censorship. I explain that the show was attacked for its fast pacing, for its picture of a racially integrated world, and for its pinko politics, and they laugh, seeing such complaints as dated. They are right, of course. *Sesame Street* has a firm and friendly foothold in our culture, and we now think of it as almost a public institution. When conservatives attack PBS funding, supporters hold up *Sesame Street* as the PBS touchstone, and newspapers feature cartoons of Big Bird standing in an unemployment line or Kermit the Frog panhandling. In light of MTV's pacing, *Sesame Street* does not seem fast anymore, and few people would really take seriously an accusation that the show is like an acid trip or encourages un-American thinking.

But *Sesame Street* can be criticized on other grounds. This chapter ventures into new critical terrain by examining the program's child-testing practices and its international production and distribution operations. The Children's Television Workshop's child-testing and global policies are ideologically linked in that both spring from faith in scientific neutrality; the CTW believes that its testing and production model is simply the best way to produce quality children's TV. The CTW's greatest claim to fame is that *Sesame Street* was the product of the "marriage," as the CTW puts it, of scientific (cognitive) research and television expertise. Never before had expert cognitive psychologists and educators worked so closely with TV producers in order to conceptualize a program. Psychologists continue to work behind the scenes of the show, testing children's responses and reporting their results to the show's producers. Through the "marriage" of social science and technological know-how, the CTW has produced the most popular children's television show on earth. In counterdistinction to other popular exported U.S. shows that some liberals interpret as cultural imperialism, *Sesame Street* is generally portrayed as a friendly presence in the global communications marketplace.

The CTW has constructed a friendly global image of *Sesame Street* without the kinds of massive and expensive ad campaigns undertaken to promote Coca-Cola or McDonald's.[1] But just because *Sesame Street* is a not-for-profit venture does not mean it should be immune to critical investigation. Close analysis of *Sesame Street*'s research, production, and distribution problematizes the show's global image, demystifying *Sesame Street* and the CTW and, I hope, opening up debate about the global politics of children's television. Since children's TV is generally articulated as a "problem" strictly in terms of its potential to make children antisocial, the political economy of mass-produced children's culture is rarely addressed.[2] For those who view *Sesame Street* as an antidote to the children's TV problem, the show's content is key. But if we concentrate on the program's production rather than consumption, a different picture emerges.

But first, picking up where the last chapter left off, we need to look at the CTW's child-testing procedures, which objectify children and narrowly define knowledge and learning. Through its child testing, the CTW produces scientific knowledge that can be fed back into its production loop in order to improve its product. Social scientific data culled from an initial group of children serves as fuel for high-tech TV production. The TV images are then tested on other children, and new data from this test group is used to produce more hi-tech images. In this way, social science and TV production form a closed circuit; responsive child test subjects are instrumental to this circuit.

Sesame Street's U.S. Testing Practices

The CTW tests children to produce facts about viewing and learning that can be used to improve the efficacy of *Sesame Street* programs. The CTW's child-testing practices are based on a number of questionable assumptions: that children's viewing practices can be translated into "data"; that their viewing can be scientifically studied without accounting for contextual aspects of television viewing and meaning making; and that memorization or recall is identical to learning.

Sesame Street engages in two kinds of research: formative and summative. Formative research is in-progress research whereby segments are tested before being aired; the segments are then reformulated in response to test results. Summative research involves postbroadcast testing of *Sesame Street's* effectivity. The CTW commissioned the Educational Testing Service to test *Sesame Street* viewers the first two years the show was on the air.[3] Since then, smaller focus groups have been tested, but most *Sesame Street* research is formative. The CTW's testing-production circuit has been coined the "CTW model." The CTW model is widely accepted by many researchers and educational-program producers around the world as the most effective means of producing quality children's programs. The model is basically a feedback loop (figure 5). First, a new curriculum objective is formulated. For example, one of the researchers comes up with the idea to teach kids about maps. It must be determined that this is not a topic that exceeds the competence of the target audience. In other words, is it too hard for three-to-five-year-olds (*Sesame Street's* primary target group)? And could it *appeal* to the target audience? Some topics might not be too hard but might be of no interest to the target audience. If it seems like a good idea, some experimental production is done: a segment is produced and tested for appeal (is it funny or compelling? do kids look at the TV when the segment is on?) and educational effectiveness (will tests show that kids got the idea of the segment?). The segment is revised in response to the formative data, and it is finally included in a broadcast show. Sometimes there is a summative postevaluation. Reactions to the new segment are brought back to curriculum developers for the next season, and they wonder where to go next: "Teaching about mountains worked last season. How about constructing a similar segment on valleys?"

   Sesame Street defines a segment as effective if it holds a child's attention and teaches him/her something. For testing purposes, learning is defined as recall. *Sesame Street* has four basic methods for measuring the effectiveness of a segment. The first is the distractor method, a "crazy Rube Goldberg style machine"[4] developed very early in *Sesame Street's* history by the program's director of research, Edward L. Palmer. In his *Sesame Street* history, Gerald Lesser reports that measuring eye movement would have produced more precise estimates of viewer attention but that such research was prohibitively expensive and placed children in "unnatural viewing conditions because of the recording equipment used."[5] As an alternative to *Clockwork Orange*–style eye movement measurement, Palmer designed a cheaper and seemingly more natural way of testing viewer attention. To

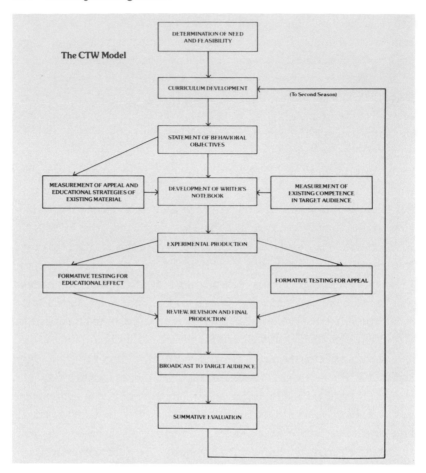

Figure 5. The Children's Television Workshop Model. *Source: Children's Television Workshop Research Notes* 4 (Fall 1983).

simulate the many "distractions" children encounter when they watch TV at home, Palmer set up a "distractor" slide projector, which he adjusted to project onto the wall beside the TV. The distractor automatically changed slides every eight seconds. Slides of "attractive scenes" such as animals and landscapes were shown.[6] To record viewing attention, a researcher in the room would depress a button when the experimental child watched the TV screen and release the button when the child looked away.[7]

The CTW's creation of the distractor as an experimental tool attests to the fact that it realizes children do not simply stare at the screen in a transfixed, hypnotic, and passive state, as some anti-TV crusaders imagine. Not unlike the producers of children's advertisements, the CTW acknowledges active and distracted child viewing and seeks to work against the latter.[8] In other words, the CTW tests, reformulates, and retests segments with the goal of increasing attention and decreasing play and distraction. The CTW views all of its testing as purely pragmatic and necessary in order to produce the best possible show, one that holds the child's attention.

CTW testers are not cruel brainwashers who want to turn children into drooling, hypnotized viewers, but they do hope to produce a particular kind of attentive viewer. CTW research is one of a multitude of institutional practices that strive to control the child in the name of a greater good (in this case, learning). Like the correctly trained body in school, church, or the military, the CTW's ideal *Sesame Street* viewer behaves in certain prescribed ways.[9] The child must focus his/her attention on the television screen, not on the distractor's images, and he/she must take in certain data—letters, numbers, and shapes—and repeat them to the tester. Knowledge and learning are defined as recall: a child sees a show focused on the letter "B," and after the show, a researcher holds up several letters and asks which is "B"; if the child correctly identifies the "B," he/she has learned what a "B" is. It is not necessary to understand what a symbol is and how symbols function in the world in order to succeed on the test. Only recognition is necessary. Test children and home viewers are not deeply and irreparably harmed by memorizing map or letter shapes without necessarily fully understanding what signs are. Besides, memorization and understanding are not mutually exclusive; they are interdependent. It can be difficult even to differentiate memorization from understanding. *Sesame Street* tests do not strive to do so.

Valeria Lovelace, a *Sesame Street* research director, reveals the central role recall plays in CTW testing when she explains that in developing a new geography curriculum, the CTW was concerned about whether or not three-to-five-year-old children could actually be taught geography on television. The CTW

developed a very simple test video, which we called the "Map Shape ID." The tape contained four segments, eight to eleven seconds in length, showing static, black-and-white maps of Hawaii, Alaska, Africa, and the United States, respectively. As each land mass appeared, a voice would identify it by name, saying twice, "This a map of Hawaii [or Alaska, Africa, or the United States of America]." . . . To our surprise, when we compared the scores of children who had viewed the segments with a control group who had not, we noticed significant differences in their ability to select the correct place. . . . Only thirteen percent of the children in the control group could correctly identify Hawaii, compared with seventy percent of the children who had viewed the tape.[10] (original brackets)

The concept of how maps symbolize land masses is a complex one (and one that is addressed on the show itself), but the researchers that Lovelace describes did not consider whether the children understood a map as an iconic sign. Rather, they tested associative memory. The children knew what shape "meant" Hawaii, but that does not mean they understood what "Hawaii" meant or what it meant to associate a particular shape with the word "Hawaii." Some CTW researchers realized the potential weakness of this research. Lovelace explains that

> [another study was] inspired by an additional set of concerns, voiced by our producers, writers, and advisers, who worried that the Map Shape ID approach came perilously close to rote teaching. Weren't we losing sight of the qualitative aspects of geography? Wouldn't children be interested in the people and the animals that live in different places? Responding to these concerns, the research staff found a segment . . . [showing] a map of Australia with pictures of animals superimposed on it. We showed this segment to children, and afterward presented them with a map of Australia and photographs of animals and asked, "Which of these photographs did you see in here?" The majority of the children correctly identified the animals.[11]

This experiment addresses the "qualitative" aspects of geography in a very limited way. Associating a kangaroo with a particular shape is not equivalent to understanding what it means for an animal to be indigenous to a country. Although the *Sesame Street* units on geography finally aired on TV do strive to explain what a map actually is, the research behind these units does not. The research produces facts that can be fed back into the CTW testing-production circuit.

Although the CTW still uses the distractor test, it also engages in three other kinds of testing. Since 1982, the CTW has used the group-viewing-attention method, whereby fifteen children sit in three rows, three-year-olds in the first row, four-year-olds in the middle, and five-year-olds in the back. A researcher sits at the end of each row wearing a headset that beeps "observation-point cues" every five seconds. When the headset beeps, the researcher scans his/her row and records "whether the children's eyes are focused on the screen."[12] Like the slide distractor, this testing environment certainly does not approximate "normal" home viewing, but then that is not the point of the test. The objective of the surveillance is to gather data about eye positioning.

In 1988, the CTW began using research video reports to measure attention. The reports are created by videotaping child viewers and then electronically inserting into the image a small box showing the program the kids are watching, in sync with their reactions. This surveillance enables researchers to see all kinds of responses to *Sesame Street*, such as clapping, singing, and repeating words. This testing method defines attention more complexly than the group-viewing-attention method, which just measures eye positioning, but like that method, the research video reports constitute one-sided observation that does not allow researcher-child interaction.

The final test type is the comprehension-testing interview, a method that does allow for researcher-child interaction. The comprehension-testing interview (like much CTW testing) functions as both formative and summative research. That is to say, it helps the CTW see what children comprehend from finished shows, which will affect how future shows are made. Although the CTW had been conducting interviews with *Sesame Street* viewers all along, it was not until 1983 that "new methods were developed to help researchers establish a better rapport with each child interviewed and to encourage children to talk more freely during the session."[13] In comprehension-testing sessions, four or five children enter a viewing room, and each child is assigned an adult researcher as a "partner." Then the children "play 'Mr. Potato Head' with their partners. This warm-up activity allows children enough time to feel comfortable and familiar with their research partners."[14] Or perhaps it merely allows the researchers to feel that the children are comfortable with them. It is certain that children are not assigned adult strangers as partners and told to play Mr. Potato Head as a preamble to their everyday, normal viewing of *Sesame Street*. After playing Mr. Potato Head, the children are given the following instructions:

Today we are going to play a game called "reporter." Do you know what a reporter is? A reporter is someone who sees something and tries to remember as much as he or she can and then tells someone else about it afterwards. To help you be a good reporter, I'm going to give you a reporter's hat [researcher mimes giving each child a hat]. Okay, everyone put your hat on and tie it under your chin [continues to mime] so that it won't fall off while you are being a reporter. We are going to be doing other things while you watch, so when you're finished watching you can tell us what you saw and what you heard on the show. Is everybody ready?[15] (original brackets)

The children then view a segment or segments of the program and "report" what they saw to their adult partners. They are allowed to role play or reproduce what they saw if they like.

This kind of scripted play is problematic, I would argue, not because it harms children. Some kids probably love it, whereas others are terrified or uninterested. Rather, it is methodologically problematic because of its rule boundedness. Children play with and against rules all the time; because their activity is *play*, the rules can be reinvented as the play progresses, or the rules can be followed exactly. The researcher, on the other hand, cannot break his/her own rules or allow the child to do so. Children often take their play very seriously, leading adults to theorize that "play is the child's work" (a homily of many play theoreticians),[16] but they do not get paid for their play. It is the discrepancy between the child's understanding(s) of play and the researchers' understanding(s) of work that problematizes the Mr. Potato Head/reporter testing scenario. The comprehension-testing session may be viewed by children as play or work (like a school test), but for the researchers, it is work. Quite simply, the children at play and the researchers gathering data have completely different and probably conflicting motives. This may be inevitable in any encounter between researchers and children, but it is crucial that researchers be aware of their own position as researchers, noticing how children respond to them as authority figures and how they interpret the interview situation.

Although all ethnography will objectify to a certain extent, some social scientific researchers have actively strived to be sensitive to their subjects as active and desiring *subjects* rather than *objects* of research. Throughout his interviews with child TV viewers, David Buckingham found children reacted to the interview situation in a variety of ways, some seeing the interview as play (a great way to get out of classes) and others seeing the situation as more stressful (like a test). As he collected data from the children, Buckingham questioned his own role as interviewer and examined how the children responded to the interview dynamics. Similarly, sociologist Patricia Palmer framed the parameters of her study of child TV viewers by responding to early feedback from kids. She used their concerns to shape her study. Ultimately, it was her study, but the point is that she attempted to shape the study around what kids thought was important about TV. The CTW has specific goals it must accomplish in its testing. This leaves little room for flexibility. Children must be objectified to produce the kind of empirical data that is useful to the CTW testing-production circuit.

The CTW understands that children often "multitask" or view TV in a distracting, busy home environment. In fact, on some PBS stations, a homework hotline number rolls across the screen during *Sesame Street* broadcasts, the assumption being that older kids watching the show are doing their homework at the same time. The distractor test seems to acknowledge that children watch TV while surrounded by other stimuli or while performing other tasks, but CTW tests such as the group-viewing-attention method, in which researchers wearing headsets conduct surveillance, position viewing as a desocialized laboratory phenomenon. The CTW recognizes distracted viewing, but its goal is to produce a show that reduces distraction.

Interestingly, the CTW labors against the same kind of distracted viewing that many cultural studies scholars have valorized. A number of cultural studies researchers have argued that TV cannot be fully understood through close analysis of particular TV shows/texts. In their daily lives, viewers' understanding of TV is dependent upon specific viewing contexts. Some people play with toys or cook dinner while the TV is on. Some people watch sports because they enjoy rooting for their favorite team, and some watch because their spouses monopolize the remote control. What viewers get out of shows is bound up in varied reception contexts, and viewers are not ineluctably positioned by texts (shows), according to this line of thought. Conversely, a "textually positioned" spectator is placed in a particular subject position by a TV show. To give a simple example, soap operas constantly move from story to story. If you believe that viewers are ineluctably positioned by texts/shows, you might conclude that soap opera viewers are as "distracted" as soap opera narratives are.[17] The CTW acknowledges that a viewing model that accounts for reception context (such as social interaction) is more realistic than the textually positioned viewing model, but its testing-production circuit is designed to create a textually determined spectator. The CTW's testing practices are designed to produce a show that holds attention and conveys certain lessons. In principle, the CTW sees viewers as cultural subjects embedded in complicated home or school viewing environments, but its testing-production circuit rests on a behaviorist foundation whereby CTW producers alter stimuli to produce desired responses. One *Sesame Street* researcher notes that

> changing the audio at the beginning of a segment is of great importance in regaining attention to the screen. Many children are continually deciding for themselves, "Is this interesting enough to watch?" I find this one of the most pleasing results of the attention research. It shows that children are not unwitting victims of television but independent little decision makers. This situation is preferable by far to the well-known "zombie viewing," the situation in which an attention level of 100 percent is achieved.[18]

This statement is interesting because it affirms the CTW's understanding of children as very active viewers, seeming to negate the possibility of gaining a child's undivided attention. But in terms of practical application, the point of the research is to determine how to change the audio to attract the maximum amount of attention.

Sesame Street in the Global Marketplace

Sesame Street holds up its testing and development model as its greatest achievement, proudly noting that children's TV producers around the world strive to duplicate the model. For this reason alone, it is crucial to subject the CTW model to critique. If this model has indeed caught on and is seen as the best way to produce educational children's television, the CTW's techniques are internationally influential. In effect, like many other technologies, the technology of children's television production needs to be understood as an imperialistic export product. *Sesame Street* is imperialistic not simply because the show itself is a widely distributed American cultural product but also because the technology of its production, the testing-production circuit, has been so widely disseminated and accepted by many governments as the best—indeed, the only—model for producing educational television.

Sesame Street is regularly leased to countries that cannot afford to produce their own educational programming; the show is one of many examples of TV that is produced in prosperous countries and distributed to less prosperous countries. (The reverse is virtually unheard of, with the exception of the Latin American telenovela.) Of course, in light of the massive mergers that have taken place, it has become increasingly difficult to label export products by country. Transnational corporations defy the unidirectional country-to-country understanding of imperialism that once seemed to make sense. As Gage Averill explains, "The emergence of transnational capitalism has, naturally, been haunted by the ghost of corporate nationality past, but transnational corporations have long sought ways of strategically positioning their 'nationality' to maximize their appeal in global markets. Locally owned subsidiaries, globally traded shares of publically owned stock, franchises, and other tactics allow transnationals to transcend their national origins in the quest for global free flow." [19] To maximize appeal in global markets, global brands are customized for particular countries. The actual product can be customized (Kellogg's proposes to market Basmati Flakes in India), or customizing can happen at the level of packaging, marketing, or simply name (Diet Coke is Coca-Cola Light in France). One might say that Sesame Street is an internationally customized brand created through franchises. Unlike transnationals, though, the CTW remains a privately owned, not-for-profit, U.S. corporation. Also, Sesame Street earnestly attempts to be profoundly sensitive to cultural differences rather than "playing to a thin or superficial version of cultural difference as a means of establishing globally uniform habits of consumption," [20] as big profit-driven corporations do. Sesame Street is not customized simply in order to increase profits. The CTW will not allow its franchisers to air Sesame Street with commercials, and the only profit it makes from the foreign Sesame Street is from toy sales. Strictly speaking, this is not really profit, as it is all pumped back into researching and producing new U.S. programs or deposited into the CTW's large endowment.

Although foreign countries purchase the rights to use filmed Sesame Street segments and the Sesame Street logo, the CTW never portrays the dissemination of Sesame Street as a business transaction.[21] Rather, the CTW persistently portrays *Sesame Street* as a utopian bridge across cultures. To illustrate its contention that it is on a global goodwill mission, the CTW notes that *Sesame Street* is even watched by political foes: Arabic children watch *Iftah Ya Simsin*, and Israeli children watch *Rechov Sumsum*. As I explained in chapter 5, the CTW sees cognition as a cultural leveler, so this might be one way to explain why it makes sense to it that both Arab and Israeli children watch *Sesame Street*. However, when the CTW notes that both Arab and Israeli children watch the show, it does not draw on developmental psychology to explain the phenomenon. Usually, the fact is mentioned, and then a strange fantasy about adults ensues. Cooney tells the story this way, half jokingly, half seriously: "My fantasy has always been that one day during a tense meeting of Arabs and Israelis at a negotiating table, one side will throw out a line from a Bert and Ernie routine, and the other side will pick it up, and the two sides will go back and forth until laughter and peace break out in the Middle East."[22] The Arab and Israeli versions of *Sesame Street* are different from the U.S. version; they include Ernie and Bert, plus new Muppets designed specifically to appeal to Arab and Israeli children. But it is the U.S.-created characters Ernie and Bert that enable the peace negotiation in this fantasy. This scenario illustrates what appeals to the CTW about the global distribution of *Sesame Street*. The show taps into what are perceived as universal child (and, implicitly, adult) needs and desires, and in this way, it is an ambassador across cultures. From the CTW's perspective, the bickering Ernie and Bert have no American qualities; their middle-class American clothing, apartment, and furniture are all neutral. Yet I would argue that, notwithstanding the CTW's efforts to respect cultural differences, *Sesame Street* is not just any ambassador. It is a specifically U.S. ambassador. In the course of producing the first combined Israeli-Palestinian *Sesame Street* segments in 1998, even the CTW could not ignore the show's status as a U.S. presence. The segments were shot in studios guarded by soldiers with automatic weapons, and there were disagreements about how fearful the puppets should be of each other. In general, both Israelis and Palestinians saw the project as naïve. As the CTW's emissary tells it, however, it did eventually work out: "The puppets, after a short, nervous introduction, became as friendly as Arafat and Rabin on the White House Lawn."[23]

The CTW has repeatedly stated that it only sends the show to countries that ask for it, but it never explains who does the inviting. Is the

CTW invited by elected government officials, military or religious rulers, TV producers, educators, or citizens? In Chile, the anti-Allende Catholic church simultaneously collaborated with the Central Intelligence Agency and the CTW. By emphasizing its invited status, the CTW absolves itself of imperialistic intent and distinguishes itself from uninhibited imperialists like Viacom, Coca-Cola, and McDonald's. The exporters of other globally popular U.S. shows like *Dallas* and *Baywatch* do not care whether or not they are imperialistic; they just want to make a buck. This makes them different from the CTW. But like *Sesame Street*, *Dallas* and *Baywatch* do have permission from somebody to be broadcast outside the United States. They were either invited like *Sesame Street*, without solicitation on the part of a U.S. producer or distributor, or they were pitched to a foreign broadcaster, who then chose to lease the shows for broadcast. With the exception of illegal transborder broadcasting, such as the United States' TV and Radio Martí (illegally broadcast to Cuba), all internationally distributed programs are "invited" by somebody.

How Global *Sesame Street* Production Works

It is not unusual for other countries to develop their own versions of popular U.S. shows. The French both imported *Dallas* and created new shows clearly modeled on *Dallas*. One thing that makes *Sesame Street* unusual, though, is that it participates in the development of foreign versions of itself.[24] *Sesame Street* has two different kinds of foreign formats. The euphemistically titled "Open Sesame" format is made up entirely of pieces of U.S.-produced program material chosen by the host country from a leased footage library. Only the opening and closing title sequence is locally produced. This is the most common type of foreign format. The CTW does not discuss it very much, emphasizing instead the second format: the coproduction. Coproductions are comprised of some material from the U.S. series and some locally produced material. In 1975, *Sesame Street* coproductions were made in four different languages for distribution to sixty-nine different countries.[25] By 1988, there were fifteen coproductions,[26] and the number of coproductions has remained at about this level. The CTW is vocal about its desire that other countries contribute to *Sesame Street* production and explains that host countries formulate their own curriculum goals.

Coproductions pass through four stages. First comes research and curriculum development. The country puts together a research team, which is sent to New York City to be trained in conducting formative research (child-testing methods such as the distractor). Summative research is generally too expensive to be undertaken by coproducers.[27] Second, the country goes into preproduction, making some pilots to test for appeal and comprehension. At the third stage, it responds to test results from the second stage, and in the fourth stage, it finally completes all of the original live-action and animated sequences. Typically, the country makes three hours of original animation and three hours of live-action footage *per season* of 130 half-hour shows.[28] By contrast, in the United States, the CTW produces 120 new one-hour shows each year, with approximately twenty-two to twenty-four minutes of new live-action and animated material *per show*.[29]

After the curriculum is developed at stage two, indigenous Muppets are produced by Henson Productions in New York City. Big Bird retains his personality in all of his incarnations, but his species may change. He is a parrot in Mexico and a porcupine in Israel. The fact that all Muppets are produced in the United States undercuts the CTW's argument that indigenous Muppets are precisely what makes Muppets in foreign countries not an imperialistic presence. Not just any puppet will do; the new characters must be real, U.S.-produced Muppets. On the practical side, making the Muppets in the CTW's U.S. facilities reduces costs for the coproducing country. To illustrate how appealing these U.S.-produced Muppets are, Lesser has noted that when Iraqis invaded Kuwait in 1991, they stole Kuwait's Muppets.[30]

The CTW requires that its quality standards be upheld. If a country can produce only 10 percent of the show with the highest quality sound, the CTW would want the country to produce only that amount. Notwithstanding the CTW's quality specifications, it does appear that, overall, foreign segments are often cheaper in sound and image than U.S. segments. Lesser has explained that the CTW has incorporated some non-U.S. material into the leased footage library that foreign producers draw from but that the U.S. version of *Sesame Street* does not use any foreign material (except a little bit of Canadian *Sesame Street*) because foreign production quality is not high enough to fit into the U.S. version of the show.[31] Again, although the CTW is not a transnational, for-profit corporation, it has something in common with transnational entertainment producers. As Averill explains,

"[T]ry as they might, cultural workers in the rest of the world have been structurally prohibited from achieving the same results as state-of-the-art studios in the West (and Japan) — that is, unless they turn over an essential stage in the production process to the transnationals."[32]

The main economic constraint for foreign coproducers is that they must set up the same testing-production circuit as is used in the United States. This is so expensive that some coproductions only run for one season. Then production must stop until enough money is raised to fund the researchers and testers needed for the testing-production circuit to continue. Germany and the Netherlands are able to produce a new season every year, whereas the Latin American Plaza Sésamo had only four seasons as of 1993.[33] The last directional arrow of the CTW model (see figure 5), "to second season," is null and void in most countries. The circuit is in effect broken by economic constraints. This means that the CTW model, which is perceived worldwide as the best way to produce children's TV, only fully functions in the handful of countries that can afford it.

In both the coproduction and the Open Sesame format, host countries pick the bulk of their program material from the CTW's leased library of "culturally neutral" Sesame Street footage. The CTW has never explained how segments are chosen for the library, and we can only guess that "neutral" Sesame Street segments avoid overt reference to American culture. Of course, the problem is that Sesame Street in and of itself is American culture. Weeding out Sesame Street segments that parody American rock singers or movie stars cannot make the program segments neutral.

Except in countries where English is the official school language or in Japan, where viewers used to watch Sesame Street to learn English, both Open Sesame producers and coproducers dub new soundtracks over their "neutral" leased footage. Since Sesame Street is meant to prepare kids for school, the show is produced in the country's official school language. Plaza Sésamo, the Latin American coproduction, is produced in "neutral" Spanish[34] and distributed to eighteen Spanish-speaking countries in South and Central America and the Caribbean.[35] (The CTW has never publicly explained what "neutral Spanish" means.) MAD artist Jack Davis illustrated a 1976 article by Rose K. Goldsen and Azriel Bibliowicz attacking the CTW, "Plaza Sésamo: 'Neutral' Language or 'Cultural Assault'?" (figure 6). The image is overcrowded, and the children seem excessively happy. There's a lot of action but no educational activity. The adults are infantilized: one

Figure 6. Cartoon by MAD artist Jack Davis illustrating a 1976 article attacking the Children's Television Workshop. *Source:* Rose K. Goldsen and Azriel Bibliowicz, "Plaza *Sésamo:* 'Neutral Language' or 'Cultural Assault'?" *Journal of Communication* 26.2 (Spring 1976): 124–125. Reproduced by permission of Oxford University Press.

has a bird on his head and holds a bouquet of flowers, another chases a balloon, and two others play on a swing. A child in the forefront has her back turned to the viewer, and her bloomers are showing. Although the image does not directly comment on the show's "neutral language," it does seem to bolster the article's argument that Plaza *Sésamo* is a "cultural assault." MAD's cynical image leads the reader to take this cartoon as a trenchant critique of Plaza *Sésamo*. The same artist had illustrated MAD's harsh 1971 *Sesame Street* parody.

The CTW explains that education experts from many different Latin American countries decided that "neutral" Spanish that avoided localisms was an economic necessity; it would not be feasible to produce separate versions of Plaza *Sésamo* in different dialects. Spanish is not the first language of many Plaza *Sésamo* viewers, but apparently Amerindian language experts were not invited to the Caracas seminars at which Plaza *Sésamo* was planned. "Neutral" Spanish is thus doubly problematic: it is unfair to both speakers of various non-neutral Spanish dialects and those who speak Spanish as a second language, if at all.

Rua Sesame is another coproduction with complicated language politics. Produced in Portuguese, Rua Sesame is shown not only in Portugal but also in African countries formerly colonized by Portugal: Angola, Mozambique, Guinea-Bissau, Cape Verde, and São Tomé. Portuguese is the official language in all of these countries. The educational director of Rua Sesame praises the program because "in these countries, not only [do] less than ten percent have access to preschool education, but also they get to primary school, where the teaching is done in Portuguese, knowing very little Portuguese—so the failure rates are, not surprisingly, enormous."[36] Rua Sesame presumably helps guard against such "failure"; the director does not consider the possibility that in this postcolonialist situation, it is not African children who fail school but rather Portuguese school that fails children. The CTW is uninterested in the politics of the language chosen for foreign versions of Sesame Street. Since the show is designed to prepare kids for school, using the official school language simply makes sense to the CTW.

Like Rua Sesame and Plaza Sésamo, the Arabic Iftah Ya Simsin is a widely distributed coproduction. As of 1989, it was sent to fourteen countries. The program is broadcast in classical Arabic, the official school language of the Arab world. Abdelkader Ezzaki, an education professor from Morocco, argues that "there is a wide gap between the language of home socialization and the language of the school, and . . . this program contributes significantly to the bridging of that gap."[37] Ezzaki explains that "the style and philosophy of CTW—and that is the philosophy of teaching through fun— does not merely serve the cause of learning, but also the cause of classical Arabic, the [popular] perception of classical Arabic."[38] But what causes does the popularization of classical Arabic serve? Of what value is the "language of home socialization"? Does the language of home socialization differ among the fourteen countries where Iftah Ya Simsin is distributed? In these fourteen countries, to what extent is the language of the home culturally coded as feminine and the language of the public sphere of the school coded as masculine? Are girls sent to school in all of these countries? Such pressing questions are never asked by Ezzaki or by the CTW, and Ezzaki never elaborates on the specifics of domestic language use. These silences are typical of discussions of foreign productions of *Sesame Street*. Language politics are never at issue because the CTW and its foreign collaborators see *Sesame Street* as a goodwill emissary to a global village.

Pedagogical theorist Paulo Freire has argued that literacy cannot be emancipatory if native languages are not used in literacy programs. (This argument begs several questions: How should native language be defined? In a postcolonial situation, must a former colonizer's language be purged? If so, how? In Morocco, should *Rua Sesame* be in French instead of in classical Arabic?) Freire further argues that the sociopolitical structures of a society and the act of reading are interrelated and that "the exclusion of social and political dimensions from the practice of reading gives rise to an ideology of cultural reproduction, one that views readers as 'objects.' It is as though their conscious bodies were simply empty, waiting to be filled by that word from the teacher." [39] The CTW objectifies children, in Freire's sense, when it accepts that a culturally neutral film library is possible and that the dubbing of official school languages in foreign versions of *Sesame Street* is merely a practicality. To the CTW, the social dimensions inherent in the cognitive act of learning letters in a politically charged, postcolonial situation, in which the former colonizers' language may still be in use, are not at issue. The CTW thus addresses children of all nations as identically capable of learning letters and numbers regardless of the possible affect bound up in the chosen teaching language.

The CTW tends to understand children as paradoxically unique yet universal. The unique child's needs can be met through cultural sensitivity, which means collaborating with educators in other countries to devise curriculum goals. The universal child will then find his/her needs met by *Sesame Street*, the cognitive equalizer. The CTW sees that the children of the world who view *Sesame Street* come from different cultures, but it does not see how such differences could conflict with the CTW's testing-production circuit, that instruction language is a politically charged issue, or that its own scientific idea of cognitive development, in which all children pass "through a series of fixed, value-free, and universal stages of development," [40] is not a politically neutral idea.

Foreign Testing of Sesame Street

Foreign *Sesame Street* coproducers test child viewers using the CTW's techniques. To show the success of *Sesame Street* with non-U.S. audiences, the CTW often cites tests undertaken in Jamaica and Mexico in the early seventies. The Jamaica study was funded by the Ken Foundation and the Markle Foundation; the Mexico tests were partially funded by the Ford Foundation.

Using the language of objective scientific research, here's how CTW researchers Edward L. Palmer, Milton Chen, and Gerald S. Lesser describe the Jamaica experiment. In 1972, "[t]elevision was brought for the first time to children in mountainous and non-electrified regions [of Jamaica]. Using a mobile videocassette system, researchers played videotapes of *Sesame Street* to the children, simultaneously recording their reactions on videotape, and later analyzed the tapes for attention patterns. The study found that special effects, animation, and music frequently characterized popular segments."[41] Not surprisingly, Marxist communications scholar Armand Mattelart describes the experiment quite differently, emphasizing its intrusive, corporate nature: "[A]rmed with a videotape system courtesy of Sony, with batteries charged by a Suzuki jeep, a team from Harvard showed *Sesame Street* in mountain villages to find out the reactions of people who had never before seen television. The findings from this groundwork were used at Harvard by the Children's Television Research Centre, established jointly by the CTW and the Harvard education department, thanks to funding from the Ford and Carnegie Foundations."[42] Using Suzuki jeeps designed to power videocassette players and video equipment developed by Sony, the Harvard University team set up mobile viewing sites in four villages and a stationary viewing site in a fifth village. At the fifth site, a video camera was mounted above the television set, and groups of children were recorded viewing *Sesame Street* programs.

At this fifth site, the viewing situation was considered noncoercive because the child viewers had options besides watching the television; instead of viewing, they could get up and move around the room, talk to each other, or look at the images cast by a distractor unit. The distractor's U.S.-produced images of circus animals, bicycles, and ice cream cones might indeed have proved distracting to rural Jamaican children, who were presumably no more familiar with slides than they were with television.

One hundred hours of videotapes were made, and these videos were then studied at Harvard. Researchers paused the tapes every few seconds in order to record viewers' attention, which was measured by whether or not they were looking at the television set. Comprehension was not measured. U.S. researchers noted whether children in three age groups paid attention to details such as different kinds of sounds, images, and characters.

Harry M. Lasker's report on the Jamaica study only briefly mentions the four nonstudy sites, but the report does note that "for the Sony and Suzuki Corporations, the project would afford an opportunity to test their equipment and to observe the general reactions of villages to mobile television." [43] Since mobile television sites were set up only at the four villages the Harvard team did not study, it is fairly clear that Sony and Suzuki were engaged in their own studies in those villages. Whatever their true purpose may have been, according to Lasker's report, the Sony/Suzuki mobile units did succeed in appealing to both children and adults in nonelectrified villages. Lasker notes that the reception of the mobile video units was "warm and enthusiastic" and that Jamaicans eagerly gathered around the mobile viewing units (figure 7). The researchers interpreted the Jamaicans' interest in TV in purely positive terms. According to them, the children and adults were "delighted" and "fascinated" by the mobile programs and "anxious" for the vehicles to return.[44] Presumably the Jamaicans were not asked if they would also like the distractor units to return, since distractor images were assumed to be neutral scientific tools. And needless to say, no one asked the Jamaican villagers if they would be interested in producing their own TV shows.

Why did Harvard researchers decide to go to Jamaica to expose village children to *Sesame Street*? Emphasizing the exotic appeal of the endeavor, Lasker describes the area: "Remote villages perch high atop mountainous ridges and overlook precipitous mountain gorges which drop hundreds of feet to the valley floor below. The towns are accessible only on winding dirt roads which swollen rivers make impassible during the rainy season. . . . Pine trees, banana trees, coffee bushes and poinsettias stretch upward in a silence broken only by the echoing horn blasts of trucks negotiating hairpin turns. Here was a remote site well-suited for the proposed experiment." [45] On a more practical note, Jamaica was chosen because it was conveniently close to the United States and because it was "an English-speaking country where *Sesame Street* had been shown in previous years

Figure 7. Jamaicans watch TV for the first time on a Sony/Suzuki mobile viewing unit.
Source: Children's Television Workshop Research Notes 4 (Fall 1983).

and had been well received, yet one which had remote areas without television."[46] Presumably, previous favorable reception of *Sesame Street* would make the Jamaican government more open to participation in the study. According to Lasker's report, the point of the study was to measure the attention of "media-illiterate" children in the hope that such a study would provide data useful in considering how to adapt *Sesame Street* to other countries. Lasker concluded that "the distractor studies have shown that the attention patterns of children who have never before viewed television is high and comparable in overall intensity to attention levels of more media literate children."[47] This finding reinforces the idea that children all over the world share the same cognitive capabilities. If young children in Jamaica share a similar "attention level" with young children in the United States, then theoretically *Sesame Street* could serve Jamaican children as well as it serves U.S. children.

However, Lasker carefully warned that the results of the study should be applied with caution to other countries and that this study should be the first of many. In other words, the Jamaican attention levels should not be assumed to be identical to the attention levels of other media-illiterate children. Although some of his results were unexpected, most of them confirmed the validity of the child-development model he believed in before the study was conducted. For example, he found that older viewers appreciated complicated backgrounds more than younger viewers and older children tended "to make higher order connections between the sound and visual track rather than experiencing them as somewhat independent phenomena."[48] Nodding to two of the study's major backers, Lasker also concluded that the experiment had demonstrated the viability of the Suzuki and Sony equipment.

The ethical ramifications of the Jamaica experiment are astounding. At no point did the researchers consider whether they had the right to introduce a new technology to a culture. They did, however, note that "electric power was scheduled to reach the villages soon, so we felt [the Jamaican villagers] would not be *tantalized* by something they could never see again" (my emphasis).[49] The implication here is that what is questionable is not introducing TV but rather introducing it and then unfairly taking it away. In fact, the Harvard team noted that "at the end of the project it was clear that our intervention, particularly at the stationary site, had *whetted such an appetite* for television that we felt obliged to leave a viewing capacity at sites where we had done substantial showing. Thus, for example, at the stationary site we left a generator and a television so that children could continue viewing after the experiment was over" (my emphasis).[50] The researchers portrayed television as simply irresistible. They reported that individual viewers were "tantalized" by such programming, making no comment on the potentially "whetted" appetite of Jamaican broadcasters. The Harvard researchers probably intended to whet an appetite only for *Sesame Street*, but encouraging a taste for the program meant encouraging a taste for a certain American television style. The experiment promoted *Sesame Street*, an export product that the CTW could lease to Jamaican broadcasters, while also planting the desire for U.S. communications products in general.

I am not suggesting that the *Sesame Street* experiments are solely to blame for the introduction of American culture to the mountains of Jamaica; with or without the Jamaica experiment, American TV would probably have found its way to the Jamaican villagers. But I would argue that, like the Ford Foundation's more extensive Samoa experiment (which I discuss later), the Jamaica experiment was intrusive and unethical: the U.S. researchers presumed they had *the right* not only to introduce a new technology to the Jamaican villagers but also to videotape and measure their responses. Medical research protocols require that human subjects used in experiments must give voluntary informed consent, and subjects must be allowed to stop an experiment at any point. When children participate in experiments, they are assumed to be incapable of giving informed consent, so their parents must give consent for them. Did the Jamaican parents fully understand the nature of the experiment, so that they could give informed consent? It seems unlikely that these subjects, who lived without electricity and had never viewed television, fully understood what it meant to be videotaped. How could they know if they wanted their children to participate in or drop out of the experiment?[51] We may never know what kind of research Sony and Suzuki conducted in Jamaica, but it seems clear that, technically, Lasker and his associates took only one thing from the Jamaican children: their images. This cannot compare to the kind of physical harm U.S. corporations have caused people in other countries (the Dalkon Shield comes to mind). But the ethical question remains: Did the Harvard researchers have the right to use the Jamaican subjects in their experiments?

The CTW has always felt that foreign productions are carried out not in the name of U.S. corporations or culture but in the name of cultural autonomy. Commenting on the Jamaica experiment, Palmer, Chen, and Lesser conclude that "the research done to date suggests that a common factor behind the popularity of Sesame Street in its different versions abroad is the degree to which the program is integrated with local or regional culture and language. Tailoring the idiom and tone of the program to local or regional culture, social and educational values also appears to enhance its appeal in adopting countries."[52] The question of how a TV program can be crafted in "idiom and tone" in a way appropriate for a non-TV culture remains unanswered. The Jamaica research affirmed for the CTW that children the world over could pay attention to (and therefore learn from) Sesame Street. Again, this implies that the Sesame Street viewer is, paradoxically, both unique and universal. Ten years later, another researcher would drive this point home by comparing the Jamaica data to data culled from observing U.S. children viewing the same program segments the Jamaican children had seen. This study carries acultural developmental psychology to an absurd extreme. The researcher, William George Husson, compares the three-to-five-year-olds in the Jamaican mountains to a group of three-to-five-year-olds in Troy, New York, explaining that "since these groups are at the same level of cognitive development, they differ mainly in their amount of previous exposure to television."[53] Husson refers to the U.S. subjects as "experienced child viewers" and the Jamaican subjects as "naive child viewers." With its emphasis on cognition ("attention") and its blindness to cultural issues, the Jamaica data certainly did nothing to discourage Husson's bizarre appropriation.

The CTW considered the Jamaica study a success. Likewise, it cites successful Mexican test results. Rogelio Diaz-Guerrero and his colleagues twice undertook summative testing on *Plaza Sésamo*, the Mexican coproduction. The first experiment was considered successful. In 1971, 221 three-to-five-year-olds from lower-class day-care centers were divided into two groups. The test group watched *Plaza Sésamo* for six months, whereas the control group watched unspecified "cartoons and other non-educational TV programs." Afterward, the children were tested for specific cognitive gains such as knowledge of numbers and letters, the ability to sort and classify, and the ability to identify embedded figures. The *Plaza Sésamo* viewers scored higher than the non–*Plaza Sésamo* viewers. As with *Sesame Street* testing in all countries (including the United States), this testing evaluated only intended effects. Since *Plaza Sésamo* producers did not explicitly set out to change viewers' attitudes about American television, they were not interested in testing for changes in such attitudes. Likewise, they were not interested in discovering what the cartoon viewers might have learned that *Plaza Sésamo* viewers did not learn, so no testing was performed toward this end. The cartoons, like the images cast by the distractor, were considered neutral. They were the control media, whereas only *Plaza Sésamo* programs were thought capable of producing effects in viewers.

The second *Plaza Sésamo* study went less smoothly. (As late as 1993, the CTW referred to positive test results in Mexico,[54] presumably referencing only the first study.) The 1971 test had been conducted when *Plaza Sésamo* was fairly new to Mexico. By the time the second study began in 1974, enough urban children had seen the program that it was impossible to find a control group of children who were "uncontaminated" (as the researchers put it) by *Plaza Sésamo* viewing. However, the broadcast of the initial version of the program, *Plaza Sésamo I*, stopped six months before the experiment began, so it was possible to control exposure to the show, even if the control group was "contaminated" by previous viewing experience. Again, the control group was shown unspecified cartoons, whereas the experimental group was shown Plaza Sésamo. Then several unforeseen problems arose that compromised the experiment. One-third of the children dropped out of the study because, the researchers lamented, "on September first, when the school year began, many parents enrolled their children prematurely in the first grade, an illegal practice that is nevertheless widespread."[55] The researchers' frustration is ironic given that one of the primary goals of Sesame Street, and its foreign equivalents, has always been to provide preschool education to those who would otherwise be denied it. It seems odd to disparage children for going to school instead of watching a show that prepares them for school. Another problem was that one month before the experiment began, Plaza Sésamo unexpectedly came back on the air. Although the experimenters kept the control children from seeing the program during the experiment, they could not prevent viewing during the preexperiment month. Nor could they control viewing during the Christmas holidays. To counteract these factors, the researchers explained, the control children were "purified." Children who could recognize any of the Plaza Sésamo characters, beyond the two most popular ones, were eliminated from the experiment.

After a year, all the children were tested, and the results were disastrous. Across all socioeconomic groups,[56] virtually no differences could be detected between the viewers of Plaza Sésamo and the viewers of "neutral" cartoons. The researchers noted that the rural children did particularly badly, even though the rural control children were not "contaminated" by previous knowledge of Plaza Sésamo (since they had no access to TV). Diaz-Guerrero et al. hypothesized that part of the problem was the rural children's poor attendance at Plaza Sésamo screenings. In other words, it was their fault. The researchers conclude their section on the rural children by saying that "in fairness to the producers of Plaza Sésamo, it should be emphasized that rural children never were the target population of Plaza Sésamo programming" (my emphasis).[57] The researchers make no similar concessions in fairness to any of the children who participated in their study, who are simply purified or contaminated objects. This experiment is a stellar example of the way that poor social scientific studies can objectify child viewers. In their conclusions, the Plaza Sésamo researchers reiterate the problem of "ambitious mothers who pushed their children illegally into the first grade" and the problem of rural child viewer absenteeism, again blaming their objects of study for the failure of the experiment. The researchers are not interested in examining how their own methods might be "contaminated." Nor are they concerned with investigating socioeconomic factors that might make parents send their children to school early and might keep rural children from regularly traveling to an urban center to view a television program. Perhaps such poor performance was an appropriate response to the experimenters' methods.

The Broader Context of Communications Imperialism

Plaza Sésamo was initially supported by a grant from the Xerox Corporation. The CTW sees critiques of Xerox sponsorship as misguided because Xerox merely received a credit before and after each broadcast of *Plaza Sésamo*. Xerox had no influence over the production or distribution of the show, but the Xerox insignia marked the program as the product of an American-based multinational, regardless of whether or not Xerox had any creative control.[58] According to one researcher, people commonly refer to the version of *Sesame Street* broadcast in Spain as "the Xerox Program."[59] Regardless of the language *Sesame Street* is broadcast in, citizens of most non-U.S. countries (especially those who watch the Open Sesame format, with very little locally produced material) see *Sesame Street* as a U.S. product, one of many dubbed U.S. programs.

Communications scholar Tapio Varis has explained that U.S. programming constitutes the majority of imported TV in many countries. Of the countries Varis studied in 1973 and 1983, Latin America had the lowest output of domestic programming (54 percent of its total programming in 1983). Thirty-five percent of the programs in Latin American countries came from the United States. The United States is not the only exporting culprit, of course. The most prosperous countries are the biggest exporters of communications products. Export trends also reflect postcolonialist hegemony. Varis notes, "Although American and British programs dominate in English-speaking Africa, the French have a strong influence in francophone Africa. In Senegal, for example, sixty percent of imported programs originate in France and only five percent in the United States."[60] In general, Varis found a "one-way traffic from the big exporting countries to the rest of the world, and a dominance of entertainment material in the flow."[61] *Sesame Street* has loftier intentions than noneducational entertainment programming, but it remains part of the unidirectional flow of U.S. programming. The vast majority of countries use the Open Sesame format, not the coproduction format, which means that the only locally produced material in most countries is the opening and closing title sequences. Although coproducing countries do shoot some of their own material and formulate their own curriculum goals, most of their programs are composed of material culled from the "neutral" library of U.S.-produced material.

As explained earlier, *Sesame Street* is like other internationally distributed U.S. shows in that it is "invited" to foreign countries. The show is different in that it is given a unique spin in some countries. This makes *Sesame Street* less like *Baywatch* and other internationally popular shows and more like international advertisements, which are crafted to suit the countries in which they are shown. Take the Coca-Cola Company, for example. Bottles of Coca-Cola arc not simply sent to foreign countries by the United States. Rather, franchises are purchased in each country. Former Coca-Cola executive Ira Herbert explains that "around the world . . . [Coke] is marketed and developed and invested in by mostly independent businessmen who are indigenous to the country in which we are marketing."[62] The product is identical in each country, which makes Coke different from *Sesame Street*, but consider Herbert's description of the specialization of Coke advertising for each country: "We developed pattern advertising that could be adjusted [by local franchisers] to fit the local environment, the local culture, the local language, and could be changed or edited as long as the concept wasn't changed—as long as the feel wasn't changed—as long as the sound wasn't changed. The feel of the commercial had to come out according to pattern."[63] Local Coca-Cola franchisers adjust advertisements to be as appealing as possible to local viewers, but the essence of the product must remain intact in the ad. Similarly, foreign versions of *Sesame Street* are required to retain key *Sesame Street* elements.[64] Big Bird may be a porcupine or a parrot in some countries, but his character, that of a quizzical six-year-old, must remain the same. Likewise, it would be unacceptable if an educator in Mozambique rejected the vignette format or suggested that cheap sock puppets be used instead of expensive muppets. Nor can one change the title so that it does not reference the U.S. title or alter the introductory song, which has the same tune the world over. Likewise, overt politics are not allowed, and any religious instruction must be carefully

Table 3. Ten Leading Transborder Radio Broadcasters, 1988

Rank	Country	No. of Languages	Hours per Week
1	United States[a]	50	2,277
2	USSR	81	2,247
3	China	47	1,493
4	Taiwan	17	1,091
5	West Germany	37	821
6	Egypt	30	816
7	United Kingdom	36	751
8	Trans World Radio[b]	61	526
9	Voice of the Andes[c]	14	500
10	Albania	21	451

Source: Sydney W. Head and Christopher H. Sterling, *Broadcasting in America: A Survey of Electronic Media*, 6th ed. (Boston: Houghton Mifflin, 1990), 507.

[a] Includes Voice of America, Radio Martí (1,199 hours), Radio Free Europe (630 hours), Radio Liberty, and Radio Free Afghanistan (448 hours).

[b] Religious broadcaster with transmitters in Guam, Monaco, Netherlands Antilles, Sri Lanka, Switzerland, and Uruguay.

[c] Religious broadcaster with transmitters in Quito, Ecuador.

framed as "legends, tradition, or folklore."[65] Deviations from these guidelines would violate "the feel" of *Sesame Street*.[66]

Historically, the U.S. government and U.S. foundations have used broadcasting to disseminate U.S. culture worldwide, and the CTW must be understood in this context. The CTW is one of many organizations that have participated in communications imperialism, although it is certainly one of the smaller, less malevolent players. Not surprisingly, one of the CTW's original funders was the Ford Foundation, which began promoting the use of telecommunications to educate poor children in the post–World War II years. In 1951, the foundation launched projects in Washington, D.C., in a Latino community in New York City, and in the United States' Pacific possessions, particularly Samoa. Samoa became a site for testing how uneducated populations react to tele-education projects. Televisions were installed in Samoan classrooms; during the day, programs were educational, while at night, U.S. films and series were shown. In 1972, an expert from the foundation proudly reported that Samoans were starting to eat foreign foods: "No one can live on coconuts, papayas and bananas forever." [67] Samoans had become interested in washing machines, automobiles, and mopeds and had abandoned their old custom of giving their money to the head of the village. The researcher exclaimed that "the Samoan system has been hailed as the most successful educational television in the world." [68]

The U.S. government, another former CTW backer, is a major disseminator of imperialist communications. The United States broadcasts more programming outside of its boundaries than any other country in the world, as table 3 illustrates for radio. In 1988, the Voice of America (VOA) radio program, an arm of the U.S. Information Agency (USIA), was broadcast in fifty languages in addition to English. The Reagan administration appreciated the VOA's power as a disseminator of U.S. policy, and between 1981 and 1988, the USIA budget was doubled. Old VOA facilities were renovated, and new ones were built. "The V.O.A. added languages and increased the number of overseas relay transmitters, especially in the Caribbean and Central America, where it set up standard AM transmitters to reach listeners with ordinary (non-short-wave) receivers." [69] The U.S. government uses broadcasting very deliberately to spread the kinds of information that suits its purposes. Unlike the government, the CTW does not engage in illegal transborder broadcasting. If the CTW disseminates information that could be labeled "propaganda"—propaganda for developmental psychology and for U.S. technologies of educational TV production—it does so without malicious intent. The CTW sees its global endeavors merely as examples of practicing what it preaches so often on *Sesame Street:* "co-op-er-a-tion."

"No Better than *Underdog* or *The Flintstones*"?

As television violence is repeatedly debated in Congress and broadcasters, pressure groups, and parents fight over the v-chip and revisions to the Children's Television Act of 1990, *Sesame Street* functions as a highly charged symbol. Proregulation forces wish there were more programs like *Sesame Street,* whereas antiregulation factions such as the networks preach the need for all kinds of programming, not just the educational kind. The industry uses *Sesame Street* as a trump card against complaints about overcommercialization, arguing that if reformers want to remove all the programs that help sell toys, *Sesame Street* would have to go too since its products are a multimillion-dollar industry. Some parents fear the v-chip will make TV more violent, sexual, and commercialized than ever before since programmers will reason that they can broadcast anything if viewers can block out whatever they do not want to see. This leads parents to fear that soon *Sesame Street* will be one of the few programs their kids can watch. For these concerned parents, the show has become a symbol of what good TV means.

Sesame Street functions as a powerful symbol for conservative politicians too. Although it no longer receives government funding, conservatives attack the show (and PBS) as an unfair burden on taxpayers. Laurence Jarvik of the right-wing Heritage Foundation has argued that "*Sesame Street* is just another kids' show. . . . No better than *Underdog* or *The Flintstones*. What did the taxpayers get for their investment in *Sesame Street*? A generation of kids who spray graffiti on the walls of New York City. If *Sesame Street* was so effective, why do we have such a literacy problem?" [70] *Sesame Street* may be like other shows, such as *The Flintstones*, in terms of its marketability and exportability, but that does not make it the same as *The Flintstones* any more than *The Flintstones* is the same as *Underdog*, as Jarvik seems to imply. All three shows have different narratives, different conventions, and different intentions, and none of them are the cause of street art or illiteracy. Jarvik targets *Sesame Street* because the CTW makes a lot of money on toys, but all of this money goes back into producing the show or into the CTW's endowment. Licensing income and the endowment enable the CTW to produce its shows without government money, and Jarvik thinks other PBS shows should finance themselves in a similar manner. But *Sesame Street* and *Barney and Friends* are the exceptions on PBS, not the rule. Is there a fortune to be made in Charlie Rose coffee mugs and Bill Moyers sweatshirts? U.S. taxpayers spend as much money on military marching bands as they do on PBS. Defunding PBS is a symbolic statement about privatization, not a genuine means of reducing the deficit.

Jarvik's assault aside, since the seventies, *Sesame Street* has become virtually immune to attack. Luckily for PBS, Jarvik makes a huge tactical error in targeting the program, because in doing so, he evokes a knee-jerk pro-PBS response from many Americans. If this knee-jerk reaction will help PBS continue, I am all for it. But *Sesame Street* and the CTW should not be off-limits to critical investigation. *Sesame Street*'s symbolic stature discourages media critics from putting the show under their analytic microscopes, but it is precisely because the show is such a potent cultural symbol that it must be subjected to close analysis. By investigating *Sesame Street*'s testing practices and foreign productions, I have tried to open up this program for critical inquiry. Just as violent and commercial cartoons may actually contain progressive elements, good programs may not be so common-sensically above reproach. It is crucial to critically examine all kinds of children's television programs, considering all phases of their production, distribution, and reception.

Hey, Hey, Hey, It's "Good" TV

Fat Albert, CBS, and Dr. William H. Cosby

7

Like *Sesame Street*, Bill Cosby's CBS show *Fat Albert and the Cosby Kids* tried to teach children while entertaining them. However, whereas *Sesame Street's* producers used their scientific research and PBS status as proof that the show was high quality, *Fat Albert* was a low-budget network cartoon, and cartoons usually have no cachet in the middle-class market of educational TV. Constantly attacked for not providing enough quality TV for children, broadcasters see a children's show that is well received by adults as a godsend. These are the programs that seem immune to censorious agitators. Such shows can hopefully help counterbalance the "bad" shows that many adults—parents, congressional representatives, communications researchers—find objectionable. When *Fat Albert* came to be widely accepted as quality Saturday morning fare, it was a public relations coup for both CBS and Bill Cosby. The networks and the mainstream press defined *Fat Albert* as "good" not only on its own merits but also relative to other programming. *Fat Albert* was good precisely because other programs were deemed so bad by groups such as the recently formed Action for Children's Television and the scientists who prepared the 1972 report to the surgeon general on television violence.[1] CBS used *Fat Albert* as a volley against the 1974 Congressional Subcommittee on Communications, which, in response to the report to the surgeon general, severely criticized cartoons as empty and worthless entertainment. The network held up the didactic *Fat Albert* as proof that cartoons could be educational. CBS hoped that other new programs, which like *Fat Albert* were produced with Ph.D. advisers, could ride *Fat Albert's* uncensorable coattails.

This chapter explains how both Cosby and CBS used *Fat Albert*. My goal, most emphatically, is not to expose CBS and Cosby as charlatans who exploited little children for their own ignoble ends. Rather, the story of *Fat Albert* illustrates the extent to which successful "children's" television has little to do with children. Children were largely absent from both CBS's and

Bill Cosby's evaluations of *Fat Albert*'s quality. Children participated neither in the study of the show's effectiveness that Cosby undertook for his dissertation, nor (arguably) in the program's ratings evaluations. CBS had children take multiple-choice tests designed to prove *Fat Albert*'s effectiveness as a teacher of moral lessons, but those tests were used not to understand how children read the program but rather as publicity for the show.

This chapter does not attempt to fill in a perceived gap by accounting for how child viewers really felt about *Fat Albert*. Rather, my purpose is closer to Jacqueline Rose's in her Peter Pan study. To reiterate some of the points made in the introduction, Rose has argued that "literature for children" is impossible. Examining the tenuousness of the "for" in "literature for children," Rose shows that children's literature is always permeated with adult fantasies and desires. In this sense, children's literature is actually produced for adults. "Children's" television is likewise impossible. By studying adult reactions to (and use of) *Fat Albert*, this chapter strives to further problematize the "for" in "television for children." As the preceding chapters have demonstrated, adults plan and execute children's programming, and adults judge whether or not those shows succeed. A network executive may decide that a program is successful because it sells many toys, whereas parents may judge a show successful because *they* find it clever or funny. Activists hated product-based shows, but the TV industry loved them. Developmental psychologists hated *Sesame Street* when it premiered, but parents loved it. *Fat Albert* is unique in its success because it seemed to please virtually every adult who saw it. The show's success was due in no small part to executive producer Bill Cosby's talent and reputation.

Dr. Cosby and *Fat Albert*: A Symbiotic Relationship

Cosby is a high-profile, well-known media figure. Producer, writer, and star of *The Cosby Show* (NBC, 1984–1992) and a best-selling author, he has also been a successful spokesperson for Coca-Cola, Jell-O, Ford, Texas Instruments, Kodak, and E. F. Hutton. Throughout the eighties, advertisers saw him as a good investment because he was widely viewed as paternal and trustworthy. As one advertising executive who tested mothers' attitudes toward Jell-O ads put it: "They think he's a good guy, wholesome, good with kids. They see him as a sort of surrogate parent for their kids, though they don't put it in those words."[2] In consumer testing undertaken by the Ford Motor Company, Cosby rated high, below only two other paternal figures: "When Cosby's name and reputation were test-marketed by Ford with 30 other famous personalities, the sample groups of consumers ranked him above everyone except, according to a Detroit account executive, God and Walter Cronkite."[3] The trustworthy Cosby is additionally known as the pro-education philanthropist who gave Spelman College $20 million and as the businessperson who attempted to negotiate the purchase of NBC in 1993 for over $3 billion. Cosby's image is that of a rich, powerful entertainer who has a doctoral degree in education to boot, as we know from his credit on *The Cosby Show* as "William H. Cosby, Ed.D."

It was perhaps Cosby's 1986 best-seller *Fatherhood* that finally clinched his paternal image, but his pro-education image certainly predates the eighties. The foundation of Cosby's educated persona was constructed in the seventies, in part via *Fat Albert*. Cosby's pro-education reputation continues today and was reinforced by his donation to Spelman, by *The Cosby Show*'s narratives, and even by his public sporting of university sweatshirts. In the seventies, Cosby's educated image grew as a result of his attainment of degrees and his association with his Saturday morning cartoon. Cosby's persona validated the program as educational and therefore good for children and uncensorable. Conversely, the program sealed Cosby's educated image. It also reinforced his reputation for producing "color-blind entertainment" since *Fat Albert* was about kids who, as Cosby often (but not always) said, "just happened to be black." Cosby has been criticized throughout his career for eliding racial issues in his entertainment. In 1992, for example, Sut Jhally and Justin Lewis published a *Cosby Show* audience study in which they argue that the program reinforces white viewers' belief that racism is a problem of the past.[4] Jhally and Lewis's study offers empirical evidence that confirms what many have intuited—that *The Cosby Show* was in many ways symptomatic of Reagan-era racial and economic politics.

Fat Albert came out of an earlier era in Cosby's career. From 1965 to 1968, Cosby costarred on *I Spy* (NBC), the first dramatic series with an African American lead character. He won three Emmys for portraying Scotty, a Rhodes scholar who spoke eight languages fluently. After *I Spy* was canceled, Cosby participated in a series of shorter-lived TV programs. He had won a Grammy for his 1964 comedy album, but his albums did not fare as well during the post-*I Spy* period. On his records, Cosby told wholesome tales of his youth, avoiding controversial topics such as race, drugs, and sex. In 1973, he lost the Grammy to the confrontational and risqué Cheech and Chong. In 1974, Richard Pryor won with his album *That Nigger's Crazy*. Cosby seemed woefully out of date. His 1977 album *Disco Bill* was not drawing the *Saturday Night Fever* crowd. As he put it in a 1985 interview with *Playboy* magazine: "In the early seventies, when the younger culture went into a kind of LSD period, a lot of legitimate showbiz people — Bill Cosby, Harry Belafonte, Andy Williams, even Johnny Mathis — began to feel like tumbleweed rolling through the back of the theaters. The economy was in a dip, our fans were becoming parents, the time seemed wrong." [5]

In his interviews throughout the late sixties, Cosby had persistently claimed that when he retired from show biz, he would like to be a teacher. So it was no surprise when Cosby turned to television teaching in the seventies. He did guest spots on *Captain Kangaroo* and *Sesame Street*, he worked extensively on *The Electric Company*, and he conceived the first educational cartoon to appear on network television, *Fat Albert and the Cosby Kids*. The show featured a cast of poor, black, inner-city kids based on the childhood characters from Cosby's stand-up routines.[6] Each *Fat Albert* episode was introduced and concluded by Cosby, who would clarify the show's lessons: do not steal, do not play hooky, do not lie to your friends. Cosby not only hosted the show but also was billed as its executive producer. He was the first African American, as far as my research has found, to get such billing on a national network television program.

There is no question that *Fat Albert* was legitimized as an educational cartoon, at least in part, by the educators involved in the show's production. The scripts were reviewed by a panel of sociologists, educators, and psychologists, all Ph.D.'s credited in each episode. The involvement of both a panel of Ph.D. experts and the former Scotty differentiated this program from the "trashy" cartoons opposed by parents, public pressure groups, and the Congressional Subcommittee on Communications.[7] The intellectual clout of the people who worked on *Fat Albert* helped establish the show as quality entertainment in spite of its status as a TV cartoon.

Cosby's educator image was sealed by his 1976 dissertation, *An Integration of the Visual Media via "Fat Albert and the Cosby Kids" into the Elementary School Curriculum as a Teaching Aid and Vehicle to Achieve Increased Learning*.[8] To research his dissertation, Cosby mailed *Fat Albert* questionnaires to teachers who showed the program in their classes. They all evaluated the show positively, which is not surprising since they had already chosen to use the program before Cosby contacted them. (Plus, some teachers might have been reluctant to tell superstar Bill Cosby they did not like his show.) The group was self-selected: 25 percent of the teachers initially contacted did not offer to participate in the study. The teachers who agreed to participate indicated which shows they thought were most successful in communicating their messages to children; they did not indicate how their students had actually responded.

The *Fat Albert* cartoons sent to the teachers in Cosby's study were distributed by the McGraw-Hill textbook company. These cartoons differed in several ways from the *Fat Albert* cartoons shown on TV. The cartoons are marked as educational from the very beginning, as they open with the McGraw-Hill logo. The next title reads, "Learning Values with Fat Albert and the Cosby Kids, Starring Bill Cosby." On TV, Cosby was marked as the star, but viewers were not advised that they were about to "learn values." The McGraw-Hill films do not have commercial breaks, which makes them seem more educational than they would be on TV since most adults feel commercialism taints children's programs. McGraw-Hill's *Fat Albert* prints do not list the Ph.D. advisers involved in the show, but this does not detract from their educational message since no end credits are listed at all. Without credits, the show comes across as authored only by Cosby. The Ph.D. panel is gone, but so is the show's status as an industrial product. In small print, Filmation and Cosby are discretely listed as copyright holders, but no animators, voice artists, or musicians are cited. The lack of end credits strips the shows of their production history and their status as TV cartoons, making them into pure educational texts suitable for classroom use. Today teachers use videos and TVs in the classroom; during the pre–home video era, the fact that McGraw-Hill's *Fat Albert* shows were films, not TV, further marked them as educational.[9]

In asking teachers about their classroom use of *Fat Albert* films, Cosby's intention was to examine how educational media could be used to address America's grave educational crisis. In particular, Cosby was concerned that African American children were receiving the short end of the educational stick. Cosby found that most teachers responded favorably to *Fat Albert*, and he concluded that the show could be a useful tool for teachers. But this finding is less interesting to me than the dissertation itself and what it might have meant to adult *Fat Albert* viewers. Producing a dissertation on *Fat Albert* helped validate the show to parents, journalists, and legislators by illustrating that it was worthy of extensive study. Previously, the only children's shows that had been subjected to lengthy academic study were all PBS productions such as *Sesame Street*, *Mister Rogers' Neighborhood*, and *The Electric Company*. The Children's Television Workshop realized that PBS's elitist, white image might limit viewership, and it had set up programs in inner cities to encourage mothers to watch *Sesame Street* with their kids. But its efforts were not enough to dispel PBS's "classy" image. Most viewers continue to associate the networks with trashy cartoons and PBS with high-quality, mostly live-action children's educational programs. Producing an educational *network* cartoon takes daring because agitators for better children's programming tend to judge network cartoons more severely than they do PBS programs and live-action programs in general. In fact, one network executive privately acknowledged to me that it was difficult to develop new educational cartoons that would win ACT approval because "Peggy [Charren] has something against cartoons."[10]

Fat Albert is the only cartoon program to have ever been the focus of a dissertation, and it is one of the few cartoons to have been almost universally embraced as effectively educational, good programming. The program certainly could have been successful without the dissertation. But there is no doubt that Cosby's high-profile back-to-school publicity increased people's interest in the show. The show's association with Cosby and the Ph.D. consultants may not have given it the same high-class cultural prestige as PBS programs have, but it did raise it far above noneducational seventies network cartoons like *Scooby-Doo, Where Are You?* (CBS, 1969–1976; ABC, 1978).

To understand how unique *Fat Albert* was, one must consider it in the historical context of adult protest of network children's television. Since television's installation in U.S. homes in the fifties, parents, teachers, and social scientists have condemned television cartoons as "bad" for children because of their violence, sexism, racism, and/or commercialism. Adult notions of "taste" and "quality" have been paramount in the condemnation of children's cartoons. Animated programs have been harshly criticized not only for what middle-class and intellectual adults have perceived as their excesses—of violence, of gender stereotyping, of commercialism—but also for their low production values in comparison to thirties and forties theatrical cartoons. Like other cartoons of the period, *Fat Albert* was fairly minimally animated, often recycling cels of actions and backgrounds.[11] However, because of its pedagogical nature, its Ph.D. advisers, and its association with Cosby, *Fat Albert* was almost universally praised as a high-quality, healthy, and uncensorable cartoon. Only the ever-crotchety Cornell University sociologist and media critic Rose K. Goldsen rejected the program's preachiness and dared to point out that *Fat Albert* was as minimally animated as other TV cartoons: "The series still shows the same hard-outline, jerkily moving, two dimensional creatures of the animated world. But the change this time is that these stick figures don't fall off cliffs, fool around with Doomsday machines or get blown to smithereens."[12]

A sure sign that the network saw *Fat Albert* as a quality cartoon was the fact that network censors seem to have cut the program some slack. In fact, *Fat Albert* characters were equally if not more likely to fall off cliffs than characters in less prestigious contemporary shows, programs widely disdained by adults such as *Speed Buggy* (CBS, 1973–1975; ABC, 1975–1976; NBC, 1976–1977; CBS, 1978) and *Josie and the Pussycats in Outer Space* (CBS, 1972–1974; NBC, 1975–1976). As with all TV cartoons, *Fat Albert* scripts and storyboards were most certainly submitted to Standards and Practices, but it seems that the program was allowed representations that Standards would have red penciled in other shows. The kids on the show engaged in so-called imitable acts such as building their own vehicles, toys, and ski ramps out of junk and, on several occasions, riding motorcycles recklessly. These acts would have been eliminated from less didactic programs in order to avoid network liability for possible dangerous imitation. The Cosby Kids' high jinks might have somehow seemed less imitable than standard cartoon violence. They rode motorcycles on telephone lines, but they did not drop anvils on each other or play with dynamite.

Although *Fat Albert* violence (rough-and-tumble football games, for example) was generally played for comic effect, in at least one program, the violence is tragic, drawing on cinematic conventions of drama and suspense rather than slapstick and farce. In an episode titled "Talk Don't Fight," Tito, a friend of Fat Albert's, has an older brother who is in a gang. Tito is shot and killed while trying to save his big brother from getting involved in a gang war. Tito runs toward his death in dramatic lap dissolves, as a heartbeat rises on the soundtrack.[13] The pointed gun is shown, and the shot is heard (but not seen), followed by a close-up of the smoking gun. Such a dramatic depiction of death was not unheard of in some sixties action cartoons such as *Jonny Quest* (originally shown during prime time on ABC, 1964–1965), but by the time *Fat Albert* came on the air in 1972, cartoon representations of death were strictly taboo. *Fat Albert* seems to have had a limited dispensation from network censorship because of the program's prosocial, educational image and, in the case of "Talk Don't Fight," because of its strong antigang message. In addition, Standards personnel might have tolerated depictions of actions that some critics would have termed "violent" because of Cosby's celebrity status and educator image and also because they might have been fans of his albums' comic style, which could be seen in the programs.

Like "Talk Don't Fight," "Dope Is for Dopes" addressed a difficult topic for a Saturday morning cartoon. In this episode, the kids have a friend named Franny who always has lots of money. The money comes from his brother Muggles, who turns out to be a dope dealer. As in "Talk Don't Fight," the story makes the criminalized character a brother of a friend so that the Cosby Kids are not actually friends with a criminal. Unlike Tito in "Talk Don't Fight," however, Muggles's downfall is not directly represented. He is simply arrested, but no gritty details of the bust are shown. Muggles gives Fat Albert a package to deliver. Fat Albert is caught by the police and is shocked to hear that Muggles is a drug pusher. Viewers less naive than Fat Albert would not be surprised since Muggles's flashy outfit and apartment code him as a pusher (or even pimp), echoing a common stereotype in contemporaneous blaxploitation films. After Fat Albert agrees to help the cops catch Muggles, he briefly discusses the situation with his parents and asks Franny if he knows what his brother does for a living. (He does not.) These two awkward scenes do not fit in the cartoon, and they are not the kind of scenes that would have been suggested by a Standards and Practices department, since Standards focuses almost exclusively on regulating violent, sexist, or racist images. It seems quite likely that these two scenes were added at the request of the show's Ph.D. advisers. In a show teaching about values, the panel would have thought it important that Fat Albert tell his parents he was helping the cops with a drug bust. As for the other scene, Franny must be clearly absolved of guilt so that it is acceptable for him not to be punished. For film censorship scholars, the addition of these awkward scenes evokes the kind of censorship executed by the Studio Relations Committee, the predecessor to Hollywood's self-censoring Production Code Administration. Like the Studio Relations Committee, the Ph.D. panel attacks details more than narrative structure, and its censorious additions often stand out like sore thumbs. Since *Fat Albert* was cut slack by Standards and Practices, the show may have been censored more by its own Ph.D. panel than by CBS, although the network did change the title "Dope Is for Dopes" to "Mister Big Timer" in its 1973 fall press release on *Fat Albert*, perhaps to temper potentially adverse reactions to a Saturday morning cartoon about drugs. (This was ten years before "just say no" came on the scene.)

Cosby's role as teacher on *Fat Albert* demonstrated to both Standards and Practices and the public that he was a respectable educator who made respectable cartoons, in spite of the fact that he has never been an educator in the traditional sense. Cosby received a master's degree in education in 1972, a doctorate in education in 1976, and a bachelor's degree in physical education from Temple University around 1977.[14] Cosby engaged in little coursework to earn his degrees. According to a bitter professor who served on his dissertation committee, Cosby invited the committee members to his home, gave them a complete tour (including his wife's fur coat closet), and fed them dinner before they discussed his project. The professor claims that a month later Cosby submitted a proposal, two months after that he submitted his first three chapters, and two months after that he defended his dissertation.[15] (These claims seem bitterly hyperbolic, and I have not been able to confirm them.) Cosby took a few special weekend courses but no semester-long courses. He got most of his credits for "practicums" and "independent studies." In other words, he got credit for his appearances on *The Electric Company*, and he submitted *Fat Albert* scripts as papers. Cosby's degree program might be interpreted as nontraditional schooling, which would make sense since his dissertation advocates the nontraditional use of media as an educational tool in the classroom. But his dissertation notwithstanding, Cosby generally opposes nontraditional higher education. He is against the "trend" of students choosing their own curriculums and condemns nontraditional courses, which he parodies as "The History of Western Belching." He laments that when he attended college, he would occasionally cut classes to go to the movies, but today instead of learning the "basic classroom skills," "the movies themselves have become the class, or as it is commonly termed, 'the film experience.' "[16] *Cosby Show* viewers will recall that when one of the Huxtable daughters was failing her college classes, she was getting good grades in only one class. The punch line? It was a film class. Given Cosby's disdain of the academic study of visual texts, it seems ironic that he earned credit for his own TV teaching. When the validity of his degrees is questioned, Cosby asserts that he fulfilled all the requirements the university gave him, which is absolutely true.

Regardless of how rigorous Cosby's doctoral studies were, what I am interested in is how the media has *used* Cosby's education. Almost every Cosby interview has mentioned his dissertation, often citing the tongue-twister title in its entirety. The media has constructed Cosby as highly educated, and his educated image strengthens his persona as a credible spokesman for family-oriented products. Cosby's educator/educated image strongly contributed to the "tasteful," extremely trustworthy image that made him one of the most sought-after, highly paid spokespeople in America throughout the eighties.[17] In a 1984 ad for Coke, Cosby appeared with basketball player "Dr." Julius Irving. The ad's playful hook was that "two out of two doctors agree" on the merits of drinking Coke.[18] The joke here is that Cosby and Dr. J. are not the kind of doctors who are qualified to recommend brands of toothpaste or pain reliever. But they are, nonetheless, credible and trustworthy African American cultural icons.

Fat Albert's child viewers may have seen Cosby as the teacher/authority figure on the show, but it is doubtful that they thought the show was good because Cosby had a Ed.D. Cosby's Ed.D. would have been of value only to adults. Cosby's wife recognized the centrality of Cosby's educated image when she advised him, in response to his original proposal that he portray a chauffeur on *The Cosby Show*, that "nobody is going to believe that you're a chauffeur. Your image has always been Temple University, college, grad school."[19] Camille Cosby reasoned that Cosby's Scotty/Rhodes scholar image from the sixties was so firmly entrenched that viewers would not accept him as working class in the eighties. In the seventies, child viewers of *Fat Albert* might have thought he was a junkyard worker (this was my interpretation), but for adults, he was an educator who just happened to be in a junkyard. Of course, for some adults, Cosby was first and foremost a *black* man in a junkyard. My research indicates widespread Cosby appeal among adults, but it must also be noted that Cosby was an early black presence on TV, and one which racist viewers would have rejected. Certainly, some adults did not respond favorably to *Fat Albert* because they did not want their children to watch a cartoon, or any other kind of program, featuring African Americans.

The theories of French sociologist Pierre Bourdieu may help clarify why Cosby's educator image would matter to many adult *Fat Albert* viewers. Bourdieu argues that by imposing titles such as "doctor of philosophy," the educational system attributes status or "academic capital" to people. Academic capital carries with it an "entitlement effect," whereby certain practices (or texts) derive their value from their author's title. "The holders of educationally uncertified cultural capital can always be required to prove themselves, because they *are* only what they *do*," whereas "the holders of titles of cultural nobility . . . only have to be what they are, because all their practices derive their value from their authors" (original emphasis).[20] For example, because Bourdieu is an *authority* on issues of taste and class and is often cited in scholarly publications, some readers may find that by citing Bourdieu, I have automatically strengthened my analysis of the public reception of Cosby's educated image. By citing an intellectual authority more established than myself, I add clout to my own argumentation. Although what I say about Bourdieu also matters, his words will be perceived as having some value by virtue of what he *is*, a famous sociologist. Dissertations and Ph.D.'s constitute academic capital because they carry with them authority and power, not just because of what they do (what a dissertation argues, what a person with a Ph.D. actually knows) but because of what they are. The logic is tautological: people with Ph.D.'s have authority because they have Ph.D.'s. *Fat Albert* may well have had educational value for actual viewers because of what the show did, but it clearly also derived much of its value from what it *was*—the product of a Ph.D. panel and the subject of a doctoral thesis by Dr. Cosby.

Cosby and *Fat Albert's* Race Politics

In his dissertation, Cosby examines how urban schools have failed to meet minority children's educational needs, and he also analyzes how *Fat Albert*, *Sesame Street*, and *The Electric Company* attempt to fight institutional racism. Cosby argues that

> *Fat Albert* has demonstrable value as a success model for inner-city and low-income children. He is a positive character, the Cosby Kids are posi-

tive characters. They are black. They live in the ghetto. No other show previously on television has concerned itself so much with identifying with black children. For the first time black children have the opportunity to see themselves through the animated characters of *Fat Albert*. A very important part of the series is that it serves as a vehicle to help eliminate the adverse effects of racism.[21]

Cosby's commitment to eliminating the effects of racism may sound incongruous since he has so often been criticized for his "color-blind" approach to comedy. However, offstage Cosby has always been fairly outspoken about racial issues and has tried to open up the TV industry to blacks. His 1969 *Playboy* interviewer notes that "Bill has been the subject of a series of limpid interviews. . . . [W]riters and editors have often deleted his more trenchant off-stage observations about the black man's place in America. Almost to the point of making him seem like an Uncle Tom."[22] Cosby counteracted his Uncle Tom image with this interview, in which he expressed doubts about the effectiveness of nonviolent resistance and spoke of the dystopian possibility of blacks being herded into concentration camps. More Malcolm X than Uncle Tom, Cosby said: "[T]he black man is not going to take any more bullshit. . . . [B]lack people will actually go to war if they're driven to it. Not all black people, but the ones who feel they're willing to give up their lives in order to mess up this country, to bring America to its knees. I'm not talking about just burning some buildings but about black guerrillas cutting wires, darkening the cities, ending communications. All-out war."[23] In this interview, Cosby showed that he was not apolitical, as the media often portrayed him. But he also said, "I'm not trying to win converts on stage. . . . I don't think an entertainer can win converts. I've never known any kind of white bigot to pay to see a black man, unless the black man was being hung. So I don't spend hours worrying how to slip a social message into my act; I just go out and do my thing."[24] In *Fat Albert*, Cosby actually did slip social messages into his act, even if those messages often seemed rather tame. The explicit messages were simple ones about not showing off or the value of cooperation, but the implicit message was, like *Sesame Street*'s "hidden curriculum," about racial politics. Like *Sesame Street*, *Fat Albert* offered viewers black characters to identify with. There were few representations of black children elsewhere on TV.

Considered in the context of Cosby's other "color-blind" entertainment projects, *Fat Albert* seems radical: it is about poor black kids whose playground is a junkyard and who make their playthings out of old tin cans and other garbage. Given the economic status of many people of color in the United States at the time, *Fat Albert* seems like a more realistic portrayal of seventies black lifestyle than *The Cosby Show*'s Reagan-era picture of fully achieved upward mobility. This is not to say that *Fat Albert* showed an America on the verge of civil war, the America Cosby described in 1969. In fact, although he argued for the importance of the characters' race in his dissertation, elsewhere Cosby stated that the characters' class and race were irrelevant: "[M]y cartoon kids . . . happen to be black kids from the ghetto. But their color, or where they live, that doesn't make them any different from the wealthy ten-year-old who lives in Beverly Hills." [25]

Although *Fat Albert* narratives may support Cosby's claim that the show addresses universal, cross-racial children's issues, such as peer pressure to play hooky or to lie, the cartoons' background drawings show garbage, decrepit buildings, and junk shops, which may work against such color-blindness.[26] Each show opens with an introduction by Cosby in a junkyard. The junkyard is cluttered but not dirty, rather like the squeaky clean inner city pictured on *Sesame Street*. After the titles and Cosby's introduction, the first animated sequence in each show is a simulated crane shot of the ghetto the kids live in. The shot shows laundry hanging on a line, decrepit TV antennas, and finally the junkyard the kids use as their playground. Since this stock introductory shot is used in every show, it is finely produced, but throughout the rest of the show, the images are of varying quality. In some cases, the background is very sparse or nonexistent, which indicates both the cheapness of the cartoon and a poverty of image consistent with the poverty of the show's characters. However, *Fat Albert*'s narratives play down the potential despair or poverty of those background images. The kids' creative junkyard play sends two very different messages: first, that "poverty is fun" and, second, that ghetto kids have agency and do not have to turn to violence or drugs to cope with their lives. *Fat Albert* was about poor black kids, which made it a radical innovation on Saturday morning TV, but the show had difficulty addressing the kids' poverty, except at the level of background design. Although the backgrounds evoked *Fritz the Cat*'s (Bakshi, 1972) stylized, gritty realism, *Fat Albert*'s narratives rarely connected with these stark backgrounds.

But would it be desirable for a kid's cartoon to address tough African American issues? And in 1972, what would this mean, a cartoon version of *Shaft?* Fat Albert and the Cosby Kids were black but distinctly different from the African Americans in contemporaneous blaxploitation movies like *Super Fly*, films whose representational politics Cosby did not approve of. For the adult audience, Cosby offered *Uptown Saturday Night*, a non-exploitative all-black gangster movie. *Fat Albert* was the kiddie version of *Uptown Saturday Night*.

Like *Uptown Saturday Night*, *Fat Albert* does not portray an integrated world. *Fat Albert*'s police officers, schoolteachers, and shopkeepers are all black. When the kids go to a theater to rehearse their production of *Moby Dick*—with Fat Albert as the eponymous star—even the posters on the theater walls show black ballerinas and black Romeos and Juliets. In this all-black world, stories addressing tensions between different races are rare. In an episode in which the kids have misconceptions about Indians, their attitudes are articulated as merely a matter of misinformation, not of racism. The show ends not with a condemnation of racism but with an homage to education and the library, where the kids "checked out" the "truth" about Indians. In another show, the kids encounter some Latino, Asian, and white kids at summer camp. This is the only *Fat Albert*, besides the Indian episode, that features non–African American characters. This is also the only episode that does not take place in the all-black inner city. As the kids drive up to the camp out in the country, stereotypical Indian drums and "powwow" music play, and we see that the kids will be sleeping in teepees. The Cosby Kids bristle when they meet the other camp kids because they are "different," but they do not remark on the teepees as different. Apparently, the teepees are included in the episode not to teach a lesson about difference or tolerance but rather to signify the adventurous spirit of summer camp. The story quickly veers away from the racial differences between the campers, and the main source of tension ends up being that one of the white kids is a bully. When one of the Cosby Kids gets lost, all the kids pull together to face the crisis, and the problem of difference is solved. The Cosby Kids sing a song called "One World": "Look at the people. They come in all kinds of colors, but they're no different from each other. No, they're all the same." This message of sameness is belied, however, by the stereotypical Indian signifiers that recur throughout the show.

Blacks, Anglos, Asians, and Latinos all get along in this show, whereas Native Americans remain the exotic other.

As for the perceptions of contemporary *Fat Albert* viewers, it is impossible to say unequivocally that *Fat Albert* was or was not "color-blind." The show only occasionally explicitly addressed racial issues, but one could argue that implicitly it always addressed race by virtue of the fact that it pictured an all–African American cast. After all, this was the first all-black TV show since *Amos 'n' Andy* (CBS, 1950–1953), a show that also did not address racial issues explicitly but that no one would argue was simply color-blind. Although *Fat Albert*'s original child audience cannot be reconstituted, some clues indicate how adults theorized child reception at the time. Many journalists reporting on *Fat Albert* focused more on Cosby than on hypothetical viewers, but the black magazine *Jet* speculated on how children would respond to the show, suggesting that the show both was and was not color-blind, depending on the viewer's race: "Black children can easily transport their own experiences into Fat Albert's shoes. White youngsters, on the other hand, can see the universality of colorless adolescent adjustments." The *Jet* writer asserts that blacks can identify with the Cosby Kids directly; they can stand in the Cosby Kids' black, lower-class shoes. White viewers, conversely, will not stand in the Cosby Kids' shoes but will instead understand them as examples of universal childhood. Implicitly, the white viewer does not see the Cosby Kids as black or lower class at all. The black viewer's ethnicity, in this reading, enables his/her identification with the characters as black characters, whereas the white viewers' ethnicity means that he/she will "get" the show and enjoy it through age-based identification. Cosby had problematically elided class differences when he said the ghetto Cosby Kids were the same as Beverly Hills kids. *Jet* says that Beverly Hills adolescents are the same as ghetto kids because Fat Albert merely represents universal adolescence but that ghetto kids are *not* the same as Beverly Hills kids because they identify with Fat Albert directly, not with his status as "universal" adolescent.

It is impossible to say how kids actually identified with the program, but the *Jet* prognosis does not seem completely off base. Our culture sees whiteness as normal and invisible and blackness as an always visible deviation from the norm. Whites occupy a comfortable place of pseudononethnicity, even when an entertainment text forces them to identify across ethnicities. Blacks rarely have the luxury of invisibility. If *Fat Albert* was really "color-blind," this would imply that blackness was "normal" and invisible on the show. That this was not the case is indicated by the fact that viewers had to be identified as white or black by the *Jet* writer. After all, no one in the white or black press felt the need to say that *Scooby-Doo* was a show about white kids that black kids could nonetheless get into because the show addressed universal issues. *Scooby-Doo* was color-blind because it showed only white, the color many viewers—and TV producers—could see only as "normal," not as a color.

CBS's Use of *Fat Albert*

Fat Albert was literally and symbolically profitable for not only Cosby but also CBS. When *Fat Albert* premiered in 1972, CBS executives might have privately seen the show as an answer to the censorious voices of ACT and other TV protesters. However, the network did not go public about the program's merits until after it had been on the air, with strong ratings, for two years. Although the expert Ph.D. panel members had been credited for their involvement all along, it was not until 1974 that CBS took out a full-page ad for the show in the *New York Times*, describing it as "an extraordinary experiment in television education, created under the direct, detailed supervision of a panel of noted scholars and educators." The ad stated that *Fat Albert*'s purpose was "to expand the child's understanding of self and the world, through the imaginative, unorthodox use of television." It cited data from "A Study of Messages Received by Children Who Viewed an Episode of *Fat Albert and the Cosby Kids*," a survey of 711 children interviewed by the Gene Reilly Group for CBS. According to the survey, 89.3 percent of the child subjects who had viewed *Fat Albert* "received one or more prosocial messages." In other words, in a multiple-choice test, eight out of nine children picked *Fat Albert* messages such as "lying is bad" that they had "received" from the program. The study demonstrated only that the kids could *recall* what they viewed, not that they had necessarily "learned" prosocial messages. CBS released these study results in February 1974 and ran the public relations advertisement for the show on 1 April. The *New York Times* ad included the address of CBS's Office of Social Research, where anyone could request a copy of the Reilly study. It is clear from both the full-page advertisement on the back page of the *Times* and the invitation to interested readers to receive a free copy of the study that CBS sank a substantial amount of money into its *Fat Albert* public relations efforts.

Also during the first week of April 1974, not coincidentally, executives from the three networks testified before Senator John Pastore's Subcommittee on Communications, where they were required to explain what they had done in response to the 1972 report to the surgeon general on television violence. Specifically, they were asked to explain how they had addressed the study's conclusion that viewing television representations of violence *might* make *some* children more aggressive. At Pastore's first hearings on television violence in 1972, the networks had promised to change children's programming in response to the surgeon general's report. Or rather, they affirmed that they would respond to Pastore and the media's *interpretation* of the report, for the report's findings actually were not as conclusive as Pastore led people to believe. Compare Pastore's view of the report to the report itself:

> Pastore: . . . [W]e now know there is a causal relation between televisual violence and antisocial behavior which is sufficient to warrant immediate remedial action. It is this certainty which has eluded men of good will for so long.[27]

> Surgeon General's Scientific Advisory Committee on Television and Social Behavior: . . . [T]here is a convergence of the fairly substantial experimental evidence for short-run causation of aggression among some children by viewing violence on the screen and the much less certain evidence from field studies that extensive violence viewing precedes some long-run manifestations of aggressive behavior. This convergence of the two types of evidence constitutes some preliminary indication of a causal relationship, but a good deal of research remains to be done before one can have confidence in these conclusions.[28]

Both the networks and the public at large bought Pastore's interpretation of the investigative committee's tentative conclusions.

Between the 1972 Pastore hearings on the surgeon general's report and the 1974 follow-up hearings, the networks hired social scientists to perform tests on children in order to produce data that could be used as ammunition against government-funded studies of television violence. The networks' social scientists produced hard copy that could be flashed not only to Pastore but also to ACT or any other citizens who complained about children's programming. For two years, all three networks aired a variety of new children's programs. CBS took *Fat Albert* as a model for un-censorable TV and produced other programs with Ph.D. advisers. Earlier TV cartoons such as *Herculoids* (CBS, 1967–69) and *Jonny Quest* might have inadvertently taught conservative lessons about family values, but it was only in the seventies that overt didacticism became a crucial trope of TV cartoons. Hanna-Barbera cofounder Joe Barbera often lamented that he could not produce a cartoon in which a cat chased a mouse unless they suddenly stopped to give lessons in basket weaving or glassblowing.

The case of *Fat Albert* and other didactic shows bolsters Annette Kuhn's claim that censorship is productive, not merely repressive, of texts.[29] We conventionally imagine that censorship produces gaps and fissures where naughty bits have been excised from a text. Textual gaps constitute censorship's most obvious effects, but censorship can also provoke generic restructuring. Were it not for the threat of government censorship, academic-consultant shows filled with educational messages would not have come into existence. Network use of Ph.D.'s in cartoon production was clearly a response to government pressure and fear of censorship. The September after the 1974 hearings, CBS released six new Saturday morning series, five of which credited academic consultants. To throw a sop to Pastore, the other networks also looked to Ph.D. advisers. NBC hired a linguist to create a Neanderthal language for its *Land of the Lost* series (1974–1977), and ABC employed a special consultant for its *New Adventures of Gilligan* (1974–1977) to ensure that the program had "story lines concerning peer-group pressure, prejudice, ecology and other themes bearing on social behavior and attitudes."[30] ABC also consulted with the Bank Street School of Education on *Devlin* (1974–1976), a new program that "substitut[ed] a healthy family relationship for overt violence" and presented motorcycle safety tips.[31] When facing Pastore, the networks emphasized not only that they had hired Ph.D. consultants but also that they had canceled some cartoons and replaced them with new live-action programs.[32] Live action was apparently assumed by all to be inherently less dangerous to children than animation.[33]

In spite of its status as a cartoon, *Fat Albert* could be flaunted at the 1974 hearings. It had been on the air spreading moralistic "prosocial" messages for two years, with high ratings and a consulting Ph.D. panel, and the show's creator, executive producer, and star was perceived as a respected educator. With such a trustworthy icon backing the show, it was quite easy for CBS to use *Fat Albert* as ammunition against the censorious Pastore. Plus, anyone criticizing the show might have risked being labeled a racist. With the exception of *Good Times*, which had premiered in 1974, *Fat Albert* was the *only* all-black show in a sea of white shows.

Just before CBS released its *New York Times* advertisement and the Reilly study, *Fat Albert*'s animation company, Filmation, published a public relations book about *Fat Albert*. The hardback book has a brown leather-colored cover, and the gold-embossed title, in "classy" script, reads, *Personal, Parental, and Peer-Group Value Conflicts as Catalysts of Complex Educational and Psychological Issues Confronting Children in a Contemporary Society or. . . .*[34] Opening the book reveals the alternate title, *Fat Albert and the Cosby Kids*, and a brightly colored picture of the whole gang playing their junkyard instruments. The cover title indicates the show's serious intentions, but those intentions are debunked as intellectual mumbo jumbo by the second, down-to-earth title.[35] The text is in large print and is illustrated like a children's book, but its language is clearly addressed to adults. This makes the book an interesting symbol of how *Fat Albert*, ostensibly for children, also offered itself to adult readers. The book's design is childlike, but its language is adult, not unlike the contrast between the Cosby Kids' entertaining animated adventures and Cosby's anticlimactic live-action lessons at the end of each show. The short book explains that the program is innovative in three ways: by virtue of its Ph.D. panel, its inner-city setting, and its being "invested with the special sharp reality of comedian-educator Bill Cosby's imagination and memory" of his childhood in Philadelphia.[36] Since he was working on his doctorate at the time, Cosby is credited as "the twelfth scholar involved with the show." The book ends with an homage to CBS's commitment to producing high-quality children's programming, and although no author is credited for the book and only Filmation and Cosby are listed as copyright holders, it seems likely that CBS had a hand in producing this book. The book lists other children's programs that CBS is proud of, concluding that "an effort like *Fat Albert and the Cosby Kids* is important not only for itself, but for its place in the larger framework of CBS Television Network programming experiments for children." [37] Such "experiments for children" were clearly bids for survival on the part of the networks; these bold new experiments in television programming appeared only after the surgeon general's report was released in 1972.

CBS surely won points with congressional investigators for producing a show with black characters at a time when protest groups were agitating for more representations of people of color on television. The show's black characters made it more respectable and helped it to be taken seriously as an educational program dealing with "real-life" issues even though it was a cheap, minimally animated cartoon. Such a program could certainly have been construed as serving "the public interest, convenience, and necessity." However, the fact that it did not explicitly deal with racial issues would have been in its favor as well. The program was serious but not propagandistic or "too political" for a child audience. The *Fat Albert* book addresses the program's racial politics briefly by saying that "the fact that the kids are black is neither minimized nor exploited. And the behavior problems they confront are universal. . . . [Racial] stereotyping is to be avoided" in the form of "characters whose physical features, coupled with movement and/or language style, will offend children and parents in all racial groups." [38] The show's images were carefully constructed to conform to these mandates: the backgrounds had to show poverty but without conveying the message that all blacks are destitute, so middle-class black characters were worked into the program as extras, such as police officers and storekeepers. The characters were designed to look "realistically" black, with larger lips and more flattened noses than whites. Designing "realistic" cartoon representations of black people might have been difficult for the Filmation animators, given the history of cartoon images of blacks. What graphic tradition could they draw on? In truth, the majority of popular cultural representations of blacks up to that point had used a cartoony style of exaggeration. [39] Perhaps to compensate for this, the *Fat Albert* characters ended up looking less cartoony than other Saturday morning characters.

Their speech was carefully coded as inner-city black but in an understated way; standard white English with black-coded intonations and some rhyming jive talk were used to create a modified black English. [40] One of the scholars on the advisory panel addressed this issue:

The use of malapropisms or inaccurate vocabulary such as "excravation" . . . raises a general issue. Most educators feel that children should not be exposed to inaccuracies without a correction being made. However, its use in the context of this series presents another and possibly more serious problem: namely, the stereotyping of black children as verbally inept or inferior. We recognize the distinction between differences in dialect among white and black children, and differences in verbal competence. *But we're not sure that the children in the audience can make this distinction.*[41] (my emphasis)

In other words, black English is not a problem for informed adults, but "children in the audience" might not understand that different people speak different kinds of English. These hypothetical child viewers seem to be white middle-class kids (Nielsen ratings kids). Would a black inner-city child, persistently exposed to the midwestern white English most commonly heard on television, really not understand that there were differences in dialect between some white and black children? The speech on *Fat Albert* is very carefully designed to sound unlike the typical white English on other cartoons (and, indeed, most of TV) but to avoid vocabulary and grammar that white middle-class children might construe as evidence of "verbal ineptness" or inferiority. A child who usually said "I be going to the store" would not construe a cartoon character using "be" in a similar way to be verbally inept. Avoiding constructions characteristic of black English was one way in which the characters' blackness was "neither minimized nor exploited." It was the show's persistent middle-ground position (neither unblack nor too black), in part, that made it both a good show to parade before Congress and a ratings success among white, middle-class Nielsen families.

In all the testing done by social scientists hired by the networks after the 1972 Pastore hearings, little data was collected that addressed racial issues. In fact, only two studies examined the issue, and both were of CBS programs. In a 1975 study, 687 children were asked questions about *The Harlem Globetrotters' Popcorn Machine.* When the children were asked, "Suppose some friend didn't know anything about the Harlem Globetrotters. What would you tell that friend about them?" and "What kind of people are they?," only 22 percent mentioned that the Globetrotters were black. Three-quarters of the total number of children in the study were white and one-quarter were black, but the racial breakdown of the 22 percent is unknown. The *New York Times* reported that the 1974 Reilly *Fat Albert* study had found similar results: 29 percent of the *Fat Albert* sample mentioned the gang's race. In the *Fat Albert* study, "race was most referred to by white children of middle-income status and least referred to by blacks from lower-income families. The same group of black children expressed greater enjoyment of the show than did the same group of white children." [42] From this data, the *Times* concluded, as its headlines declared, "Children in CBS Study Largely Indifferent to Race" [43] and "Children Don't See TV as Black or White." [44] This apparently was good news to the networks, who claimed that for years they had not produced programs with black leads because "most viewers would be unable to 'identify' with black leads" and "some would reject programs starring blacks for racist reasons." [45] The studies thus strangely proved to the networks that it was okay to have programs with black characters but only if most viewers did not notice the characters were black. With *Fat Albert*, CBS could have its cake and eat it too. Nielsen viewers were retained because they did not find the show's race politics off-putting; a Congress (and Federal Communications Commission) deluged with demands for fairer treatment of blacks on TV could congratulate CBS on a show that not only taught moral lessons but also did it with an all-black cast.

It is worth noting that *Fat Albert* was useful to CBS as a response to the 1972 Pastore hearings not only because of its black cast and prosocial message but also because it was perceived as less commercial than other Saturday morning programs. Being less commercial made it seem more educational. Other programs that had high ratings were fairly widely merchandised to companies producing lunch boxes, toys, records, and books. Norm Prescott, Filmation coowner, explained that *Fat Albert* was initially widely merchandised, but Filmation decided to stop on ethical grounds: "When we saw Fat Albert suddenly emerge as a meaningful character who carried a lot of weight with the kids and *grownups* and became a symbol for good things, we never renewed those contracts. We said the hell with it, we're not interested in just making money and jeopardizing what this character has become" (my emphasis). [46] Although Prescott may have been speaking in earnest here, I would hypothesize that Filmation realized the immensity of *Fat Albert*'s symbolic weight, with grown-ups in particular, around the time of the 1974 Pastore hearings. Once Filmation started to license out the *Fat Albert* characters more selectively, it focused on educational, adult-approved products. One key contract was with McGraw-Hill, which distributed *Fat Albert* films and teachers' guides to elementary and grammar schools. Another contract was with the Dell Publishing Company, which produced books based on episodes from the show. Prescott stressed that Dell "agreed to novelize the show; not with picture or coloring books but making novels out of our scripts."[47] Clearly novels would have had higher adult approval than merely entertaining picture books. Finally, Prescott reported a third, ill-fated project, "Fat Albert cookies, which on the surface sounds like crass commercialism. But they have no preservatives, only wholesome ingredients like honey with a low, very low, sugar content. We hope it will spark a line of Fat Albert health foods."[48] Given Fat Albert's hefty appetite for junk food, this project was doomed from the start. This ill-conceived idea indicates a desire to please tasteful, middle-class grown-ups, not children. With Fat Albert health foods, Filmation and CBS attempted to appeal to the very adult health-food and antisugar movements of the seventies, somehow not considering that a tremendously obese character would not be the ideal spokesperson for a line of health foods.

No Class!

The Cosby Kids often played a cleaned-up version of the dozens, one-upping each other with insults. "They oughta call you school during summer vacation," one kid might say. The other would ask, "Why?," and the rejoinder would always be, "No class!" "No class!" was the lowest insult imaginable; someone with class would never act like an irritating jerk. Of course, it would be impossible for anyone literally to have no class, just as one cannot be "tasteless." Everyone has class or taste.

In the case of *Fat Albert*, the "no class" rejoinder is interesting because the characters are all poor and black, whereas the characters on the rest of TV are mostly well-off and white. It is they who have "no class" and ethnicity in that their class and ethnicity are supposed to be invisible. No network executive would conduct research to make sure viewers would not be turned off by characters because they were white and middle class. After all, these are considered desirable qualities by TV executives. In the TV world, the white middle class is simply normal. So *Fat Albert* was a careful balancing act of entertainment and didacticism, black-coded language and

Oxford grammar, dilapidated mise-en-scène and stories that could have taken place on *Leave It to Beaver*. It seemed to somehow please virtually every audience, from censorious legislators and activists to parents looking for something educational besides *Sesame Street*.

In writing the history of African Americans on television, scholars generally point to a small group of programs featuring black characters: *The Beulah Show, Amos 'n' Andy, The Nat King Cole Show, Julia, I Spy, Good Times,* and *The Jeffersons*. That *Fat Albert and the Cosby Kids*, one of the longest-running all-black shows ever on TV, has been deleted from television histories is symptomatic of how adults view children's cartoons. *Fat Albert* was highly praised and satisfied many adult needs, but in the long run, it was still "just a cartoon." The ultimate irony of cartoons "for" children is that adults both overinvest and underinvest in them. On the one hand, they imagine the shows to corrupt, deprave, and endanger child viewers or, rarely, to edify, educate, and enlighten children. On the other hand, adults are dismissive of cartoons because, regardless of their potential for good or evil, they simply do not count as TV in the same way that live-action adult shows do.

Conclusion

Talking across Boundaries?

The politics of childhood are a touchy subject. The ideal of childhood innocence is so sacred, it is very difficult to even question the political use-value it has for adults. In the course of the 1996 presidential election, for example, Bill Clinton attracted conservative, "profamily" voters by advocating the policing of children. Clinton had already passed Megan's Law to crack down on "child molesters" (a broad category that can include rapists, consenting transgenerational lovers, and eighteen-year-olds who have sex with seventeen-year-olds). As the election approached, Clinton came out in favor of curfews, school uniforms, and mandatory drug tests for minors applying for driver's licenses. Imagine the dip in his popularity that would have occurred if Clinton had called for mandatory drug testing, work uniforms, or curfews for adults. This would have been seen as an egregious violation of civil rights. But denying adolescents their civil rights was perceived as reasonable. Clinton cleverly tapped into adult voters' anxieties about the preservation of childhood innocence and purity. As citizens advocating a democratic society, we need to be able to expose this kind of political manipulation, but it is extremely difficult to advocate changes in policies toward children. No legislator wants to open up discussion of age-of-consent laws, for example. It would be political suicide. In a society that obsessively invokes free speech as a doctrine, certain topics are nonetheless off-limits. This makes it difficult to discuss the ways that adults speak for children to achieve certain political ends.

I have no illusions that adults will stop speaking for children, and, politically, it is not altogether desirable that they should. Since children do not vote and do not have the same citizen status as adults, adults will always speak for them, and often this is a good thing. When the Reagan administration said that pickles and ketchup should count as vegetables in school lunches, adults protested for children. When Channel One is shown in public schools, adults protest for children.[1] When school districts lose state funding for textbooks, adults protest for children.

Adults do not need to let children simply fend for themselves, but they do need to be honest about their own motivations in speaking for children and to take into account what effect such reflection could have on the political efficacy of their campaigns for both children *and* adults. As a number of critics have noted, protesting Channel One is not just about keeping kids safe from ads; it is about deciding whether education should be public or private, whether it should serve the community or the bottom line. When some people focus simply on the ethics of selling kids tennis shoes and cheeseburgers in school, they speak in terms that are not particularly threatening to Channel One or the advertisers who fund it; the purveyors of Channel One respond by explaining that it teaches crucial current events, making kids into informed members of a democratic society.

One goal of this book has been to show that "children's" issues need to be looked at more broadly. Should Channel One stay out of schools *only* because kids should not be coerced into buying Milky Way candy bars? Is the child audience the *only* audience that could profit from re-regulation? Is TV regulation and deregulation really *just* about children's television, as most public discussion of the Children's Television Act and the v-chip seems to imply? The v-chip, a small part of the Telecommunications Act of 1996, will enable parents to block out programs they do not want their kids to see. Meanwhile, the rest of the act allows virtually unlimited media conglomeration. By focusing only on the act's import for child viewers, we lose sight of its important, broader implications. Someday v-chip kids will grow up and find that Disney and Turner own all of the media. What kinds of programs will Disney and Turner choose to block out? This is a crucial question and one that cannot be asked if our discussion of the act focuses only on what we (adults) presume to be children's needs.

These are the kinds of issues I have tried to raise in this book. In the process of writing the book, I have presented parts of it to diverse audiences of communications researchers: lawyers, policy specialists, rhetoricians, TV producers, filmmakers, radio station managers, organizational behavioralists, social scientists, and ex-commissioners of the FCC. The sometimes puzzled (and sometimes hostile) feedback from researchers trained in methods radically different from my own demonstrates the variety of responses a book like this can evoke. For example, just as I have found myself incapable of cracking the code of quantitative research, a number of the social scientists I have encountered do not understand how I can argue anything about children's television without performing tests on child subjects. In one instance, an effects researcher interested in correlating how blood pressure changes in response to media images asked me, "So, um, you do *content analysis?*" This person had no training in reading images closely or in studying industrial history, just as I have no training in statistics or blood pressure analysis. We both studied communication, but our different interests and backgrounds made communication almost impossible.

In another instance, a policy specialist asked about the "policy implications" of my work. I had just given a talk drawn from chapter 3 on Action for Children's Television's FCC reception and the cultural climate of seventies TV regulation. I knew what the political and social stakes of regulation and deregulation were, but I did not know what "policy implications" meant. Later, I figured out that this question basically meant, "If you presented your research to the FCC or to Congress, of what use would it be? What policies would your research indicate a need for?" Where children's television is concerned, Congress and the FCC are mainly interested in useful data that prove something "new." Since my research analyzes previously existing data and does not produce new data (statistics), it probably does not have policy implications, at least in terms of what the person asking the question meant. Here again, I had trouble communicating with someone with different training from my own. Unfortunately, this was a job interview, and *our* communication difficulties were perceived as *my* problem.

The fact that I simply could not get the import of the question about policy implications is symptomatic of how difficult dialogue across disciplines can be. On one level, *Saturday Morning Censors* is interdisciplinary because of the wide range of materials and methods it draws on. In the course of developing this book, I have seen it as comfortably fitting under the rubric of cultural studies, television studies, women's studies, and even film studies since it was within the context of film studies that I first learned how to "do" industrial history and formal analysis. But in the course of presenting the material and encountering both policy researchers who did not understand why my research had any use-value and social scientists who could understand it only as content analysis, I realized that writing an interdisciplinary book is not the same thing as engaging in cross-disciplinary dialogue. Cross-disciplinary dialogue is hard work. Given the difficulty of communicating across disciplines within academia, the idea of communicating ideas in a university press book to nonacademic readers (whether teachers, FCC commissioners, members of Congress, or simply the broad category "parents") seems overwhelmingly daunting. That is, if crossing disciplinary boundaries is so difficult, how can one expect to traverse the academic/public sphere divide? If you cannot communicate an idea to someone across the seminar table, you cannot expect to communicate that idea to your neighbor across the street.

But the academic/nonacademic divide is not as intransigent as it may seem. The divide's seeming intransigence depends, in part at least, on mistakenly thinking that the university exists apart from the public sphere. In recounting her attempts to bring cultural studies research to nonacademic audiences, Constance Penley explains that she is striving to address "other public spheres":

> I say "other public spheres" because, of course, there are more than one, and to oppose the kind of thinking (too often coming from the left) that does not consider the university to be a significant public sphere. . . . [T]he university is not so much an ivory tower as it is the muddy trenches. After all, everyone from Stuart Hall to Patrick Buchanan insists that we are in a state of cultural war and the university, in both its public and private versions, has been a site of some of the messiest skirmishes and prolonged battles. I do not imagine . . . [my] traveling, then, to consist of trips "out from" or "beyond" the university but as a to-ing and fro-ing between and among public spheres. . . . I operate on the principle that public spheres do not so much exist as have to be made.[2]

The notions that, first, we move to and from multiple public spheres and, second, public spheres are made, not simply found or intruded upon, are quite useful to someone who wants to communicate both within and beyond the muddy trenches of academia. Notwithstanding the difficulties of cross-disciplinary dialogue, research on children's television does offer more opportunities for provoking discussion with "nonspecialists" than, say, particle physics. Not everyone has an opinion on particle physics, but practically everyone not only has an opinion on children's television but also is eager to share it and to hear what you have to say. Children's television provokes strong feelings in almost everybody. It demands dialogue and, often, disagreement; it demands that those of us researching children's TV from within the muddy trenches communicate with people in other trenches.

When academics see themselves as trepidatiously venturing as intruders into the Public Sphere, they propagate a binaristic situation to which they claim to be merely responding. I will illustrate how difficult it can be to overcome such binaristic thinking with a personal example. In working on a public-access video on children's television censorship, I thought I was making a foray into a public sphere, doing something very different from presenting my work at a conference or giving a job talk. Being on public-access TV in New York City, on a video that would then be for sale, is not the same thing as being on CBS, but it does allow for a much wider audience than many academics are used to addressing. The video was produced by Paper Tiger Television, which has been producing critical, leftist readings of the mainstream media for twenty years. I know some skeptics dismiss public access as speaking only to the converted, but I found that producing a show on children's TV complicated what "the converted" meant. Many on the left think of TV as inherently dangerous to children; by summarizing some of this book's key arguments in the video, I thought I had a strong response to this kind of thinking. I wrote a script and brainstormed on it with the Paper Tiger collective, and then we shot it and edited a preliminary rough cut.

The images and ideas were good, but to my horror, I found that my vocal delivery was a terrible melding of TV news anchor and flight attendant. It sounded kind of like I was presenting a conference paper. To my even greater horror, I discovered that the rough cut was ten minutes shorter than it should have been. I had written a script, accompanied by short video clips, that ended up being eighteen minutes long: the length of a conference paper. In attempting to do something totally new, I had somehow replicated an old genre: the conference presentation. In this first cut of the video, my clips were too short, and I had not allowed any time for the audience to catch their breath. In writing the script, I had tried to be as straightforward as possible, avoiding academic jargon, but my delivery betrayed my anxiety about what my academic peers would think of my presentation. I had replicated the very academic/nonacademic division I was trying to overcome by doing the project in the first place.

The video was not a disaster. In fact, it came out fine.[3] So what if my delivery remains stilted? I sound no worse than Connie Chung, and I have more interesting things to say than she does. But those moments of horror remain with me as a reminder that as one goes to and fro between public spheres, the models of one sphere will not simply mesh with the parameters of other spheres. Discussing the politics of childhood and children's media is important enough, though, that it is worthwhile to keep trying until you find a fit between spheres that seems to work.

Not long ago, I had the disconcerting experience of being told by a journalism professor, "It's too bad your book is out of date before it even comes out, because of the v-chip." This comment represents more than sheer rudeness or a misunderstanding of my research. The comment itself is hyperprofessional, in the most insidious sense, since it implies that books go out of date almost immediately, that academic thoughts have only academic value, that ideas and "hot" authors displace each other just as the Mighty Morphin' Power Rangers displaced the Ninja Turtles. The very idea that the v-chip has displaced all previous discussion of the "dangers" of children's television demonstrates that, although adults often claim it is *children* who suffer from shortened attention spans (because of TV), it is censorious *adults* who cannot train their attention on the more complicated issues at hand. Whether the most current debate is about FCC regulation, the Children's Television Act, or the v-chip, the fact remains that it is adults who decide what constitutes an innocent child and what constitutes an innocent program.

Meanwhile, children continue to get up every Saturday at the crack of dawn to see their favorite shows. Will the v-chip change the Saturday morning viewing experience? Well, let's just say that while parents are groping for the snooze buttons on their alarm clocks, their kids will be nimbly investigating the workings of the v-chip. Barring a power outage, it's likely that the average Saturday morning viewer will continue to outwit the average Saturday morning censor.

Notes

Introduction: Adults, Children, and Censorship

1 Annette Kuhn, *Cinema, Censorship, and Sexuality, 1909–1925* (New York: Routledge, 1988) 2.

2 Kuhn 46.

3 See Lea Jacobs, *The Wages of Sin: Censorship and the Fallen Woman Film, 1928–1942* (Madison: U of Wisconsin P, 1991).

4 Jacqueline Rose, *The Case of Peter Pan, or, the Impossibility of Children's Fiction* (London: Macmillan, 1984).

5 In its October 1993 media campaign against violent television programs, Focus on the Family quotes Hillary Clinton: "I don't think there's anything wrong with parents' groups or other groups calling for people to boycott certain kinds of entertainment. That's advocacy, education, and choice." Hillary Clinton, "When It Comes to Family Values . . . I Worry about Television," *Parade Magazine* 11 Apr. 1993: 10.

6 *Children and Television*, 3 filmstrips, 3 audiocassettes, U of Wisconsin Extension, 1982.

7 Cited in Carlin Romano, "Between the Motion and the Act," *Nation* 15 Nov. 1993: 567. MacKinnon further argues that men use the concept of a transhistorical masculine nature as a foil against those who would hamper their desire for pornography. "[M]en's beloved 'hard-wiring,' giv[es] them that exculpatory sense that the sexual desires so programmed are natural and so operate before and beyond their minds—got there before they did, as it were. But it is nothing more than social conditioning." Catharine A. MacKinnon, *Only Words* (Cambridge: Harvard UP, 1993) 61.

8 Pauline B. Bart and Margaret Jozsa contrast two common scientific models of viewership: the catharsis model and the imitation model. The authors find the first model inadequate and biased. On the other hand, they argue, "the imitation model . . . suggests that people learn patterns of violence from role models. Anger, frustrations, and aggression are behaviors which are acquired like any other social habits—from the examples around us. Thus, aggressive behavior is learned; therefore it is cultural rather than instinctive." Pauline B. Bart and Margaret Jozsa, "Dirty Books, Dirty Films, and Dirty Data," *Take Back the Night: Women on Pornography*, ed. Laura Lederer (New York: Bantam, 1980) 204.

9 A few examples, among many, are Neil Postman, *The Disappearance of Childhood*

(New York: Random House, 1982); Marie Winn, *The Plug-In Drug: Television, Children, and the Family* (New York: Viking, 1977); Robert M. Liebert, John M. Neale, and Emily S. Davidson, *The Early Window: Effects of Television on Children and Youth* (New York: Pergamon, 1973); Lloyd deMause, ed. *The History of Childhood* (New York: Harper and Row, 1975).

10   Stephen Kline, *Out of the Garden: Toys and Children's Culture in the Age of TV Marketing* (New York: Verso, 1993) 49.

11   A general survey (albeit dated) of scientific literature on child viewers can be found in "One Highly Attracted Public" in George Comstock et al., *Television and Social Behavior* (New York: Columbia UP, 1978).

12   See, for example, Ellen Seiter, *Sold Separately: Children and Parents in Consumer Culture* (New Brunswick, N.J.: Rutgers UP, 1993); Henry Jenkins III, " 'Going Bonkers!': Children, Play, and Pee-wee," *Camera Obscura* 17 (May 1988): 169–193; Jenkins, " 'X Logic': Repositioning Nintendo in Children's Lives," rev. of *Playing with Power in Movies, Television, and Video Games: From Muppet Babies to Teenage Mutant Ninja Turtles*, by Marsha Kinder, and *Video Kids Making Sense of Nintendo*, by Eugene F. Provenzo Jr., *Quarterly Review of Film and Video* 14.4 (August 1993): 55–70; Patricia Palmer, *The Lively Audience: A Study of Children around the TV Set* (Sydney: Allen and Unwin, 1986); and David Buckingham, *Children Talking Television: The Making of Television Literacy* (London: Falmer, 1993).

13   Chapters 1 and 2 are methodologically indebted to Eric Smoodin's work on reception, much of which focuses on government and industrial audiences. Smoodin writes a reception history using copyright documents and Library of Congress analyses as his primary sources in *Animating Culture: Hollywood Cartoons from the Sound Era* (New Brunswick, N.J.: Rutgers UP, 1993). In his Frank Capra research, Smoodin examines State Department documents, and he explains how the government anticipated *Mr. Smith Goes to Washington* would be received by Latin American audiences: "The documents tell us how State Department bureaucrats assumed the film would be received, but really show us how those bureaucrats themselves interpreted the film; and their language in discussing the film indicates a kind of unconscious anxiety about the place of the United States in global politics." Eric Smoodin, "Compulsory Viewing for Every Citizen: Mr. Smith, Film Reception, and the Discourse on Democracy," conference paper, Society for Cinema Studies, Syracuse, N.Y., Mar. 1994, 8.

14   I have found no data on the racial composition of U.S. animation workers.

15   Smoodin, "Compulsory Viewing."

16   Jackie Stacey, "Textual Obsessions: Methodology, History, and Researching Female Spectatorship," *Screen* 34.3 (Autumn 1993): 266–267.

17   Michael Holquist, "Corrupt Originals: The Paradox of Censorship," *PMLA* 109.1 (Jan. 1994): 16.

18 See Linda Williams, *Hard Core: Power, Pleasure, and the Frenzy of the Visible* (Berkeley: U of California P, 1989).

1 Attacking (TV?) Violence

1 James C. Dobson, "Countering the Culture," Focus on the Family Newsletter.

2 See chapter 4 for more on the Children's Television Act of 1990.

3 Cited in Sydney W. Head and Christopher H. Sterling, *Broadcasting in America: A Survey of Electronic Media*, 6th ed. (Boston: Houghton Mifflin, 1990) 470.

4 See Jennifer Fleissner, *The Federal Communications Commission* (New York: Chelsea House, 1991) 59.

5 Between the 1975 *Pacifica* decision and 1987, the FCC did not find anyone guilty of indecency. In April 1987, the FCC issued four indecency decisions and released a new "get tough" policy on indecency. Donald M. Gillmor et al., *Fundamentals of Mass Communication Law* (Minneapolis: West, 1996) 151.

6 Head and Sterling 489.

7 For more on audiences and ratings, see Eileen R. Meehan, "Why We Don't Count," Mellencamp 117–137, and Ien Ang's *Desperately Seeking the Audience* (New York: Routledge, 1991).

8 Robert Scheer, "Violence Is Us," *Nation* 15 Nov. 1993: 557.

9 See Toy Manufacturers of America, *Toy Industry Fact Book* (New York: Toy Manufacturers of America, 1990–1991). This publication recounts how limits have been voluntarily set on the allowable level of nitrosamines, "a controversial compound found in rubber pacifiers. . . . Limits also have been set for heavy metals, such as barium and cadmium, used as dyes and pigments in paints and surface coatings" (11). See also "Safety Patrol" in Sydney Ladensohn Stern and Ted Schoenhaus, *Toyland: The High Stakes Game of the Toy Industry* (Chicago: Contemporary Books, 1990) 203–214.

10 Fred W. Friendly, *The Good Guys, the Bad Guys, and the First Amendment: Free Speech vs. Fairness in Broadcasting* (New York: Vintage, 1977) 89.

11 Michael Morgan, Justin Lewis, and Sut Jhally, "More Viewing, Less Knowledge," *Triumph of the Image*, ed. Hamid Mowlana, George Gerbner, and Herbert I. Schiller (Boulder, Colo.: Westview, 1992) 227. On the Gulf War as national "group therapy" to work through anxieties about Vietnam, see Amanda Howell, rev. of *The Remasculinization of America: Gender and the Vietnam War*, by Susan Jeffords, *Camera Obscura* 27 (Sept. 1991): 166–173.

12 George Gerbner, "Instant History—Image History: Lessons of the Persian Gulf War," *Velvet Light Trap* 31 (Spring 1993): 8. For further discussion of Gulf War news censorship at the local and national levels, see Laura U. Marks, "Tie a Yellow Ribbon around Me: Masochism, Militarism, and the Gulf War on TV,"

Camera Obscura 27 (Sept. 1991): 55–75. Although Marks does not focus on censorship per se, she explains how local and national news narratives managed and defused certain public responses to the war and how maternity and the family were structured within such news narratives.

13   The students in my 1996 Hampshire College course, Media Censorship: World War I to the V-Chip, pointed out that regulators are often paranoid, attempting to ward off censorship that might never ensue if the regulation was removed. In some comic book stores, for example, risqué comic books that are not really pornographic are not sold to minors or are sold only with parental permission. Fear can make self-regulators overly zealous, and in this way, regulation can be more oppressive than censorship.

14   For a historical and critical account of the film bill during Hollywood's classical period, see Smoodin's "Reading the Film Bill: Features, Cartoons, and the First-Run Theatre," in *Animating Culture*.

15   For more on censorship of theatrical cartoons, see Smoodin's "Studio Strategies: Sexuality, the Law, and Corporate Competition," in *Animating Culture*. See also my "Chaste, Chased, and Erased: Betty Boop's Censorship," *Added Attractions: Histories and Theories of Film Shorts*, ed. Hank Sartin and Arthur Knight (forthcoming).

16   Since their inception at the turn of the century, films were censored at the state and municipal levels, and producers feared censorship at the federal level. The variety of images and sounds that were removed varied from state to state and city to city. By virtue of the Supreme Court decision in *Mutual Film Co. v. Ohio Board of Censors* (1915), film was not guaranteed First Amendment protection until *Burstyn v. Wilson* (1952). (The Supreme Court ruling in *Burstyn v. Wilson* "recognized for the first time that movies were 'a significant medium for the communication of ideas,' and were, therefore, protected by the constitutional guarantees of freedom of expression." Edward de Grazia and Roger K. Newman, *Banned Films: Movies, Censors, and the First Amendment* [New York: Bowker, 1982] 232. See Gerald Mast, *The Movies in Our Midst: Documents in the Cultural History of Film in America* [Chicago: U of Chicago P, 1982] 614–619, for the text of *Burstyn v. Wilson*.) To guard against consumer boycott and federal, state, and municipal censorship, in 1929, the Motion Picture Producers and Distributors of America, the industry's trade organization, set up the Studio Relations Committee as a self-regulatory body. In 1934, the Studio Relations Committee was reconstituted under new leadership as the Production Code Administration (PCA). The story of the establishment of the PCA is complex and has been extensively discussed elsewhere. (See, for example, Jacobs; Raymond Moley, *The Hays Office* [Indianapolis: Bobs-Merrill, 1945]; and Lea Jacobs and Richard Maltby, eds., *Quarterly Review of Film and Video: Rethinking the Production Code* 15.4 [1995].) The important points here

are that Hollywood began regulating itself in 1929, dramatically stepping up its regulation in 1934, and that this self-regulation came about in part because of fear of theater boycotts by pressure groups such as the Catholic Legion of Decency and in part because of fear of governmental intrusion. Self-censorship was also a means for the oligopolistic companies that controlled the industry to consolidate their power over motion pictures. Except during wartime, there has never been *official* film or television censorship in the United States on the *federal* level. At the state and city levels, on the other hand, censorship has existed more blatantly, and state and municipal film censorship boards continued to operate well into the sixties. For information on state and municipal censorship, see Ira H. Carmen, *Movies, Censorship, and the Law* (Ann Arbor: U of Michigan P, 1966).

17 Kathryn C. Montgomery, *Target: Prime Time, Advocacy Groups, and the Struggle over Entertainment Television* (New York: Oxford UP, 1989) 227.

18 See Lynn Spigel, *Make Room for TV: Television and the Family Ideal in Postwar America* (Chicago: U of Chicago P, 1992). Low ownership of television sets may have contributed to anxieties about the division of the family because viewers who did not own sets often went to communal, public viewing spaces such as bars. See Anna McCarthy, "The Front Row is Reserved for Scotch Drinkers: Early Television's Tavern Audience," *Cinema Journal* 35.4 (Summer 1995): 31–49.

19 See William Boddy, "The Seven Dwarfs and the Money Grubbers: The Public Relations Crisis of U.S. Television in the Late 1950's," Mellencamp 98–116.

20 For example, Montgomery recounts that "Laurence A. Johnson, who owned a small chain of supermarkets in upstate New York, devised a unique method of pressuring sponsors. He placed signs next to certain products on his grocery shelves, warning customers that purchasing these goods would advance the spread of Communism [because the products sponsored shows with "Communist" actors]. To ensure the cooperation of the advertising industry, he made regular trips to New York City, traveling up and down Madison Avenue to advise advertisers about whom to hire and whom not to hire. Most of the companies willingly cooperated with the system, justifying their action as good business" (14). For more on Johnson's campaign, see "Fade to Black" in Jeff Kisseloff, *The Box: An Oral History of Television, 1920–1961* (New York: Penguin, 1997).

21 Montgomery 17–19.

22 This phrase defining broadcasters' obligations is from the Communications Act of 1934, which is discussed more extensively in chapter 3.

23 Examples of positivist accounts of censorship include Gerald Gardner, *The Censorship Papers* (New York: Dodd, Mead, 1987); Moley; de Grazia and Newman; and Leonard J. Leff and Jerold L. Simmons, *The Dame in the Kimono: Hollywood, Censorship, and the Production Code from the 1920's to the 1960's* (New York: Grove Weidenfeld, 1990).

24 Jack Vizzard, *See No Evil: Life inside a Hollywood Censor* (New York: Simon and Schuster, 1970) 102.

25 Peggy Charren, phone conversation with the author, June 1993.

26 See Mark I. West, *Children, Culture, and Controversy* (Hamden, Conn.: Archon, 1988).

27 Morris L. Ernst and Pare Lorentz, *Censored: The Private Life of the Movies* (New York: Cape and Smith, 1930).

28 Wertham asks, "[W]hat are the activities in comic books which women 'indulge in on equal footing with men'? They do not work. They are not homemakers. They do not bring up a family. Mother-love is entirely absent. Even when Wonder Woman adopts a girl there are Lesbian overtones. They are either superwomen flying through the air, scantily dressed or uniformed, outsmarting hostile natives, animals or wicked men, functioning like Wonder Woman in a fascistic-futuristic setting, or they are molls or prizes to be pushed around and sadistically abused." Frederic Wertham, *Seduction of the Innocent* (New York: Rinehart, 1954) 234.

29 Muriel Cantor, "The Role of the Producer in Choosing Children's Television Content," Comstock and Rubinstein 266.

30 Thomas F. Baldwin and Colby Lewis, "Violence in Television: The Industry Looks at Itself," Comstock and Rubinstein 324.

31 Baldwin and Lewis 351.

32 Andrew Kopkind, "He's a Happening: Robert Kennedy's Road to Somewhere," *The Sense of the 60's*, ed. Edward Quinn and Paul J. Dolan (New York: Free Press, 1968) 183–194.

33 In his 1961 address to the National Association of Broadcasters (the "vast wasteland" speech), Minow said, "There are some fine children's shows, but they are drowned out in massive doses of cartoons, violence and more violence. Must these be your trademarks? Search out your consciences and see if you cannot offer more to your young beneficiaries whose future you guide so many hours each and every day." Quoted in Mary Ann Watson, *The Expanding Vista: American Television in the Kennedy Years* (New York: Oxford UP, 1990) 155.

34 Cited in Watson 156–157. Soon afterward, RFK actually participated in children's television when his children went trick-or-treating with Richard Thomas (a.k.a. John Boy Walton) on *1, 2, 3—Go!* Kennedy invited the trick-or-treaters into his home and made a plug for UNICEF.

35 Richard Harwood, "*The Washington Post*, June 8, 1968," *"An Honorable Profession": A Tribute to Robert F. Kennedy*, ed. Pierre Salinger, Edwin Guthman, and Frank Mankiewicz (New York: Doubleday, 1968) 81–82.

36 Cartoon reprinted in Harwood 166.

37 Cantor 273.

38 Roland Barthes, *Mythologies*, trans. Annette Lavers (New York: Noonday, 1990) 143.

39 This crediting of TV with the power to produce dramatic shifts in public opinion was unprecedented, with the exceptions of TV coverage of Nixon's "Checkers" speech and the 1960 Kennedy-Nixon debates. On the debates, see Theodore H. White, *The Making of the President 1960* (New York: Pocket Books, 1961), and David Culbert, "Television's Nixon: The Politician and His Image," O'Connor 184–207.

40 See Jerome H. Skolnick, *The Politics of Protest* (New York: Simon and Schuster, 1969), a report on black militancy, antiwar protest, and police brutality submitted to the National Commission on the Causes and Prevention of Violence.

41 Jerry Mander, *Four Arguments for the Elimination of Television* (New York: Morrow Quill, 1978) 46.

42 Sandra J. Parker, "L.A. TV Veterans Speak," *Emmy Magazine* Dec. 1991: 54. Parker quotes broadcast news veteran Ralph Story, but Story's mirror analogy is a cliché of broadcaster self-defense.

43 Later broadcasters feared the Nixon administration would pursue antitrust actions against the networks to retaliate against unfavorable Vietnam War coverage.

44 Cantor 270.

45 Baldwin and Lewis 351.

46 Baldwin and Lewis 343–344.

47 Robert Pekurny, *Broadcast Self-Regulation: A Participant-Observation Study of the National Broadcasting Company's Broadcast Standards Department*, diss., U of Minnesota, 1977 (Ann Arbor: UMI, 1977) 216–217.

48 See Barthes. The prohibition against pointing guns at heads and necks might be explained as a response not only to recent assassinations but also to media images of the Vietnam War. In particular, the head-neck prohibition evokes a violent image of iconic significance, the infamous *Life* magazine photograph of a South Vietnamese police chief holding a gun to a suspected Vietcong's head moments before pulling the trigger.

49 Pekurny's observations also indicate that censorship is not an infallible, Big Brother–like operation. Rather, censorship can make mistakes and be inconsistent. Censors unwittingly both forbade and permitted the representation of cross hairs. The cross hairs gaffe illustrates that censorship, like any legal or cultural expression of power, manifests itself unevenly.

2 "We Call Our Company *Motel*"

1 Vizzard 9. In their more recent censorship history, Leff and Simmons delight in boob jokes. Edward de Grazia chooses a titillating title for his book, *Girls Lean*

Back Everywhere: The Law of Obscenity and the Assault on Genius (New York: Random House, 1992). Salacious chapter titles include "I Was Getting Hard-Ons," "Like a Towel Boy in a Whorehouse," and "Any Writer Who Hasn't Jacked Off."

2   For a thrashing of women state film censors of the twenties, see Ernst and Lorentz. Carmen interviews state film censors, mostly women. Although he does not explore censorship's gender politics, his text proves a rich source of information on women's roles as censors if one "reads between the lines." In a rare moment, gender is explicitly at issue when Carmen interviews a Chicago police officer (even though the actual previewing of films in Chicago was performed by a board of six women). The officer notes that "the fact that there are no men on the bureau plus the fact that all are widows has led the press to make derogatory comments about 'policemen's widows' being in charge of movie censorship" (295).

3   Sybil DelGaudio, "Seduced and Reduced: Female Animal Characters in Some Warners' Cartoons," *The American Animated Cartoon: A Critical Anthology*, ed. Danny Peary and Gerry Peary (New York: Dutton, 1980) 212.

4   Storyboards picture a cartoon's major actions, costumes, and settings. They are produced after the script but before actual animation.

5   "Roundtable on Children's Programming," *Emmy Magazine* Fall 1979: 16.

6   The U.S. Commission on Civil Rights has produced two studies on the employment and representation of women and minorities in network television: *Window Dressing on the Set: Women and Minorities in Television* (Washington, D.C.: U.S. Commission on Civil Rights, 1977) and *Window Dressing on the Set: An Update* (Washington, D.C.: U.S. Commission on Civil Rights, 1979). The commission found that white men held the positions of greatest power in network television, and white women and women of color held the positions of least power. In 1977, at the "officials and managers" level, NBC employed 559 white men, 80 white women, 19 black men, and 5 black women. At the "office and clerical" level, NBC employed 198 white men, 685 white women, 61 black men, and 190 black women (*Update* 93).

7   A glossy hybrid of *People* and *Variety*, *Emmy* is "a general-interest magazine designed to serve both the television industry and the intelligent television viewer." All members of the Academy of Television Arts and Sciences receive a subscription with their membership. Hank Rieger, "Editorial," *Emmy Magazine* Fall 1979: 5. The magazine offers a fairly accurate gauge of how the industry perceives itself and how it wants to be perceived.

8   ABC broadcast Standards and Practices director, phone conversation with the author, 14 Apr. 1993.

9   Animators and animation historians typically describe the studios of the twenties, thirties, and forties in meritocratic terms. Young animators would start at

the bottom and work their way up based on skill. This is not how things worked for women employed in the animation studios, however. The Fleischer studio promoted only three women above the lowest echelons of the employee hierarchy. One of those three did not enjoy her position long, as she died of tuberculosis, which some Fleischer employees allege was caused by poor working conditions. Another employee, Edith Vernick, reportedly earned half as much as every other department head and only a dollar more than the top people who served under her. Harvey Deneroff, "We Can't Get Much Spinach: The Organization and Implementation of the Fleischer Animation Strike," *Film History* 1 (1987): 1–14.

10   Elizabeth Bell, "Somatexts at the Disney Shop: Constructing the Pentimentos of Women's Animated Bodies," *From Mouse to Mermaid: The Politics of Film, Gender, and Culture*, ed. Elizabeth Bell, Lynda Haas, and Laura Sells (Bloomington: Indiana UP, 1995) 107.

11   Allen J. Scott, *Metropolis: From Division of Labor to Urban Form* (Berkeley: U of California, 1988). Scott notes that unlike workers in the clothing industry, most U.S.-based workers in the animation industry, including unskilled technical workers, "are (for the present at least) usually native-born U.S. citizens with a minimum of a high-school education" (142). Ink-and-paint department women are evocative not only of garment workers but also of the female laborers employed as hand tinters of films by the live-action film industry. See illustration of "dying and retouching room" in *The American Film Industry*, ed. Tino Balio, Rev. ed. (Madison: U of Wisconsin P, 1985) 13.

12   Scott 154.

13   Scott 154.

14   Don Jurwich, interview with the author, 6 Apr. 1993.

15   Adrienne Bello, interview with the author, 7 Apr. 1993.

16   Baldwin and Lewis 325–326. These producer statements should be understood in the context of their position in the first volume of the surgeon general's report, "Media Content and Control." This volume, unlike the other four in the television violence series, is devoted to television content and production rather than television's potential "effects." It clearly behooves the authors, who are generally critical of television content, to describe the producer-network relationship as fraught with difficulty. The interview excerpts picked by the researchers illustrate that there is no rhyme or reason to content regulation, which supposedly explains why television is such a "vast wasteland." After all, given all the "asinine" underlings who come between creative cartoon makers and potentially compassionate high-level executives, how could television be anything but a wasteland? Although these reports are over twenty years old, they provide a useful context for understanding both the issues of industrial power

raised explicitly in the Scott study and those implicit in my interviews with Barbera, Jurwich, and Bello.

17   Edward L. Palmer, *Children in the Cradle of Television* (Toronto: Heath, 1987).

18   Scott 154–155. See also Barbara Basler, "Peter Pan, Garfield, and Bart—All Have Asian Roots," *New York Times* 2 Dec. 1990, sec. 2: 35–36.

19   Basler 35.

20   Basler 36.

21   See Cynthia Enloe, *Bananas, Beaches, and Bases: Making Feminist Sense of International Politics* (Berkeley: U of California P, 1989).

22   Cited in Armand Mattelart, *Transnationals and the Third World: The Struggle for Culture*, trans. David Buxton (South Hadley, Mass.: Bergin and Garvey, 1983) 111–112.

23   A. Mattelart, *Transnationals* 112.

24   Annette Fuentes and Barbara Ehrenreich, *Women in the Global Factory* (Boston: South End, 1983).

25   A. Mattelart, *Transnationals* 112. For more on runaway production, see A. Mattelart's *Multinational Corporations and the Control of Culture*, trans. Michael Chanan (Atlantic Highlands, N.J.: Humanities Press, 1979), as well as Fuentes and Ehrenreich, whose research A. Mattelart draws on in *Transnationals*. Also of interest is Erica Rand's reading of Mattel's annual shareholder report in *Barbie's Queer Accessories* (Durham, N.C.: Duke UP, 1995) 70–73.

26   Seiter, *Sold Separately* 205.

27   See, for example, the following *TV Guides* with cover stories on children and television: 22–28 Aug. 1992; 24–30 Oct. 1992; 27 Feb.–5 Mar. 1993; 30 Oct.–5 Nov. 1993; 12–18 Mar. 1994; 26 Oct.–1 Nov. 1996; 25–31 Oct. 1997; 14–20 Mar. 1998.

28   "Censor Overload," *Entertainment Weekly* 11 June 1993: 69.

29   Bello, interview with the author, 15 Apr. 1993.

30   Jurwich, the disgruntled Hanna-Barbera–Standards liaison, explains that in anticipation of censorship, the studio often contrives an "absurd gun." Joe Barbera recounts that in a cartoon with pirates, the networks said the pirates' swords would have to be eliminated. Barbera asks, "Well, what in the heck is a pirate gonna have, a banana?" Besides being an amusing phallic substitute for a sword, the banana weapon, which Barbera suggests ironically, is actually not far off the mark. A giant (and therefore "unreal" and not imitable) banana probably would be a perfectly acceptable weapon from Standards's perspective.

31   Or by reading a historical survey book on U.S. animation, such as Leonard Maltin's *Of Mice and Magic: A History of American Animated Cartoons*, rev. ed. (New York: McGraw Hill, 1987), which discusses plenty of cartoons that contemporary TV censors might find offensive.

32   See the Pee-wee dossier in Constance Penley and Sharon Willis, eds. *Male Trouble* (Minneapolis: U of Minnesota P, 1993).

33   In *Sold Separately*, Seiter has shown that toy-based cartoons are directed only at children, which frustrates parents. This frustration supports my argument: parents *expect* intergenerational appeal to be built into programs, and they bristle when they do not "get" a program. *Sesame Street*'s initial success was highly dependent on such intergenerational appeal, as chapter 5 explains.

34   Cartoon character transvestism may well have been the product of animators' homophobia, but cartoons with cross dressing in them are now shown with great success at gay and lesbian film festivals. One journalist explains that "Bugs Bunny toyed with gay themes in ways that were off limits for regular movies after the industry's Production Code banned 'sexual perversion' in 1934. . . . Bugs became a gay studies star at the University of Chicago recently when his campy cartoons opened each night of a ten week film festival exploring the depiction of homosexuality in the movies." Deb Price, "Gay Studies Show New Dimensions of the World," *Democrat and Chronicle* 3 Dec. 1992: 4C. See also Hank Sartin, "Bugs Bunny: Queer as a Three Dollar Bill," *Windy City Times* 24 June 1993, sec. 2: 79; and Sean Griffin, "Pronoun Trouble: The 'Queerness' of Animation," *Spectator* 15.1 (Fall 1994): 94–109. Although such representations were forbidden, PCA documents indicate an ongoing attempt by Hollywood producers to include gay stereotypes in their live-action films. To the *Maltese Falcon* script, the Breen office responded: "We cannot approve the characterization of [Joel] Cairo [Peter Lorre] as a pansy, indicated by the lavender perfume, high-pitched voice, and other accouterments." Gardner 39.

35   The National Gay Task Force has pressured the networks in the past to show "positive" gay representations and to avoid portraying "effeminate" or "limp-wristed" types. Montgomery, *Target* 89. The task force objected to the same kinds of TV stereotypes the children's TV censors objected to, but they wanted to change rather than eliminate gay representations. Of course, the task force was advocating "positive" gay characters on *adult* shows. It would be political suicide to advocate gay characters on a children's show.

36   Jim Mullen, "Tinky Wink Wink," *Entertainment Weekly* 17 Apr. 1998: 10.

37   For more information on lesbian and gay television activists, see Montgomery's *Target* as well as her *Gay Activists and the Networks: A Case Study of Special Interest Pressure in Television*, diss., U of California, Los Angeles, 1979 (Ann Arbor: UMI, 1979).

38   Pekurny 191–192.

39   Importantly, advertisers are much more likely to avoid specious images when producing an ad for network (as opposed to cable) television.

40   Michel Foucault, *Discipline and Punish: The Birth of the Prison*, trans. Alan Sheri-

dan (New York: Random House, 1979) 194. Applying Foucault's theorization of power as productive to film censorship, Kuhn has argued that "film censorship creates censorable films. . . . [C]ensorship operates not only prohibitively—in the regulation of a public sphere of discussion—but also productively—in the actual creation of such a sphere" (96). That is, censorship does not just cut things out of movies; it also creates genres of censorable movies and alluring "forbidden" movies that are often highly marketable.

3 Action for (and against) Children's Television

1   Peggy Charren, quoted in Gary H. Grossman, *Saturday Morning TV* (New York: Dell, 1981) 357.

2   See Robert W. McChesney, *Telecommunications, Mass Media, and Democracy: The Battle for the Control of U.S. Broadcasting, 1928–1935* (New York: Oxford UP, 1993).

3   See Aniko Bodroghkozy, " 'Is This What You Mean by Color TV?' Race, Gender, and Contested Meanings in NBC's *Julia*," *Private Screenings: Television and the Female Consumer*, ed. Lynn Spigel and Denise Mann (Minneapolis: U of Minnesota P, 1992) 143–167, and Watson's "The Chosen Instrument of the Revolution: Civil Rights," in *Expanding Vista*.

4   *Julia's* Diahann Carroll described herself in 1970 as "a black woman with a white image." Carolyn See, "Diahann Carroll's Image," *TV Guide* 14 Mar. 1970: 27. For an analysis of viewer responses to *Julia*, see Bodroghkozy.

5   Michael R. Winston, "Racial Consciousness and the Evolution of Communications in the United States," *Daedalus* Fall 1982: 178.

6   Although the focus here is on black Civil Rights activism, many other people of color were also involved in media reform in the sixties and seventies. As Chon Noriega explains, "It was in the late '60s and early '70s, during the Chicano civil rights movement and similar activities on the East Coast among Puerto Rican communities, when Hollywood's representation of Latinos became an issue, and was manifested in protests and struggles to gain access to Hollywood studios and television stations." C. Ondine Chavoya, "Images of Advocacy: An Interview with Chon Noriega," *Afterimage* 21.10 (May 1994): 6. For an account of seventies Latino media protest, see also Montgomery's "Managing Advocacy Groups," in *Target*.

7   Watson.

8   Denied access to newspapers, radio, and TV, Mississippi Civil Rights activists advocating boycott in 1962 had been forced to hand-deliver leaflets, hiding them in paper bags and umbrellas and under their coats to avoid police harrassment. See Steven Douglas Classen, "Standing on Unstable Grounds: A Reexamination of the WLBT-TV Case," *Critical Studies in Mass Communication* 11 (1991): 76.

9   Quoted in Nicholas Johnson, *How to Talk Back to Your Television Set* (New York: Bantam, 1970) 12.

10 Of course they could feel solidarity only if they had a TV. According to the U.S. Department of Commerce, in the late fifties, 66 percent of all households in Mississippi had television sets, but only 40 percent of nonwhite households had sets. The percentage of nonwhites with sets was even smaller in impoverished rural areas. Classen 85.

11 Quoted in Watson 110–111.

12 Such reports were also critical of children's television. According to one children's television historian, the National Commission on the Causes and Prevention of Violence accused children's television of being "a profitable business and a dangerous baby-sitter." Grossman 353.

13 Erik Barnouw, *The Image Empire: A History of Broadcasting in the United States from 1953* (New York: Oxford UP, 1970) 322.

14 Quoted in Johnson 13.

15 Minow's conception of "the public interest" was problematic on several counts. First, Minow assumed a *singular* public interest, as if everyone had the same concerns about television, regardless of gender, age, race, or ethnic background. Second, and relatedly, Minow's criticisms of television were painfully elitist. In his "vast wasteland" speech, he disdainfully rejected what he considered tasteless and socially worthless programming: Westerns, action-adventure shows, and cartoons. He would later retreat from his attack on entertainment programming and focus on advocating public affairs (news) programs. See Michael Curtin, *Redeeming the Wasteland: Television Documentary and Cold War Politics* (New Brunswick, N.J.: Rutgers UP, 1995).

16 Robert W. McChesney, "Conflict, Not Consensus: The Debate over Broadcast Communication Policy, 1930–1935," Solomon and McChesney 245.

17 See Spigel, *Make Room*.

18 Classen 79.

19 ACT focused on changing FCC rules and never actually petitioned to deny license renewal, which is one reason the FCC found it to be a group it could handle with relative ease. However, ACT was organized in the wake of the excitement inspired by the WLBT decision, and in retrospect, when Charren tells of the group's founding, she often mentions the "petition to deny" procedure.

20 Alice Echols, *Daring to Be Bad: Radical Feminism in America, 1967–1975* (Minneapolis: U of Minnesota P, 1989) 93–94.

21 Boston Women's Health Book Collective, *Ourselves and Our Children: A Book by and for Parents* (New York: Random House, 1978) 211.

22 Barry Cole and Mal Oettinger, *Reluctant Regulators: The FCC and the Broadcast Audience* (Reading, Mass.: Addison-Wesley, 1978) 248.

23 Cole and Oettinger 268.

24 Cynthia Alperowicz and Robert Krock, *Rocking the Boat: Celebrating Fifteen Years of Action for Children's Television* (Newtonville, Mass.: Action for Children's Television, 1983) n.p.

25 Cole and Oettinger 248.

26 Cole and Oettinger 249.

27 Cole and Oettinger 250.

28 What about adult exploitation? Lynn Spigel observes that "the only widespread challenge to commercialization of the [television] airwaves has taken place in the name of the child." Rather than making children a safety valve for feelings of disempowerment, adults need to "express their own disenfranchisement from our nation's dominant mode of communication." Lynn Spigel, "Seducing the Innocent: Childhood and Television in Postwar America," Solomon and McChesney 283.

29 Cole and Oettinger 253.

30 Cole and Oettinger 92. But by the late seventies, meetings with citizens would be much more common. Such meetings, in which citizens tried to force the FCC to act in "the public interest," were symptomatic of a widespread attitude, in the wake of Watergate and the Pentagon papers, of public mistrust of government agencies. When citizen groups clamored for meetings with the FCC, the FCC agreed largely in order to appease them. In 1975, the FCC announced open meetings with the public, ostensibly to receive greater public input but really to stave off the Government in Sunshine Act, which was under discussion and would have required all FCC meetings to be open to the public. See Cole and Oettinger 104. The act was eventually passed in 1976.

31 Cole and Oettinger 92.

32 Cole and Oettinger 93.

33 Cole and Oettinger 93.

34 Cole and Oettinger 94.

35 Cole and Oettinger 94.

36 On the anticigarette campaign, see Friendly 103–120.

37 Cole and Oettinger 97.

38 Cole and Oettinger 98.

39 The FCC later met with more moderate NOW representatives.

40 *Behind the Lines*, WNET-TV, 27 Dec. 1973, Museum of Television and Radio.

41 Johnson 188.

42 Quoted in Grossman 357.

43 "Peggy Charren and Reverend Donald Wildmon of CBTV," *Weekday*, WNAC-TV, 24 Feb. 1981, ACT Collection.

44 See Montgomery's "Cleaning Up TV," in *Target*, for a full account.

45 *Weekday.*

46 In the wake of the Pentagon papers, Watergate, and Nixon's resignation, Congress approved the Government in Sunshine Act in 1976, which required regulatory agencies to conduct their meetings in public. In practice, this meant that the FCC made all of its decisions (and did all of its arguing) in unofficial meetings and then staged argument-free public meetings in which "absolute loyalty to the Chairman" was demonstrated. Erwin G. Krasnow, Lawrence D. Longley, and Herbert A. Terry, *The Politics of Broadcast Regulation*, 3rd ed. (New York: St. Martin's, 1982) 44.

47 Cole and Oettinger 259.

48 Thomas Radecki, letter to Peggy Charren, c. 5 Sept. 1980, National Coalition on Television Violence file, ACT Collection.

49 Radecki, letter to Charren.

50 *NCTV News* 2.4 (July–Aug. 1981) and *NCTV News* 2.5 (Sept.–Nov. 1981), National Coalition on Television Violence file, ACT Collection.

51 Although CBS, NBC, and ABC were inclined to cry "Censorship!" when ACT criticized their programming, they recognized ACT as an antiboycotting ally. ACT sent anti–Coalition for Better Television petitions to the networks, all three of which sent Charren warm letters of thanks for her support of free speech and "the free exchange of ideas in a free society." Gene P. Mater, senior vice president, Policy, CBS, letter to Peggy Charren, 31 Mar. 1982, ACT Collection.

52 Quoted in Daniel R. Shaw, *A Mother's Battle against Trash TV: The Story of Terry Rakolta and Americans for Responsible Television* (n.p.: Dogwood, 1992) 48–49.

53 A. Mattelart, *Multinational Corporations* 165.

54 Anna Williams, for example, discusses some of the contradictions inherent in the ideology of the family in her argument that the "traditional family" of *America's Most Wanted* is threatened from both without and within. See Anna Williams, "Domesticity and the Aetiology of Crime in *America's Most Wanted*," *Camera Obscura* 31 (Jan.–May 1993): 97–118.

55 Cole and Oettinger 248–249.

56 Meg Schwarz, ed., *TV and Teens: Experts Look at the Issues* (Reading, Mass.: Addison-Wesley, 1982).

57 Bruce Fein, "In the Interests of Common Decency: Prudent Use of Law," *Washington Times* 2 June 1992: F1.

58 Harry A. Jessell, "High Court Agrees Ban Is Unconstitutional," *Broadcasting* 9 Mar. 1992: 35.

59 Action for Children's Television, "Action for Children's Television: How Consumers ACTivate Change," 3, ACT Collection.

60 Cole and Oettinger 249.

61 Alperowicz and Krock n.p.

62   Cited in Alperowicz and Krock n.p.

63   Action for Children's Television, "ACT and the PTA Coalition for Change," 7, To Be Integrated ACT Speeches filing cabinet, ACT Collection.

64   "Transcript the MacNeil/Lehrer Report 5/10/78," 3, To Be Integrated ACT Speeches filing cabinet, ACT Collection.

65   The problem with ACT's campaign against kid-targeted TV ads is not that children are never duped by ads (they are) but that the campaign assumed that adults are *substantially (indeed, inherently) more sophisticated, critical, and thoughtful viewers* than children. Implicit in this is the idea that adults are *better* viewers than children. Taking a cue from sociologist revisionists Allison James and Alan Prout, I would argue instead that adults are not always better or smarter viewers than children. Adults and children view *differently*, asking different questions, finding different pleasures, and, on occasion, being duped in different ways. James and Prout have criticized the common idea that childhood is an irrational, pre-adult time that is corrected by "development" (the achievement of adulthood). They argue that childhood has its own cultures, which—to the extent that it is possible for adults to do so—need to be studied on their own terms. Similarly, I would argue that children do not need to be "fixed" by learning to view TV more like adults. This is not to say that adults must take a laissez-faire attitude toward child viewers but to suggest that it is possible to discuss TV with children without simply trying to "convert" them to adult thought. See Allison James and A. Prout, eds., *Constructing and Reconstructing Childhood: Contemporary Issues in the Sociological Study of Childhood* (London: Falmer, 1990).

66   Action for Children's Television, "Speech at the American Dental Association 10/11/77," 6, To Be Integrated ACT Speeches filing cabinet, ACT Collection. ACT's concerns about the middle-class child's cavities pale if one considers other bodies hurt by sugar: the foreign poor people of color who harvest and process sugar. At the same time that ACT was pushing the FTC to ban ads for sugared products, the U.S. State Department was sending foreign service trainees to South Florida, where every year 10,000 men from the West Indies are imported to cut sugarcane. The State Department sent its trainees to these U.S. sugar plantations to acquaint them with the poverty and decay they would later encounter in Third World countries. Sugar is a globally exploitative, colonialist, racist, and sexist enterprise. See Alec Wilkinson, *Big Sugar* (New York: Knopf, 1989) 173.

67   My reading of the adult conception of "proper" eating practices is indebted to Allison James, "Confections, Concoctions, and Conceptions," *Popular Culture: Past and Present* ed. B. Waites, T. Bennett, and G. Martins (London: Croom Helm/Open UP, 1982) 294–307.

68   Seiter, *Sold Separately* 97.

69 Action for Children's Television, "How Consumers ACTivate Change," 6. On cultural capital, see Pierre Bourdieu, *Distinction: A Social Critique of the Judgment of Taste*, trans. Richard Nice (Cambridge: Harvard UP, 1984). In *Sold Separately* Seiter argues that "ACT's protest and its publicity created pervasive feelings of guilt among parents over commercial television viewing and in some ways silenced mothers, who could hardly discuss commercial children's television openly if they were supposed to have watched as little as possible" (102). ACT advocated informed or "educated" viewing over abstinence, and I would stress that it was the *publicity* around ACT protests that may have silenced mothers and made them feel guilt. ACT certainly did not intend to lay blame on parents in the same way that Winn did with her scare tactics and holier-than-thou finger pointing.

70 Seiter, *Sold Separately* 115.

71 See, for example, Lendon H. Smith, *Improving Your Child's Behavior Chemistry* (New York: Pocket Books, 1976); William Dufty, *Sugar Blues* (New York: Warner, 1975); and John Yudkin, *Sweet and Dangerous* (New York: Bantam, 1973), all discussed extensively in Elizabeth Walker Mechling and Jay Mechling, "Sweet Talk: The Moral Rhetoric against Sugar," *Central States Speech Journal* 34 (Spring 1983): 19–32.

72 Dufty 149–153.

73 See Michelle Stacey, *Consumed: Why Americans Love, Hate, and Fear Food* (New York: Simon and Schuster, 1994).

74 Anna Thomas, *The Vegetarian Epicure* (New York: Vintage, 1972) 3.

75 For example: "In the eternal order of the universe, man-refined sugar, like all other things, plays its part. Perhaps the sugar pushers are our predators, leading us into temptation, peddling a kind of sweet, sweet, human pesticide which lures greedy seekers after La Dolce Vita into self-destruction, weeding the human garden, naturally selecting the fittest for survival while the rest go down in another biblical flood—not water this time, but Coke, Pepsi, and Dr. Pepper—purifying the human race for a new age." Dufty 25.

76 Susan Willis, *A Primer for Daily Life* (New York: Routledge, 1991) 134. Henry Jenkins has pointed out that the antisugar campaign can be read as a backlash not only against perceived excesses of the sixties but also against permissive postwar childrearing practices. Permissive childrearing allows the child's food to be *fun*, not purely utilitarian as in the seventies ACT campaign.

77 Loren Baritz, *Backfire: American Culture and the Vietnam War* (New York: Ballantine, 1985) 310–311.

78 One scene in TVTV's *Four More Years*, a guerrilla television program about the 1972 Republican National Convention, illustrates my point. A World War II veteran complains that because they were "all hopped up" the U.S. soldiers in Vietnam did not watch out for each other like the soldiers in World War II had.

79   Dufty 146.

80   Dufty 18.

81   Dufty 134.

82   See Baritz.

83   Action for Children's Television, "Chester Cheetah Filing March 5, 1992," Legal Drawer III Violence Study filing cabinet, ACT Collection.

84   "Chester Cheetah" 6.

85   "Chester Cheetah" 3.

86   "TV Cartoon Plans Are Dropped," *New York Times* 31 Mar. 1992: D7.

87   Montgomery, *Target* 55.

88   Friendly 24–25.

89   Friendly 39.

90   Adult campaigns for children also tend to ignore the rights and needs of non-children. Many adult campaigns to help children are problematic, not because children are not entitled to adequate food, shelter, clothing, and health care but because campaigns for children's rights often ignore *adults*, who should also be able to live without misery. Groups such as Save the Children also tend to be mute about why the Third World child's situation is so desperate. Contrary to what such groups would have us believe, most people do not suffer from famine merely because their country has had too much or not enough rain. As wealthy transnational corporations buy up land in poor countries, cash crops come to replace staple food crops, and many of the impoverished countries where people are starving export large amounts of food to richer countries. "Even in the starving nation of Bangladesh, enough grain was produced in 1976 to feed everyone moderately well, about 2,600 calories per day. These figures show that the major problem is not one of too little food or too many people, but of the unequal distribution of the food that is produced." Brett Silverstein, *Fed Up: The Food Forces That Make You Fat, Sick, and Poor* (Boston: South End, 1984) 141. The voice-overs that accompany terrifying images of starving children do not tell us why the children are starving. Rather, Save the Children, like many other groups that try to help children, appeals to a global, borderless, and dangerously depoliticized sense of common decency.

4 Toys, TV, and Toaster Pictures

1   Tom Engelhardt, "The Shortcake Strategy," *Watching Television*, ed. Todd Gitlin (New York: Pantheon, 1986) 69.

2   Communications scholar Stephen Kline not only argues against the crass commercial intentions of product-based programming but also discusses the shows themselves in the course of a content analysis of 511 episodes of the most

popular animated shows of 1987. He concludes that the programs' stories are "blunted and maimed, truncated and sanitised to the point where they lose their healthy aspect and become mere distractions." This conclusion does a disservice to those child viewers who tapped into these programs powerfully and passionately, not as "mere distractions." Stephen Kline, "The Empire of Play: Emergent Genres of Product-Based Animations," In Front of the Children: Screen Entertainment and Young Audiences, ed. Cary Bazalgette and David Buckingham (London: British Film Institute, 1995) 163.

3   My general categories are intended to be helpful descriptions, not tidy taxonomies to be used to determine what is a true product-based show. Jem, for example, was a tremendously popular product-based program of the eighties that does not fit into any of these general categories. This unique, girl-targeted show is more like Hanna-Barbera's popular seventies show Josie and the Pussycats than like other girl-targeted product-based programs such as My Little Pony.

4   The mystical powers of muscled superheroes cause some fundamentalist Christians great concern. As Phil Phillips says in his classic fundamentalist attack on secular children's culture, Turmoil in the Toybox (Lancaster, Pa.: Starburst, 1986), "Many parents have expressed concern that their children, after watching the 'He-Man' cartoons, go running throughout the house with plastic swords held aloft shouting, 'by the power of Grayskull, I have the power!' God's Word warns us that only by the blood of Jesus do humans have any power and authority over others. There is no mention of the power of Grayskull" (89). See also Ellen Seiter and Karen Riggs, " 'Barney's Better than Jesus': TV and Conflict in the Evangelical Preschool," conference paper, Console-ing Passions, Madison, Wis., Apr. 1996.

5   Both mechanical transformers and muscled superheroes offer what the industry considers to be appealing to boy viewers: a masculinity characterized by strength and mutability. Willis argues that transforming toys represent a taming of the utopian desire for change: "What is interesting about the Transformers is the way the notion of transformation suggests spontaneity and change, while the reality of the toy teaches program and pre-programmed outcome" (36). The toy's metamorphosis is preprogrammed, Willis explains, just as social roles within capitalism are preprogrammed by the social formation. In her argument, the pleasure in such preprogrammed play may lie in the feeling of mastery that comes with the successful completion of the transformation and, perhaps more important, in the masterful feeling that comes with the endless repetition of the transforming process.

6   Kline, "Empire" 158.

7   The wild commercial success of "boys' " tie-in toys indicates an enormous number of purchasers, and it is quite possible that girls are getting in on the fun

and enjoying "boys' " toys and programs. Conversely, boys may be playing with "girls' " toys. A number of the boys in my classes at Vassar College were almost as enthusiastic about Strawberry Shortcake as they were about G.I. Joe, but when I conducted ethnographic research on Strawberry Shortcake at the University of Rochester, most boys reacted disdainfully. Spuriously, Cy Schneider interprets any interest boys might have in female characters as being motivated by heterosexual drive: "*Wonder Woman* comic books were said to be aimed at young girls, but her lack of clothing certainly must have caught boys' eyes. Gershan Legman once described Wonder Woman as having 'the drum majorette patriotism of star-spangled panties and spread-eagled breasts.' " Cy Schneider, *Children's Television: The Art, the Business, and How It Works* (Chicago: NTC Business Books, 1987) 151.

8   Marsha Kinder, *Playing with Power in Movies, Television, and Video Games: From Muppet Babies to Teenage Mutant Ninja Turtles* (Berkeley: U of California P, 1991) 122–123.

9   Note that cartoons generally are not the starting point for a supersystem. Toys, greeting cards, comics, and so forth generally come first; the cartoon then serves both to promote previously successful products and to introduce and promote new products.

10   *TV Guide* 13 June 1987: 6.

11   Emily Sacher, "Cartoon Power: Are Children Being Brainwashed to Buy Toys?," *Newsday* 17 Feb. 1985: 15.

12   Although guns, tanks, and bombs are common in all the boys' programs, the most hyperbolically militaristic program is *G.I. Joe*, which unabashedly displays Reagan-era militarism. *G.I. Joe*'s militaristic agenda is illustrated particularly well by the four-part "Synthoid Conspiracy," in which military cutbacks weaken the army. The Joe Team cannot run its drills because cutbacks have wiped out its supplies of bullets and gasoline. Without a properly equipped Joe Team, the evil Cobra terrorists can easily conquer the world. It turns out, however, that military cutbacks in and of themselves are un-American: the U.S. generals who want to reduce military spending are really synthoids—synthetic humans created by the Cobra terrorists. For an analysis of "terrorism" in the Reagan years, see Annie Goldson and Chris Bratton, "Counter Terror," Schneider and Wallis 147–159.

13   Joan E. Aitken, "The Role of Language and Gender in 'The Transformers': An Analysis of Messages in Cartoons for Children," conference paper, Organization for the Study of Communication, Language, and Gender, Oct. 1986.

14   Production company executive, conversation with the author, 7 Apr. 1993.

15   The idea that whiteness is "normal" or invisible carries over to the toy industry as well. Many girls, and Mattel, see white Barbie dolls as "normal" and "non-ethnic." See Rand. If the number of cartoon characters of color has increased

since the eighties, this may be less because of enlightened consciousness than out of a desire to placate the FCC. Although it sounds odd, I suspect broadcasters may feel that an "educational" label, needed to satisfy the mandates of the Children's Television Act of 1990, may adhere better to shows with characters of color. "Difference" is seen as inherently educational.

16   Kinder cites a study in which third graders were asked to respond to a story with animal characters and a story with human characters. Seventy-four percent preferred the story with animals, "perhaps because they were less emotionally involving and therefore aroused less anxiety about 'good' versus 'bad' (that is socially disapproved behavior)" (74). Although it may be true that animal characters arouse less anxiety about certain kinds of conflict, it is also true that animal characters are often used to mask race as an issue. I would not disallow Kinder's argument that children find great pleasure in identifying with mischievous animals in part because such identifications are "rendered safe by the distancing techniques of animation and animal masquerade" (125), but I would argue additionally that the child's "distanced" identification may represent a denial of the ways in which animality serves to mask ethnicity, gender, and other "real-life" issues.

17   Alan Bash, "Human Half of New 'Muppets' Host," USA Today 11 Apr. 1996: 3D.

18   American Greetings Corporation, Strawberry Shortcake: The First $100 Million (Cleveland: American Greetings, 1980) 147.

19   Sut Jhally and Justin Lewis, Enlightened Racism: "The Cosby Show," Audiences, and the Myth of the American Dream (Boulder, Colo.: Westview, 1992) 71.

20   Winston 178. For a different take on Amos 'n' Andy and the debates around it, see Thomas Cripps, " 'Amos 'n' Andy' and the Debate over American Racial Integration," O'Connor 33–54.

21   I am referring here of course to Donald Bogle's groundbreaking Toms, Coons, Mulattos, Mammies, and Bucks: An Interpretive History of Blacks in American Films, rev. ed. (New York: Continuum, 1990), which discusses black stereotyping and black actors who break away from that stereotyping in live-action Hollywood films.

22   George W. Woolery, Children's Television: The First Thirty-Five Years, 1946–1981, part 1: Animated Cartoon Series (Metuchen, N.J.: Scarecrow, 1983) 156.

23   X-Men, a nineties cartoon, features mutant characters who seem to be white coded, but the show occasionally addresses the issue of difference in interesting ways. Mutants are discriminated against, often by skinhead types. In one episode, the show's egghead mutant character, who is blue but apparently white coded, falls in love with a woman only to find that her father does not approve of such miscegenation: humans and mutants should not mix. In TV cartoons

in general, one of the most common "prosocial" messages is that one should not prejudge those who are different from oneself. "Difference" rarely, if ever, means racial difference.

24   On whiteness as a culturally constructed ethnic category, see Richard Dyer, "White," *Screen* 29.4 (Autumn 1988): 44–64.

25   D. A. Miller, "Anal Rope," *Inside/Out: Lesbian Theories, Gay Theories,* ed. Diana Fuss (New York: Routledge, 1991) 123–124.

26   Miller 123.

27   Grossman 357. See also Dale Kunkel, "From a Raised Eyebrow to a Turned Back: The FCC and Children's Product-Related Programming," *Journal of Communication* 38.4 (Autumn 1988): 90–108; and Edward L. Palmer, *Television and America's Children: A Crisis of Neglect* (New York: Oxford UP, 1988).

28   Address to the International Radio and Television Society, 1981, quoted in Krasnow, Longley, and Terry 47–48.

29   Schneider 182.

30   Quoted in Kirk Honeycutt, " 'Care Bears': Kids' Entertainment or an Advertising Bonanza?," *Los Angeles Daily News* 30 Apr. 1985, Life Section: n.p., clipping in Margaret Herrick Library, Academy of Motion Picture Arts and Sciences, Beverly Hills, Calif.

31   Quoted in Honeycutt.

32   On the star industry, see Christine Gledhill, ed., *Stardom: Industry of Desire* (New York: Routledge, 1991). For a history of the early marketing of cartoon stars and toy tie-ins, see Richard deCordova, "The Mickey in Macy's Window: Childhood, Consumerism, and Disney Animation," *Disney Discourse: Producing the Magic Kingdom,* ed. Eric Smoodin (New York: Routledge, 1994) 203–213.

33   Schneider 112.

34   Schneider created the commercials for two infamous Mattel toys, Barbie and the 1955 Burp Gun, the first toy that owed its success to television advertising. Schneider recalls, "[T]he Burp Gun was an automatic cap-firing machine gun modeled after the machine guns used in WWII jungle fighting" (19).

35   Schneider 115. Schneider seems to have inflated the 1987 figure, for according to many sources the licensed character had stopped being a "hot salesman" by this date. Kline gives a different set of figures. He says sales of licensed-character toys constituted 20 percent of total toy sales in 1977 and had risen to 65 percent by 1987. "Empire" 163.

36   Schneider 112.

37   Howdy Doody information from Grossman 225; Davy Crockett information from *Betty Boop to Barney: Make-Believe Characters Invade the Marketplace,* exhibition pamphlet, Strong Museum, Rochester, N.Y.

38   For a social scientific take on the dangers of host-selling, see Dale Kunkel,

"Children and Host-Selling Television Commercials," *Communication Research* 15.1 (Feb. 1988): 71–92.

39   From the consumer point of view the eighties toy-TV phenomenon was not radically new, but from the business perspective the phenomenon did entail some important structural shifts. Over the course of the eighties, there was a progressive consolidation of TV and licensing under fewer and fewer companies. See Norma Odom Pecora, *The Business of Children's Television* (New York: Guilford, 1998).

40   D. C. Denison, "The Year of Playing Dangerously," *Boston Globe* 8 Dec. 1985: 14–16+.

41   Stern and Schoenhaus 22. I criticize Stern and Schoenhaus repeatedly in this chapter not to attack *them* but because their opinions are so typical of the children's entertainment industry.

42   Stern and Schoenhaus 202.

43   Stern and Schoenhaus 198.

44   Stern and Schoenhaus 112.

45   Schneider 95.

46   Birthday parties and the crisis of forgotten birthdays are prominent in both Shortcake cartoons and books. Willis's theorization of the importance of birthdays as a child's means of assembling an "imaginary utopian social space" may explain why the narrativization of birthdays appeals to child viewers. See Willis's "Gender as Commodity," in *Primer*.

47   I elaborate on the burden placed on female subjects to emanate "proper" odors in "Is Something Fishy Going on Here? Douching and the Myth of Female Genital Odor," conference paper, Graduate Student Critical Theory Colloquium, U of Rochester, Rochester, N.Y., Apr. 1990.

48   Constance Penley, "The Cabinet of Dr. Pee-wee: Consumerism and Sexual Terror," *Camera Obscura* 17 (May 1988): 152.

49   Jenkins, " 'Going Bonkers!' " 184.

50   Seiter, *Sold Separately* 157–158.

51   Seiter, *Sold Separately* 157.

52   Stern and Schoenhaus 201. Whereas superhero and mechanical-transformer programs emphasize primary colors, nurturing-caretaker programs are persistently pastel. The programs' pastel backgrounds reinforce the idea of a "soft" program designed for a soft, feminine viewer. Pink, the ultimate feminine marker, dominates the mise-en-scène of nurturing-caretaker cartoons. Interestingly, Jane Gallop contends that pink functions as much more than a marker of femininity: "If blue, outside the infantile realm, is no longer a particularly masculine color, might not that relate to the phallocentrism which in our culture (as well as in most if not all others) raises the masculine to the universal human,

beyond gender, so that the feminine alone must bear the burden of sexual difference? Pink then becomes THE color of sexual difference, carrying alone within it
the diacritical distinction pink/blue." Jane Gallop, "Annie Leclerc Writing a Letter, with Vermeer," *The Poetics of Gender,* ed. Nancy K. Miller (New York: Columbia
UP, 1986) 138–139.

53 As Seiter has convincingly argued in *Sold Separately,* some middle-class parents
may be nauseated by frilly femininity because of the working-class connotations
of such "tasteless" excess. See her chapter on *My Little Pony* in *Sold Separately.*

54 Stern and Schoenhaus 147–148.

55 In Seiter's study, Sara, a teacher at a Montessori school, enforces strict rules
forbidding talk or play that draws on "noneducational" media: "Curiously these
rules apply much more leniently to girls, who tend to play in groups separate
from boys. Sara knows that the girls play games in secret based on *Aladdin* or
Beauty and the Beast while they are on the playground. But the girls only play
these games out of her hearing, and because the girls' games do not create dis-
ruptions, she does not intervene. Also, Sara does not enforce the no-characters
rules with the girls' clothing, allowing Jasmine and others to make their way
into the classroom on shoes, socks, t-shirts." Ellen Seiter, "Power Rangers at
Preschool: Negotiating Media in Child Care Settings" 9–10, unpublished paper,
1996.

56 Willis 24.

57 Schneider 95.

58 *Advertising Age* 8 Feb. 1993.

59 Schneider 107.

60 *Advertising Age* 8 Feb. 1993.

61 Laura Mulvey, "Afterthoughts on 'Visual Pleasure and Narrative Cinema' Inspired by *Duel in the Sun*," *Feminism and Film Theory,* ed. Constance Penley (New
York: Routledge, 1988) 72.

62 Rosalind Coward, *Female Desires: How They Are Sought, Bought, and Packaged* (New
York: Grove, 1985) 89.

63 Coward 105.

64 Stern and Schoenhaus 194.

65 See Robin Andersen, *Consumer Culture and TV Programming* (Boulder, Colo.: Westview, 1995).

66 Engelhardt 75–76.

67 Engelhardt 72–73.

68 *Strawberry Shortcake* was the first product-based blockbuster, but only a small
number of shows were produced and endlessly repeated.

69 Janet Maslin, "There's a Moral in TV Cartoons: Be Resourceful," *New York Times*
4 Oct. 1992.

70 Dale Kunkel, "Report to the Federal Communications Commission re: Mass Media Docket 93-48," *Broadcasters License Renewal Claims Regarding Children's Educational Programming* (1993).

71 Grossman 357.

72 *Advertising Age* 25 Jan. 1982: 79.

73 Vivian Gussin Paley, *Boys and Girls* (Chicago: U of Chicago P, 1984) 109.

74 The act is in some ways merely a "Band-Aid" solution. As Kinder argues: "[T]he problem of decommodifying children's television cannot be addressed simply by limiting the amount of commercial time that broadcasters can sell or by demanding a crackdown on the program-length commercial. . . . As long as children's programming is firmly embedded in the larger intertextual structures of American commercial television, it will reproduce consumerist subjects" (46).

75 For a limited ethnographic study of the scented Strawberry Shortcake dolls that draws on adult recollections, see my essay "Dolls: Odour, Disgust, Femininity, and Toy Design," *The Gendered Object*, ed. Pat Kirkham (Manchester, Eng.: Manchester UP, 1996) 90–102.

76 Such as Buckingham's and P. Palmer's work. See also the research on child media users in Thomas R. Lindlof, ed., *Natural Audiences: Qualitative Research of Media Uses and Effects* (Norwood, N.J.: Ablex, 1987), and Ellen Seiter's work on adult and child media use in *Television and New Media Audiences* (Oxford: Oxford UP, 1998).

77 Lynn Spigel and Henry Jenkins come to a similar conclusion in their study of popular memory and the *Batman* TV show, "Same Bat Channel, Different Bat Times: Mass Culture and Popular Memory," *The Many Lives of the Batman: Critical Approaches to a Superhero and His Media*, ed. Roberta E. Pearson and William Urrichio (New York: Routledge, 1991) 117–148.

5 Turned-on Toddlers and Space Age TV

1 Hilary Mills, "Pete and Joan," *Vanity Fair* Aug. 1993: 119. Henson also opposed female muppet operators, feeling it was unseemly for women to engage in what was often vigorous, athletic puppet manipulation. He also did not like the falsetto voices men had to use to do female characters. See "Sesame Street: Getting from There to Here [Joan Ganz Cooney]," 1993, Museum of Television and Radio Collection, New York, N.Y.; hereafter referred to as Cooney Seminar.

2 Richard M. Polsky, *Getting to Sesame Street: Origins of the Children's Television Workshop* (New York: Praeger, 1974) 114. Figure given is budget for preproduction and first season, 1968–1970. By 1993, the budget had risen to around $19 million. Cooney Seminar.

3 See Henry Jenkins III, " 'A Person's a Person, No Matter How Small': Grow-

ing up with Dr. Seuss and Dr. Spock," conference paper, Society for Cinema Studies, New Orleans, La., 1993, and "The All-American Handful: *Dennis the Menace, Permissive Childrearing, and the Popular Imagination*," conference paper, Console-ing Passions, Tucson, Ariz., Apr. 1994, as well as his work in progress, *No Matter How Small: Permissive Childrearing and Postwar Popular Culture.*

4 For a concise summary of education models running counter to the Montessori method, see J. McVicker Hunt's Introduction to *The Montessori Method*, by Maria Montessori (New York: Schocken, 1974) xi–xxxix. Although Montessori education had a very progressive or even hippy image in the sixties and seventies, the Maria Montessori of the twenties was not as far to the left as her later proponents might have imagined. She was no eugenicist but did give credence to craniometry and other means of biologically determining intelligence that were popular at the time. Her radicalness lay in her desire to thwart the "destiny" of children who were supposedly biologically destined to inferiority. It was a question of culture defying nature. See Stephen Jay Gould, *The Mismeasure of Man* (New York: Norton, 1981).

5 For an account of the Montessori method's potential for combating poverty, see Lena L. Gitter, *A Strategy for Fighting the War on Poverty: The Montessori Method as Applied to the Brookhaven Project* (Washington, D.C.: Fagan, 1965).

6 For a detailed account of historical shifts in psychological theory and how these shifts have been played out in learning theory, see Abram Amsel, *Behaviorism, Neobehaviorism, and Cognitivism in Learning Theory: Historical and Contemporary Perspectives* (Hillsdale, N.J.: Erlbaum, 1989).

7 Buckingham 13.

8 Two books are emblematic of the rejection of the deficit model in the late sixties: Herbert Ginsburg, *The Myth of the Deprived Child: Poor Children's Intellect and Education* (Englewood Cliffs, N.J.: Prentice-Hall, 1972) and William Labov et al., *A Study of the Non-Standard English of Negro and Puerto-Rican Speakers in New York City* (Washington, D.C.: U.S. Department of Health, Education, and Welfare, Office of Education, 1968). The latter study offers complex linguistic analyses of African American and Puerto Rican speech in order to strongly criticize educators who, largely deaf to nonstandard English, assume that poor people of color are verbally impoverished.

9 Gerald Lesser, *Children and Television: Lessons from Sesame Street* (New York: Random House, 1974) 52.

10 Lesser 52.

11 Johnson cited in Valora Washington and Ura Jean Oyemade, *Project Head Start: Past, Present, and Future Trends in the Context of Family Needs* (New York: Garland, 1987) 6.

12 Arthur R. Jensen, "How Much Can We Boost I.Q. and Scholastic Achievement?,"

Harvard Educational Review 39.1 (Winter 1969): 1–123. The uproar Jensen's article provoked is comparable to the more recent controversy surrounding Richard J. Herrnstein and Charles Murray, *The Bell Curve: Intelligence and Class Structure in American Life* (New York: Free Press, 1994). Herrnstein and Murray claim that attacks on Jensen's work drove psychometrics away from the public sphere and into an ivory tower quarantine (13). Jensen continued his work after the 1969 controversy; he is the most cited author in *The Bell Curve*'s bibliography.

13 Jensen 83.

14 See in particular the pro and con views expressed in *Harvard Educational Review* 39.2 (Spring 1969).

15 Paulo Freire and Donaldo Macedo, *Literacy: Reading the Word and the World* (South Hadley, Mass.: Bergin and Garvey, 1987) 154.

16 African Americans Ronald Edmonds et al. rebutted Jencks in "A Black Response to Christopher Jencks' *Inequality* and Certain Other Issues," *Harvard Educational Review* 43.1 (Feb. 1973): 76–91. (See also other articles in this special issue on Jencks's *Inequality*.) The authors compared Jencks to Senator Daniel Patrick Moynihan, whose report to President Lyndon Johnson, *The Negro Family: The Case for National Action* (Washington, D.C.: U.S. Department of Labor, Office of Policy Research, 1965), had been widely attacked by African Americans. Moynihan asserted that black families were held back from getting ahead in America largely because they were dominated by matriarchs. Edmonds et al. stated that, like Moynihan's report, *Inequality* suggested " 'benign neglect' of national issues of race" (77).

17 Polsky 114. Polsky also notes that 18.3% of the total funding was provided by the Carnegie Corporation and 18.7% came from the Ford Foundation.

18 Cooney Seminar.

19 Edward A. De Avila and Barbara Havassy, with Juan Pascual-Leone, *Mexican-American Schoolchildren: A Neo-Piagetian Analysis* (Georgetown: Georgetown UP, 1976).

20 Quoted in Polsky 11.

21 Quoted in Polsky 11.

22 *Laugh-In* had more than twice as many segments per show as *Sesame Street*. It was framed by its hosts as a variety show, but the frame was minimal compared to the way the neighborhood in *Sesame Street* reasserts itself as a kind of home base between fast-paced segments. Furthermore, although *Sesame Street* segments are often short, it is not unusual for the pacing within a short segment to be fairly slow, unlike on *Laugh-In*.

23 George W. Woolery quoted in Lucille Burbank, *Children's Television: An Historical Inquiry on Three Selected, Prominent, Long-Running, Early Childhood TV Programs*, diss., Temple U, 1992 (Ann Arbor: UMI, 1992) 61.

24   Big companies such as IBM and Xerox fund many PBS programs. Also, conservative foundations such as the Lynde and Harry Bradley Foundation, the Smith Richardson Foundation, the John M. Olin Foundation, the Sarah Scaife Foundation, the J. M. Foundation, and the Adolph Coors Foundation fund programming. See Josh Daniel, "Uncivil Wars: The Conservative Assault on Public Broadcasting," *Independent* Aug./Sept. 1992: 20–25.

25   Lesser's preliminary outline of *Sesame Street* curriculum goals cited in Polsky 72.

26   Dafna Lemish, "Viewers in Diapers: The Early Development of Television Viewing," Lindlof 44.

27   Quoted in Polsky 13–14.

28   Werner I. Halpern, "Turned-on Toddlers," *Journal of Communication* 25.4 (Autumn 1975): 66.

29   Winn's *Plug-In Drug* demonizes the idiot box as both a narcotic and a stimulant. Siding with the developmentalists, Winn states that *Sesame Street* contributes to "frantic behavior" because it is " 'sensory overkill' for some preschoolers, who are not developmentally equipped to handle fast-paced electronic stimulation" (14).

30   Dr. S. Hayakawa cited in Lesser 29.

31   Halpern 68.

32   Halpern 68.

33   Halpern 69.

34   Although Ivy League rivalry was never an explicit component of the *Sesame Street* versus *Mister Rogers' Neighborhood* debate, it is noteworthy that the pro-*Rogers* group was from Yale, whereas the pro–*Sesame Street* people were from Harvard.

35   Jerome Singer and Dorothy Singer, "Come Back, Mister Rogers, Come Back," *Television and American Culture*, ed. Carl Lowe (New York: Wilson, 1981) 124–128.

36   Singer and Singer 124.

37   Singer and Singer 126.

38   In practice, sometimes parents watch *Sesame Street* with their kids, and sometimes they do household chores when it is on. In Lemish's study, it is the show that most holds children's attention so that tasks can be done or leisure time can be taken. As two mothers in the study explain, "I like to put on [television] when fixing dinner because he sits and doesn't pop up all the time"; "We walk in the door, the coats come off, the TV goes on and I go to pick up the mail and do all the rest. It's kind of nice, because that's my half hour to get my things done" (43). Winn agrees that *Sesame Street* allows mothers some free time, but she thinks mothers should make their children take naps instead of using TV to "pacify" them. She is appalled that some women purposely get their kids "hooked" on *Sesame Street* (127–128).

39   Lesser 120.

40   One particularly harsh critic of the program wrote that "unlike the makers of *Barney*, Cooney and colleagues did have one indisputable stroke of genius. They made sure their program, like *The Bullwinkle Show* before it, was a kiddie show for adults. Because parents were so giddy over 'Meryl Sheep' and 'Placido Flamingo,' they felt it must be educational." Billy Tashman, "E-Z Street: Twenty-five Years and Still Counting," *Village Voice* 23 Nov. 1993: 55.

41   Seeger's appearance a few years earlier on *The Smothers Brothers Comedy Hour* had provoked a scandal. See Steven Alan Carr, "On the Edge of Tastelessness: CBS, the Smothers Brothers, and the Struggle for Control," *Cinema Journal* 31.4 (Summer 1992): 3–24, and Bert Spector, "A Clash of Cultures: The Smothers Brothers vs. CBS Television," O'Connor 159–183.

42   *Captain Kangaroo*, on the other hand, received government funding around 1968 to produce cartoon segments on nutrition, personal awareness, and growing up. According to Burbank, these segments were "designed for mental health purposes in hopes of counteracting future drug use" (31).

43   On technological determinism, see Raymond Williams, *Television: Technology and Cultural Form* (Hanover, N.H.: Wesleyan UP, 1992), especially "The Technology and the Society." Basically, technological determinism confuses technologies with their social uses. Technological determinists believe certain technologies inevitably produce certain effects. For example, they may believe TV makes people stupid because *by its very nature* it cannot do otherwise or the World Wide Web is *inherently* liberatory and promotes nonlinear, nonhierarchical thinking.

44   Michèle Mattelart, "Education, Television, and Mass Culture: Reflections on Research into Innovation," *Television in Transition*, ed. Phillip Drummond and Richard Patterson (London: BFI, 1986) 172.

45   Loretta Moore Long, *Sesame Street: A Space Age Approach to Education for Space Age Children*, diss., U of Massachusetts, 1973 (Ann Arbor: UMI, 1973) 1.

46   Long 1.

47   References to the space age were something of a TV convention at the time, so *Sesame Street* was hardly unique in this respect. Other shows that used the outer space motif in the post-*Sputnik* years included *Lost in Space*, *The Jetsons*, *I Dream of Jeannie*, and *My Favorite Martian*. For more on TV and the space program, see Watson, particularly "Hungering for Heroes: The Space Program." On TV and the New Frontier/Kennedy administration, see Curtin.

48   Lesser 177.

49   *The Councilor* (Shreveport, La.), 3–24 July 1971. Cited in Lesser 177–178.

50   Cited in Polsky 77.

51   Long 56. However, Long notes, in order to avoid controversy and make test-

ing easier, *Sesame Street*'s curriculum goals were more highly cognitive in nature during its first three seasons. In recent years, *Sesame Street* has developed overt curriculums on race relations. See Cooney Seminar.

52 Long vii.

53 Long 80.

54 Lesser also tells this story (86).

55 Long 81.

56 Long 81.

57 Long 82.

58 Buckingham 15. Buckingham criticizes this developmentalist take on children and TV. He draws an analogy between the psychological theory of child development, whereby children are deficient in comparison to adults, and socialization theory, as James and Prout have characterized it, whereby childhood is seen as a rehearsal for adulthood, as a time when children learn to conform to grown-up norms.

59 Paul Messaris, "Mothers' Comments to Their Children about the Relationship between Television and Reality," Lindlof 106.

60 Scholars trained outside the parameters of traditional social science have also produced interesting small-scale ethnographic studies of child media users. Here I am thinking particularly of Jenkins and Kinder. Jenkins's study of his son and his friends at a Pee-wee party, " 'Going Bonkers!,' " draws interesting conclusions about children's media use. In researching *Playing with Power*, Kinder took a camcorder to a video arcade and interviewed kids about their video game habits. Kinder also interviewed schoolchildren after showing them an episode of *Teenage Mutant Ninja Turtles*.

6 *Sesame Street* Technologies

1 Through advertising, multinational corporations engage in global public relations campaigns for their products. There's a huge body of literature on globalization. A few sources that I have found helpful are "Going Global: Transcript of a Report Broadcast on the *MacNeil/Lehrer Newshour* September 29, 1987, Schneider and Wallis 182–183; Gage Averill, "Global Imaginings, Ohmann 203–223; William M. O'Barr, "The Airbrushing of Culture: An Insider's Look at Global Advertising," *Public Culture* 2.1 (1989): 1–19; and Caren Kaplan, " 'A World without Boundaries': The Body/Shop's Trans/National Geographics," *Social Text* 43 (Fall 1995): 45–66.

2 Buckingham 279. One researcher who has looked at the economics of children's entertainment from the global perspective is Bernard Miège in *The Capitalization of Cultural Production* (New York: International General, 1989). See also Ariel

Dorfman and Armand Mattelart, *How to Read Donald Duck: Imperialist Ideology in the Disney Comic* (New York: I. G. Editions, 1975), and Marsha Kinder, ed., *Kids' Media Culture* (Durham, N.C.: Duke UP, forthcoming).

3   In their scandalously negative appraisal of the Educational Testing Service's (ETS) evaluation of *Sesame Street*, Thomas D. Cook et al. concluded that the positive evaluation was problematic because the children in the study were actively encouraged to watch the program. Thus, the ETS study, upon which *Sesame Street* has depended over the years as proof of its efficacy, was flawed because it measured how much "encouraged viewers" learned from *Sesame Street*, not how much viewers in general learned. Thomas D. Cook et al., *Sesame Street Revisited* (New York: Russell Sage Foundation, 1975).

4   Cooney Seminar.

5   Lesser 138.

6   Rose K. Goldsen, *The Show and Tell Machine: How Television Works and Works You Over* (New York: Dial, 1977) 197.

7   This test defines attention as looking, which is problematic on several counts. Like adults, many children frequently engage in other activities while nevertheless listening to a program. As Lemish notes, studies of young TV viewers tend to focus "almost exclusively on the development of visual attention to television" (33). On adults listening to TV, see Rick Altman's "Television/Sound," *Studies in Entertainment: Critical Approaches to Mass Culture*, ed. Tania Modleski (Bloomington: Indiana UP, 1986) 39–54.

8   The CTW's distractor child-testing method has been adopted by the television industry for testing commercials and programs on children. Goldsen, *Show and Tell* 197.

9   See Foucault, *Discipline and Punish*.

10 Valeria Lovelace, "*Sesame Street* as a Continuing Experiment," *Educational Technology Research and Development* 38.4 (1990): 23–24.

11 Lovelace 24.

12 Lovelace 20.

13 Lovelace 20.

14 Lovelace 21.

15 Lovelace 21.

16 See Brian Sutton-Smith, *Toys as Culture* (New York: Gardner, 1986), "The Toy as the Child's Work: The First Year" and "Play and Work after Infancy: The Second Year."

17 See Tania Modleski, "The Rhythms of Reception: Daytime Television and Women's Work," *Regarding Television: Critical Approaches—An Anthology*, ed. E. Ann Kaplan (Los Angeles: American Film Institute, 1983) 67–75.

18 Peter Levelt, "A Review of Research on International Coproductions of *Sesame*

Street," *Sesame Street Research: A Twentieth Anniversary Symposium* (New York: Children's Television Workshop, 1990) 57–58.

19   Averill 211.

20   Averill 203.

21   The only figures I have found on the purchase of *Sesame Street* are from 1977. According to Goldsen, in that year the Arabian Gulf States Joint Program Production Institution in Kuwait paid $7,500,000 "in return for all rights to the Arabic-language version of the first CTW series in Arabic. The Institution is funded by Gulf States to produce educational television for Bahrain, Iraq, Kuwait, Oman, Qatar, Saudi Arabia and the United Arab Emirates. Production of the Arab pilot is the first step." *Show and Tell* 408.

22   Cooney cited in Gerald Lesser Seminar, "Sesame Street: Getting from There to Here, International Co-Productions: And the Street Goes On," 1993, Museum of Television and Radio Collection, New York, N.Y.; hereafter referred to as Lesser Seminar.

23   Josh Selig, "Muppets Succeed Where Politicians Haven't," *New York Times* 29 Mar. 1998, sec. 2: 45.

24   *Wheel of Fortune* is another U.S.-based show that obliges foreign creators to follow specific guidelines. See Michael Skovmand, "Barbarous TV International: Syndicated *Wheels of Fortune*," *Media Cultures: Reappraising Transnational Media*, ed. Michael Skovmand and Kim Christian Schrøder (London: Routledge, 1992) 84–103.

25   Goldsen, *Show and Tell* 407.

26   Lutrelle Horne, "Introductory Remarks," *Sesame Street Research* 54.

27   Levelt 58.

28   Lesser Seminar.

29   Cooney Seminar.

30   Lesser Seminar.

31   Lesser Seminar.

32   Averill 213–214.

33   *Plaza Sésamo* was produced in 1972, 1974, 1983, and 1993. Lesser Seminar. In 1983, the show was funded by a grant from Latin American Bottlers of Coca-Cola. *Children's Television Workshop International Research Notes* 4 (Fall 1983): 25.

34   Rose K. Goldsen and Azriel Bibliowicz, "Plaza Sésamo: 'Neutral' Language or 'Cultural Assault'?," *Journal of Communication* 26.2 (Spring 1976): 124–125.

35   Lesser Seminar.

36   Maria Emilia Brederode, "Research on *Rua Sesamo*, the Portuguese Coproduction," *Sesame Street Research* 64.

37   Abdelkader Ezzaki, "Research on *Iftah Ya Simsin*, the Arabic Coproduction," *Sesame Street Research* 61.

38 Ezzaki 61.

39 Freire and Macedo 145.

40 Freire and Macedo 148.

41 Edward L. Palmer, Milton Chen, and Gerald S. Lesser, "*Sesame Street*: Patterns of International Adaptation," *Journal of Communication* 26.2 (Spring 1976): 118.

42 A. Mattelart, *Multinational Corporations* 183.

43 Harry M. Lasker, "The Jamaican Project: Final Report," unpublished report (New York: Children's Television Workshop, 1973) 1.

44 Lasker 58–59.

45 Lasker 3–4.

46 Lasker 3.

47 Lasker 64.

48 Lasker 56.

49 Lasker 4.

50 Lasker 6–7.

51 I realize that in emphasizing the Jamaicans' lack of exposure to technology, I risk romanticizing them as untouched "primitives." This is not my intent. I also realize that the Harvard researchers may have been wrong in their characterization of the villagers as isolated from television. I have no way of knowing if the villagers had really never encountered TV, slides, video recorders, and so forth.

52 Palmer, Chen, and Lesser 118.

53 William George Husson, *A Time Series Analysis of the Attention Patterns of Naive and Experienced Child Viewers*, diss., Rensselaer Polytechnic Institute, 1981 (Ann Arbor: UMI, 1981) 71.

54 Lesser Seminar.

55 Rogelio Diaz-Guerrero et al., "*Plaza Sésamo* in Mexico: An Evaluation," *Journal of Communication* 26.2 (Spring 1976): 149.

56 The researchers divided the children into five groups: rural children, urban lower-class four-year-olds, urban blue-collar four-year-olds, urban lower-class five-year-olds, and urban blue-collar five-year-olds.

57 Diaz-Guerrero et al. 150.

58 A. Mattelart, *Multinational Corporations*.

59 Goldsen, *Show and Tell* 409. Goldsen may be confusing the Spanish version of the show with the Latin American version.

60 Tapio Varis, "Trends in International Television Flow," Schneider and Wallis 106.

61 Varis 106.

62 "Ira Herbert: The Coca-Cola Company," Ohmann 4.

63 "Ira Herbert" 5.

64 To get some idea of how foreign versions of *Sesame Street* look, see the CTW's

1994 *Sesame Street Celebrates around the World*, a special New Year's Eve video that visits a number of foreign *Sesame Streets*, inserting into each country a foreign version of Elmo. The foreign Elmos speak English with foreign accents and are voiced by the same artist who does the American Elmo.

65   Lesser Seminar.

66   The CTW does not articulate what "feel" it is attempting to create in *Sesame Street*; this is my interpretation. I should add that, notwithstanding the CTW's rules, there is room for flexibility. For example, the program is shown in English in Curaçao, where the local dialect is Papimiento. At points when the local broadcasters thought English might not be understood, they turned down the audio and added a Papimiento voice-over. Then they turned the English audio track back up. Later, the teachers who had been doing the voice-overs were incorporated into the show to explain segments in Papimiento. This is discussed in the Lesser Seminar. Clearly, the CTW is sometimes flexible; in Curaçao, the feel of the show is definitively altered.

67   A. Mattelart, *Multinational Corporations* 159.

68   A. Mattelart, *Multinational Corporations* 160.

69   Head and Sterling 508.

70   Quoted in Bill Carter, "Conservatives Call for PBS to Go Private or Go Dark," *New York Times* 30 Apr. 1992: B4.

7 Hey, Hey, Hey, It's "Good" TV

1   George A. Comstock and Eli Rubinstein, eds., *Television and Social Behavior* (Rockville, Md.: U.S. Department of Health, Education, and Welfare, 1972).

2   William Greider, "On Television, Race No Longer Divides Us: America Finally Invented the Black and White Television," *Washington Post* 12 Apr. 1978, final ed.: A1+.

3   Greider.

4   Jhally and Lewis.

5   Lawrence Linderman, "Playboy Interview: Bill Cosby," *Playboy* 1985: 76.

6   The Saturday morning show evolved from an earlier project, a 1969 animated prime-time special called *Hey, Hey, Hey—It's Fat Albert* (NBC). The 1969 show drew very heavily on Cosby's comedy routines and seems to have been targeted at both kids and adults. It included characters later featured in the Saturday morning show, but they looked different, especially Fat Albert, who was much fatter, literally bulging out of his clothing. The TV-special backgrounds were a weird amalgam of UPA-style minimalism and Ralph Bakshi's artsy realism. The program can be viewed at the Museum of Television and Radio in New York, N.Y.

7   Since *Fat Albert*, hiring Ph.D.'s to consult on cartoons has become practically de
rigueur. Listing Ph.D's in the credits helps a show defend itself against adult
critics.

8   William Henry Cosby Jr., *An Integration of the Visual Media via "Fat Albert and the
Cosby Kids" into the Elementary School Curriculum as a Teaching Aid and Vehicle to Achieve
Increased Learning*, diss., U of Massachusetts, 1976 (Ann Arbor: UMI, 1976).

9   Interestingly, the cartoons' pure educational function for *adults* is reinforced by
the University of Massachusetts, where Cosby wrote his dissertation. The university houses the films in its library's Special Collections department. Following
McGraw-Hill's explicit directions, the university will not show researchers the
16mm film prints. Instead, researchers are allowed to see only black-and-white
videotaped copies of the films. McGraw-Hill stipulates that "the videotapes are
to be used only as documentation of the Bill Cosby thesis and as a historical
record." Josephine Chessare, executive editor of McGraw-Hill Book Company,
letter to Katherine Emerson, University of Massachusetts archivist, 17 July 1978.
In their black-and-white, duplicated format, the videos are designated as having
pure use-value to adult researchers. Of course, since their color has been purposely removed, their use-value to scholars has been lessened.

10   In a 1990 speaking engagement at the Museum of Television and Radio, Charren actually praised a number of cartoons, all of which were expensively produced, video-only releases. Charren's gripe was against mass-produced, cheap,
and (she implied) "tasteless" cartoons.

11   Such money-saving tactics were not new to TV animation, of course. Throughout the thirties and forties—the pretelevision cartoon days that many animation aficionados see as a "Golden Age"—animators found they could recycle
cells and reduce drawing time (by putting moving body parts on cells separate from nonmoving body parts, for example) to save money. More dramatic
money-saving tactics were devised by television animators. Hanna-Barbera is
widely credited as the inventor of "limited animation" for television. As Maltin
describes it, in the dismissive manner typical of animation historians and children's TV reformers such as ACT: "Limited animation, as it came to be known,
paved the way for a systematic destruction of the cartoon art form. By reducing
movement to a bare minimum, eliminating personality animation and nuance,
and emphasizing slickly made sound tracks, this form of production earned the
nickname 'illustrated radio' " (344). It is precisely this style that Generation X
TV viewers now look on nostalgically as a Golden Age style, making them an
ideal target audience for the seventies classics shown on Ted Turner's Cartoon
Network.

12   Rose K. Goldsen, "Engineering Children," *A Personal Perspective on Broadcasting*,

WVBR, Ithaca, N.Y., 27 Apr. 1974; WHCU, Ithaca, N.Y., 29 Apr. 1974, 2. Goldsen took a familiar disdainful intellectual stance toward children's television, rejecting *Fat Albert* in particular for its use of didactic "messages" and arguing that "in the long run, what is 'good for children' can only be authentic art and literature and all the other expressive materials children need." *Show and Tell* 204.

13   Technically, one should describe these lap dissolves as simulated. Marks of cinematic punctuation such as dissolves and wipes are generally created directly on the animation cel (or on a computer). On camera-movement simulation in cartoons, see Kristin Thompson, "Implications of the Cel Animation Technique," *The Cinematic Apparatus*, ed. Teresa de Lauretis and Stephen Heath (New York: St. Martin's, 1980) 106–120.

14   Cosby had dropped out of Temple during his sophomore year. Temple neither labeled its degree honorary nor required Cosby to finish his remaining two years of course work.

15   Reginald G. Damerell, *Education's Smoking Gun: How Teacher's Colleges Have Destroyed Education in America* (New York: Freundlich, n.d.).

16   Larry Kettelkamp, *Bill Cosby: Family Fun Man* (New York: Simon and Schuster, 1987) 100–101.

17   Cosby's endorsements dried up in the nineties. His 1992 Service Merchandise campaign was a big flop.

18   Damerell 217.

19   Linderman (1985) 78.

20   Bourdieu 22–24. Bourdieu argues that the combination of "cultural capital inherited from the family" (of which Cosby had little, given his poor, working-class background) and academic capital produces an "entitlement effect." Bourdieu cannot, however, imagine one accruing much academic capital without the right kind of "cultural transmission from the family." In other words, he writes off class mobility via the accruing of academic capital.

21   Cosby 67.

22   Lawrence Linderman, "Playboy Interview: Bill Cosby," *Playboy* 1969: 74.

23   Linderman (1969) 86.

24   Linderman (1969) 76.

25   James T. Olsen, *Bill Cosby: Look Back in Laughter* (Mankato, Minn.: Creative Education, 1974) 23.

26   Cosby was certainly familiar with slum conditions and with the racism that kept blacks in the slums: "How many winters have white people spent with rats scurrying around their apartments at night, with windows boarded up but not keeping out the cold, and with no heat? Try to get a ghetto slumlord to fix up an apartment and you'll know what frustration and bitterness is." Linderman (1969) 170.

27   Pastore cited in Eli A. Rubinstein, "The TV Violence Report: What's Next?" Journal of Communication 24.1 (Winter 1974): 80.

28   Comstock and Rubinstein, eds., Television and Social Behavior, cited in Rubinstein 82.

29   Kuhn, Cinema.

30   Les Brown, "Children Don't See TV as Black or White," New York Times 4 Apr. 1974: 83.

31   Woolery 81; Goldsen, Show and Tell 202–203.

32   In fact, in response to Pastore's hearings, as well as ACT pressure and broad cultural anxieties about violence (as described in chapter 1), animation production fell off so much that animators felt the crunch. A screen cartoonist's union representative noted in April 1974 that "new programming is where we lost out. Renewals are more or less the same . . . but 50% of the new programs are live-action." Steve Toy, " 'Suspended' Animation: Hard Times for Cartoonists as TV Webs Taper Off," Variety 3 Apr. 1974: 68.

33   The adults debating children's television in the seventies had grown up either without television (the so-called good old days) or watching live-action Golden Age programming such as Howdy-Doody, The Soupy Sales Show, Captain Midnight, Kukla, Fran, and Ollie, and Ding Dong School. Minimally animated fifties shows such as Crusader Rabbit and Ruff and Reddy were conveniently forgotten by nostalgic seventies reformers. Reformers attacking contemporary programs on the grounds that they were lacking in comparison to their childhood live-action favorites also elided the fact that in 1954 the Senate juvenile-delinquency hearings attacked much live-action programming as objectionable. Programs singled out for objectionable violence included Captain Midnight, The Bowery Boys, Captain Video and His Video Rangers, and Dick Tracy. See Grossman 20–25.

34   Filmation Associates and William H. Cosby Jr., Personal, Parental, and Peer-Group Value Conflicts as Catalysts of Complex Educational and Psychological Issues Confronting Children in a Contemporary Society or . . . Fat Albert and the Cosby Kids (Los Angeles: Filmation Associates, 1972).

35   This book might be read as a response to PBS rhetoric about its high-quality programming. The book makes a bid to put Fat Albert in the same class as Sesame Street and Mister Rogers' Neighborhood while subtly critiquing PBS's high-class pretensions. Compare Smoodin's analysis of a 1939 public relations ploy by Warner Bros. in which the studio flaunted its self-censorship policies. Smoodin reads this move as an attempt to gain the kind of high-class legitimacy and "quality" image Disney had a monopoly on. Animating Culture 11–17.

36   Filmation and Cosby 4.

37   Filmation and Cosby 38.

38   Filmation and Cosby 11, 20.

39   See Marlon Riggs's video, *Ethnic Notions* (1986).

40   "Black English" is a problematic way to describe African American speech be-
     cause, of course, all African Americans do not speak the same way. However,
     I cannot find a better phrase for the style of speech *Fat Albert*'s producers con-
     sciously chose to work both with and against.

41   Filmation and Cosby 30. Fear of making the children appear verbally inept or
     inferior may also explain why the Mushmouth character, who had a speech im-
     pediment, was so carefully handled. In my discussions with others who viewed
     Fat Albert as children, Mushmouth is almost always mentioned or imitated, and
     he seems to have been a favorite character of many viewers. Yet after re-viewing
     the series, I found that Mushmouth's presence was actually quite minimal, un-
     doubtedly because of the scholarly panel's fear that his speech impediment
     might reinforce racist sentiment in some viewers. In fact, Mushmouth is virtu-
     ally absent from some episodes. In one show, all the kids except for Mushmouth
     spend a day with their dads at work. As the dads share their sons' key physi-
     cal and character features, it is my guess that Mushmouth was excluded to
     avoid addressing the problem of the father's speech. This problem is implicitly
     addressed when it is stated that Mushmouth's dad is a tour bus guide, thus
     someone who must have good verbal skills.

42   Les Brown, "Children in CBS Study Largely Indifferent to Race," *New York Times*
     12 June 1975: 75.

43   Brown, "Children in CBS Study" 75.

44   Brown, "Children Don't See TV as Black or White" 83.

45   Brown, "Children in CBS Study" 75.

46   Quoted in Grossman 245–247.

47   Quoted in Grossman 247.

48   Quoted in Grossman 247.

Conclusion

1   See Ann De Vaney, ed., *Watching Channel One: The Convergence of Students, Technology,
    and Private Business* (Albany: State U of New York P, 1994).

2   Constance Penley, "From NASA to *The 700 Club* (with a Detour through Holly-
    wood): Cultural Studies in the Public Sphere," *Disciplinarity and Dissent in Cultural
    Studies*, ed. Cary Nelson and Dilip Parameshwar Gaonkar (New York: Routledge,
    1996) 236.

3   *Mighty Morphin' Censorship: Who's Watching Children's Television?* is available from
    Paper Tiger Television, 339 Lafayette Street, New York, NY 10012; phone: 212-
    420-9045; e-mail: Tigertv@bway.net; Web site: www.papertiger.org.

Action for Children's Television. "ACT and the PTA Coalition for Change." To Be
	Integrated ACT Speeches filing cabinet. ACT Collection.
———. "Action for Children's Television: How Consumers ACTivate Change." ACT
	Collection.
———. "Chester Cheetah Filing March 5, 1992." Legal Drawer III Violence Study
	filing cabinet. ACT Collection.
———. "Speech at the American Dental Association 10/11/77." To Be Integrated ACT
	Speeches filing cabinet. ACT Collection.
Action for Children's Television (ACT) Collection. Gutman Library. Harvard Univer-
	sity, Cambridge, Mass.
Aitken, Joan E. "The Role of Language and Gender in 'The Transformers': An Analysis
	of Messages in Cartoons for Children." Conference paper. Organization for the
	Study of Communication, Language, and Gender. 1986.
Alperowicz, Cynthia, and Robert Krock. Rocking the Boat: Celebrating Fifteen Years of Action
	for Children's Television. Newtonville, Mass.: Action for Children's Television, 1983.
Altman, Rick. "Television/Sound." Studies in Entertainment: Critical Approaches to Mass Cul-
	ture. Ed. Tania Modleski. Bloomington: Indiana UP, 1986. 39–54.
American Greetings Corporation. Strawberry Shortcake: The First $100 Million. Cleveland:
	American Greetings, 1980.
Amsel, Abram. Behaviorism, Neobehaviorism, and Cognitivism in Learning Theory: Historical
	and Contemporary Perspectives. Hillsdale, N.J.: Erlbaum, 1989.
Andersen, Robin. Consumer Culture and TV Programming. Boulder, Colo.: Westview, 1995.
Ang, Ien. Desperately Seeking the Audience. New York: Routledge, 1991.
Averill, Gage. "Global Imaginings." Ohmann 203–223.
Baldwin, Thomas F., and Colby Lewis. "Violence in Television: The Industry Looks at
	Itself." Comstock and Rubinstein 290–373.
Balio, Tino, ed. The American Film Industry. Rev. ed. Madison: U of Wisconsin P, 1985.
Baritz, Loren. Backfire: American Culture and the Vietnam War. New York: Ballantine, 1985.
Barnouw, Erik. The Image Empire: A History of Broadcasting in the United States from 1953.
	New York: Oxford UP, 1970.
Bart, Pauline B., and Margaret Jozsa. "Dirty Books, Dirty Films, and Dirty Data." Take
	Back the Night: Women on Pornography. Ed. Laura Lederer. New York: Bantam, 1980.
	201–215.
Barthes, Roland. Mythologies. Trans. Annette Lavers. New York: Noonday, 1990.

Bash, Alan. "Human Half of New 'Muppets' Host." *USA Today* 11 Apr. 1996: 3D.

Basler, Barbara. "Peter Pan, Garfield, and Bart—All Have Asian Roots." *New York Times* 2 Dec. 1990, sec. 2: 35–36.

Bell, Elizabeth. "Somatexts at the Disney Shop: Constructing the Pentimentos of Women's Animated Bodies." *From Mouse to Mermaid: The Politics of Film, Gender, and Culture.* Ed. Elizabeth Bell, Lynda Haas, and Laura Sells. Bloomington: Indiana UP, 1995. 107–124.

Betty Boop to Barney: Make-Believe Characters Invade the Marketplace. Exhibition pamphlet. Strong Museum, Rochester, N.Y.

Boddy, William. "The Seven Dwarfs and the Money Grubbers: The Public Relations Crisis of U.S. Television in the Late 1950's." Mellencamp 98–116.

Bodroghkozy, Aniko. " 'Is This What You Mean by Color TV?' Race, Gender, and Contested Meanings in NBC's *Julia*." *Private Screenings: Television and the Female Consumer.* Ed. Lynn Spigel and Denise Mann. Minneapolis: U of Minnesota P, 1992. 143–167.

Bogle, Donald. *Toms, Coons, Mulattos, Mammies, and Bucks: An Interpretive History of Blacks in American Films.* Rev. ed. New York: Continuum, 1990.

Boston Women's Health Book Collective. *Ourselves and Our Children: A Book by and for Parents.* New York: Random House, 1978.

Bourdieu, Pierre. *Distinction: A Social Critique of the Judgment of Taste.* Cambridge: Harvard UP, 1984.

Brederode, Maria Emilia. "Research on *Iftah Ya Simsin*, the Arabic Coproduction." *Sesame Street Research: A Twentieth Anniversary Symposium.* New York: Children's Television Workshop, 1990. 63–67.

Brown, Les. "Children Don't See TV as Black or White." *New York Times* 4 Apr. 1974: 83.

———. "Children in CBS Study Largely Indifferent to Race." *New York Times* 12 June 1975: 75.

Buckingham, David. *Children Talking Television: The Making of Television Literacy.* London: Falmer, 1993.

Burbank, Lucille. *Children's Television: An Historical Inquiry on Three Selected, Prominent, Long-Running, Early Childhood TV Programs.* Diss. Temple U, 1992. Ann Arbor: UMI, 1992.

Cantor, Muriel. "The Role of the Producer in Choosing Children's Television Content." Comstock and Rubinstein 259–288.

Carmen, Ira H. *Movies, Censorship, and the Law.* Ann Arbor: U of Michigan P, 1966.

Carr, Steven Alan. "On the Edge of Tastelessness: CBS, the Smothers Brothers, and the Struggle for Control." *Cinema Journal* 31.4 (Summer 1992): 3–24.

Carter, Bill. "Conservatives Call for PBS to Go Private or Go Dark." *New York Times* 30 Apr. 1992: A1+.

"Censor Overload." *Entertainment Weekly* 11 June 1993: 69.

Chavoya, C. Ondine. "Images of Advocacy: An Interview with Chon Noriega." *Afterimage* 21.10 (May 1994): 5–9.

Children and Television. 3 filmstrips, 3 audiocassettes. University of Wisconsin Extension, 1982.

Children's Television Workshop International Research Notes 4 (Fall 1983).

Classen, Steven Douglas. "Standing on Unstable Grounds: A Reexamination of the WLBT-TV Case." Critical Studies in Mass Communication 11 (1991): 73–91.

Clinton, Hillary. "When It Comes to Family Values . . . I Worry about Television." Parade Magazine 11 Apr. 1993: 10.

Cole, Barry, and Mal Oettinger. Reluctant Regulators: The FCC and the Broadcast Audience. Reading, Mass.: Addison-Wesley, 1978.

Comstock, George, et al. Television and Social Behavior. New York: Columbia UP, 1978.

Comstock, George A., and Eli A. Rubinstein, eds. Television and Social Behavior: Reports and Papers. Vol. 1: Media Content and Control. Rockville, Md.: U.S. Department of Health, Education, and Welfare, 1972.

Cook, Thomas D., et al. Sesame Street Revisited. New York: Russell Sage Foundation, 1975.

Cosby, William Henry, Jr. An Integration of the Visual Media via "Fat Albert and the Cosby Kids" into the Elementary School Curriculum as a Teaching Aid and Vehicle to Achieve Increased Learning. Diss. U of Massachusetts, 1976. Ann Arbor: UMI, 1976.

Coward, Rosalind. Female Desires: How They Are Sought, Bought, and Packaged. New York: Grove, 1985.

Cripps, Thomas. " 'Amos 'n' Andy' and the Debate over American Racial Integration." O'Connor 33–54.

Culbert, David. "Television's Nixon: The Politician and His Image." O'Connor 184–207.

Curtin, Michael. Redeeming the Wasteland: Television Documentary and Cold War Politics. New Brunswick, N.J.: Rutgers UP, 1995.

Damerell, Reginald G. Education's Smoking Gun: How Teacher's Colleges Have Destroyed Education in America. New York: Freundlich, n.d.

Daniel, Josh. "Uncivil Wars: The Conservative Assault on Public Broadcasting." Independent Aug./Sept. 1992: 20–25.

De Avila, Edward A., and Barbara Havassy, with Juan Pascual-Leone. Mexican-American Schoolchildren: A Neo-Piagetian Analysis. Georgetown: Georgetown UP, 1976.

deCordova, Richard. "The Mickey in Macy's Window: Childhood, Consumerism, and Disney Animation." Disney Discourse: Producing the Magic Kingdom. Ed. Eric Smoodin. New York: Routledge, 1994. 203–213.

de Grazia, Edward. Girls Lean Back Everywhere: The Law of Obscenity and the Assault on Genius. New York: Random House, 1992.

de Grazia, Edward, and Roger K. Newman. Banned Films: Movies, Censors, and the First Amendment. New York: Bowker, 1982.

DelGaudio, Sybil. "Seduced and Reduced: Female Animal Characters in Some

Warners' Cartoons." *The American Animated Cartoon: A Critical Anthology*. Ed. Danny Peary and Gerry Peary. New York: Dutton, 1980. 211–216.

DeMause, Lloyd. *The History of Childhood*. New York: Harper and Row, 1975.

Deneroff, Harvey. "We Can't Get Much Spinach: The Organization and Implementation of the Fleischer Animation Strike." *Film History* 1 (1987): 1–14.

Denison, D. C. "The Year of Playing Dangerously." *Boston Globe* 8 Dec. 1985: 14–16+.

De Vaney, Ann, ed. *Watching Channel One: The Convergence of Students, Technology, and Private Business*. Albany: State U of New York P, 1994.

Diaz-Guerrero, Rogelio, et al. "*Plaza Sésamo* in Mexico: An Evaluation." *Journal of Communication* 26.2 (Spring 1976): 145–154.

Dorfman, Ariel, and Armand Mattelart. *How to Read Donald Duck: Imperialist Ideology in the Disney Comic*. New York: I. G. Editions, 1975.

Dufty, William. *Sugar Blues*. New York: Warner, 1975.

Dyer, Richard. "White." *Screen* 29.4 (Autumn 1988): 44–64.

Echols, Alice. *Daring to Be Bad: Radical Feminism in America, 1967–1975*. Minneapolis: U of Minnesota P, 1989.

Edmonds, Ronald, et al. "A Black Response to Christopher Jencks' *Inequality* and Certain Other Issues." *Harvard Educational Review* 43.1 (Feb. 1973): 76–91.

Engelhardt, Tom. "The Shortcake Strategy." *Watching Television*. Ed. Todd Gitlin. New York: Pantheon, 1986. 68–110.

Enloe, Cynthia. *Bananas, Beaches, and Bases: Making Feminist Sense of International Politics*. Berkeley: U of California P, 1989.

Ernst, Morris L., and Pare Lorentz. *Censored: The Private Life of the Movies*. New York: Cape and Smith, 1930.

Ezzaki, Abdelkader. "Research on *Iftah Ya Simsin*, the Arabic Coproduction." *Sesame Street Research* 60–62.

"The FCC's New (and Greater) Forfeiture Schedule." *Broadcasting* 5 Aug. 1991: 24.

Fein, Bruce. "In the Interests of Common Decency: Prudent Use of Law." *Washington Times* 2 June 1992: F1.

Filmation Associates and William H. Cosby Jr. *Personal, Parental, and Peer-Group Value Conflicts as Catalysts of Complex Educational and Psychological Issues Confronting Children in a Contemporary Society or . . . Fat Albert and the Cosby Kids*. Los Angeles: Filmation Associates, 1972.

Fiske, John. *Television Culture*. New York: Methuen, 1987.

Fleissner, Jennifer. *The Federal Communications Commission*. New York: Chelsea House, 1991.

Foucault, Michel. *Discipline and Punish: The Birth of the Prison*. Trans. Alan Sheridan. New York: Random House, 1979.

Freire, Paulo, and Donaldo Macedo. *Literacy: Reading the Word and the World*. South Hadley, Mass.: Bergin and Garvey, 1987.

Friendly, Fred W. *The Good Guys, the Bad Guys, and the First Amendment: Free Speech vs. Fairness in Broadcasting.* New York: Vintage, 1977.

Fuentes, Annette, and Barbara Ehrenreich. *Women in the Global Factory.* Boston: South End, 1983.

Gallop, Jane. "Annie Leclerc Writing a Letter, with Vermeer." *The Poetics of Gender.* Ed. Nancy K. Miller. New York: Columbia UP, 1986. 137–156.

Gardner, Gerald. *The Censorship Papers.* New York: Dodd, Mead, 1987.

Gerbner, George. "Instant History—Image History: Lessons of the Persian Gulf War." *Velvet Light Trap* 31 (Spring 1993): 3–13.

Gettas, Gregory J. "The Globalization of *Sesame Street*: A Producer's Perspective." *Educational Technology Research and Development* 38.4 (1990): 55–63.

Gillmor, Donald M., et al. *Fundamentals of Mass Communication Law.* Minneapolis: West, 1996.

Ginsburg, Herbert. *The Myth of the Deprived Child: Poor Children's Intellect and Education.* Englewood Cliffs, N.J.: Prentice-Hall, 1972.

Gitter, Lena L. *A Strategy for Fighting the War on Poverty: The Montessori Method as Applied to the Brookhaven Project.* Washington, D.C.: Fagan, 1965.

Gledhill, Christine, ed. *Stardom: Industry of Desire.* New York: Routledge, 1991.

"Going Global: Transcript of a Report Broadcast on the *MacNeil/Lehrer Newshour* September 29, 1987." Schneider and Wallis 182–183.

Goldsen, Rose K. "Engineering Children." *A Personal Perspective on Broadcasting.* WVBR, Ithaca, N.Y. 27 Apr. 1974. WHCU, Ithaca, N.Y. 29 Apr. 1974.

———. *The Show and Tell Machine: How Television Works and Works You Over.* New York: Dial, 1977.

Goldsen, Rose K., and Azriel Bibliowicz. "Plaza Sésamo: 'Neutral' Language or 'Cultural Assault'?" *Journal of Communication* 26.2 (Spring 1976): 124–125.

Goldson, Annie, and Chris Bratton. "Counter Terror." Schneider and Wallis 147–159.

Gore, Tipper. *Raising PG Kids in an X-Rated Society.* Nashville, Tenn.: Abingdon, 1987.

Gould, Stephen Jay. *The Mismeasure of Man.* New York: Norton, 1981.

Greider, William. "On Television, Race No Longer Divides Us: America Finally Invented the Black and White Television." *Washington Post* 12 Apr. 1978, final ed.: A1+.

Griffin, Sean. "Pronoun Trouble: The 'Queerness' of Animation." *Spectator* 15.1 (Fall 1994): 94–109.

Grossman, Gary H. *Saturday Morning TV.* New York: Dell, 1981.

Halpern, Werner I. "Turned-on Toddlers." *Journal of Communication* 25.4 (Autumn 1975): 66–70.

Harwood, Richard. "*The Washington Post*, June 8, 1968." *"An Honorable Profession": A Tribute to Robert F. Kennedy.* Ed. Pierre Salinger, Edwin Guthman, and Frank Mankiewicz. New York: Doubleday, 1968. 81–82.

Head, Sydney W., and Christopher H. Sterling. *Broadcasting in America: A Survey of Electronic Media*. 6th ed. Boston: Houghton Mifflin, 1990.

Hendershot, Heather. "Chaste, Chased, and Erased: Betty Boop's Censorship." *Added Attractions: Histories and Theories of Film Shorts*. Ed. Hank Sartin and Arthur Knight. Forthcoming.

———. "Dolls: Odour, Disgust, Femininity, and Toy Design." *The Gendered Object*. Ed. Pat Kirkham. Manchester, Eng.: Manchester UP, 1996. 90–102.

———. "Is Something Fishy Going on Here? Douching and the Myth of Female Genital Odor." Conference paper. Graduate Student Critical Theory Colloquium. U of Rochester, Rochester, N.Y. Apr. 1990.

Herrnstein, Richard J., and Charles Murray. *The Bell Curve: Intelligence and Class Structure in American Life*. New York: Free Press, 1994.

Holquist, Michael. "Corrupt Originals: The Paradox of Censorship." *PMLA* 109.1 (Jan. 1994): 14–25.

Honeycutt, Kirk. " 'Care Bears': Kids' Entertainment or an Advertising Bonanza?" *Los Angeles Daily News* 30 Apr. 1985, Life Section: n.p. Clipping in Margaret Herrick Library, Academy of Motion Picture Arts and Sciences, Beverly Hills, Calif.

Horne, Lutrelle. "Introductory Remarks." *Sesame Street Research*. 54.

Howell, Amanda. Rev. of *The Remasculinization of America: Gender and the Vietnam War*, by Susan Jeffords. *Camera Obscura* 27 (Sept. 1991): 166–173.

Hunt, J. McVicker. Introduction. *The Montessori Method*. By Maria Montessori. New York: Schocken, 1974. xi–xxxix.

Husson, William George. *A Time Series Analysis of the Attention Patterns of Naive and Experienced Child Viewers*. Diss. Rensselaer Polytechnic Institute, 1981. Ann Arbor: UMI, 1981.

"Ira Herbert: The Coca-Cola Company." Ohmann 3–17.

Jacobs, Lea. *The Wages of Sin: Censorship and the Fallen Woman Film, 1928–1942*. Madison: U of Wisconsin P, 1991.

Jacobs, Lea, and Richard Maltby, eds. *Quarterly Review of Film and Video: Rethinking the Production Code* 15.4 (1995).

James, Allison. "Confections, Concoctions, and Conceptions." *Popular Culture: Past and Present*. Ed. B. Waites, T. Bennett, and G. Martins. London: Croom Helm/Open UP, 1982. 294–307.

James, Allison, and A. Prout, eds. *Constructing and Reconstructing Childhood: Contemporary Issues in the Sociological Study of Childhood*. London: Falmer, 1990.

Jenkins, Henry, III. "The All-American Handful: *Dennis the Menace*, Permissive Child-rearing, and the Popular Imagination." Conference paper. Console-ing Passions. Tucson, Ariz. Apr. 1994.

———. " 'Going Bonkers!': Children, Play, and Pee-wee." *Camera Obscura* 17 (May 1988): 169–193.

———. " 'A Person's a Person, No Matter How Small': Growing up with Dr. Seuss and Dr. Spock." Conference paper. Society for Cinema Studies. New Orleans, La. Mar. 1993.

———. " 'X Logic': Repositioning Nintendo in Children's Lives." Rev. of *Playing with Power in Movies, Television, and Video Games: From Muppet Babies to Teenage Mutant Ninja Turtles*, by Marsha Kinder, and *Video Kids Making Sense of Nintendo*, by Eugene F. Provenzo Jr. *Quarterly Review of Film and Video* 14.4 (August 1993): 55–70.

Jensen, Arthur R. "How Much Can We Boost I.Q. and Scholastic Achievement?" *Harvard Educational Review* 39.1 (Winter 1969): 1–123.

Jessell, Harry A. "High Court Agrees Ban Is Unconstitutional." *Broadcasting* 9 Mar. 1992: 35.

Jhally, Sut, and Justin Lewis. *Enlightened Racism: "The Cosby Show," Audiences, and the Myth of the American Dream*. Boulder, Colo.: Westview, 1992.

Johnson, Nicholas. *How to Talk Back to Your Television Set*. New York: Bantam, 1970.

Kaplan, Caren. " 'A World without Boundaries': The Body/Shop's Trans/National Geographics." *Social Text* 43 (Fall 1995): 45–66.

Kettelkamp, Larry. *Bill Cosby: Family Fun Man*. New York: Simon and Schuster, 1987.

Kinder, Marsha. *Playing with Power in Movies, Television, and Video Games: From Muppet Babies to Teenage Mutant Ninja Turtles*. Berkeley: U of California P, 1991.

———, ed. *Kids' Media Culture*. Durham, N.C.: Duke UP, forthcoming.

Kisseloff, Jeff. *The Box: An Oral History of Television, 1920–1961*. New York: Penguin, 1997.

Kline, Stephen. "The Empire of Play: Emergent Genres of Product-Based Animations." In *Front of the Children: Screen Entertainment and Young Audiences*. Ed. Cary Bazalgette and David Buckingham. London: British Film Institute, 1995. 151–165.

———. *Out of the Garden: Toys and Children's Culture in the Age of TV Marketing*. New York: Verso, 1993.

Kopkind, Andrew. "He's a Happening: Robert Kennedy's Road to Somewhere." *The Sense of the 60's*. Ed. Edward Quinn and Paul J. Dolan. New York: Free Press, 1968. 183 194.

Krasnow, Erwin G., Lawrence D. Longley, and Herbert A. Terry. *The Politics of Broadcast Regulation*. 3rd ed. New York: St. Martin's, 1982.

Kuhn, Annette. *Cinema, Censorship, and Sexuality, 1909–1925*. New York: Routledge, 1988.

Kunkel, Dale. "Children and Host-Selling Television Commercials." *Communication Research* 15.1 (Feb. 1988): 71–92.

———. "From a Raised Eyebrow to a Turned Back: The FCC and Children's Product-Related Programming." *Journal of Communication* 38.4 (Autumn 1988): 90–108.

———. "Report to the Federal Communications Commission re: Mass Media Docket 93-48." *Broadcasters License Renewal Claims Regarding Children's Educational Programming* (1993).

———. "Young Minds and Marketplace Values: Issues in Children's Television Advertising." *Journal of Social Sciences* 47.1 (1991): 57–72.

Labov, William, et al. *A Study of the Non-Standard English of Negro and Puerto-Rican Speakers in New York City*. Washington, D.C.: U.S. Department of Health, Education, and Welfare, Office of Education, 1968.

Lasker, Harry M. "The Jamaican Project: Final Report." Unpublished report. New York: Children's Television Workshop, 1973.

Leff, Leonard J., and Jerold L. Simmons. *The Dame in the Kimono: Hollywood, Censorship, and the Production Code from the 1920's to the 1960's*. New York: Grove Weidenfeld, 1990.

Lemish, Dafna. "Viewers in Diapers: The Early Development of Television Viewing." Lindlof 33–57.

Lesser, Gerald. *Children and Television: Lessons from Sesame Street*. New York: Random House, 1974.

Levelt, Peter. "A Review of Research on International Coproductions of *Sesame Street*." *Sesame Street Research* 55–59.

Liebert, Robert M., John M. Neale, and Emily S. Davidson. *The Early Window: Effects of Television on Children and Youth*. New York: Pergamon, 1973.

Linderman, Lawrence. "Playboy Interview: Bill Cosby." *Playboy* 1969: 73+.

———. "Playboy Interview: Bill Cosby." *Playboy* 1985: 75+.

Lindlof, Thomas R., ed. *Natural Audiences: Qualitative Research of Media Uses and Effects*. Norwood, N.J.: Ablex, 1987.

Long, Loretta Moore. "*Sesame Street*": A Space Age Approach to Education for Space Age Children. Diss. U of Massachusetts, 1973. Ann Arbor: UMI, 1973.

Lovelace, Valeria. "*Sesame Street* as a Continuing Experiment." *Educational Technology Research and Development* 38.4 (1990): 17–24.

MacKinnon, Catharine A. *Only Words*. Cambridge: Harvard UP, 1993.

Maltin, Leonard. *Of Mice and Magic: A History of American Animated Cartoons*. Rev. ed. New York: McGraw-Hill, 1987.

Mander, Jerry. *Four Arguments for the Elimination of Television*. New York: Morrow Quill, 1978.

Marks, Laura U. "Tie a Yellow Ribbon around Me: Masochism, Militarism, and the Gulf War on TV." *Camera Obscura* 27 (Sept. 1991): 55–75.

Maslin, Janet. "There's a Moral in TV Cartoons: Be Resourceful." *New York Times* 4 Oct. 1992, sec. 4: 2.

Mast, Gerald. *The Movies in Our Midst: Documents in the Cultural History of Film in America*. Chicago: U of Chicago P, 1982.

Mater, Gene P. Letter to Peggy Charren. 31 Mar. 1982. ACT Collection.

Mattelart, Armand. *Multinational Corporations and the Control of Culture*. Trans. Michael Chanan. Atlantic Highlands, N.J.: Humanities Press, 1979.

———. *Transnationals and the Third World: The Struggle for Culture.* Trans. David Buxton. South Hadley, Mass.: Bergin and Garvey, 1983.

Mattelart, Michèle. "Education, Television, and Mass Culture: Reflections on Research into Innovation." *Television in Transition.* Ed. Phillip Drummond and Richard Patterson. London: BFI, 1986. 164–184.

McCarthy, Anna. "The Front Row Is Reserved for Scotch Drinkers: Early Television's Tavern Audience." *Cinema Journal* 35.4 (Summer 1995): 31–49.

McChesney, Robert W. "Conflict, Not Consensus: The Debate over Broadcast Communication Policy, 1930–1935." Solomon and McChesney 222–258.

———. *Telecommunications, Mass Media, and Democracy: The Battle for the Control of U.S. Broadcasting, 1928–1935.* New York: Oxford UP, 1993.

Mechling, Elizabeth Walker, and Jay Mechling. "Sweet Talk: The Moral Rhetoric against Sugar." *Central States Speech Journal* 34 (Spring 1983): 19–32.

Meehan, Eileen R. "Why We Don't Count." Mellencamp 117–137.

Mellencamp, Patricia, ed. *Logics of Television: Essays in Cultural Criticism.* Bloomington: Indiana UP, 1990.

Messaris, Paul. "Mothers' Comments to Their Children about the Relationship between Television and Reality." Lindlof 95–107.

Miège, Bernard. *The Capitalization of Cultural Production.* New York: International General, 1989.

Miller, D. A. "Anal Rope." *Inside/Out: Lesbian Theories, Gay Theories.* Ed. Diana Fuss. New York: Routledge, 1991. 119–141.

Mills, Hilary. "Pete and Joan." *Vanity Fair* Aug. 1993: 116+.

Modleski, Tania. "The Rhythms of Reception: Daytime Television and Women's Work." *Regarding Television: Critical Approaches — An Anthology.* Ed. E. Ann Kaplan. Los Angeles: American Film Institute, 1983. 67–75.

Moley, Raymond. *The Hays Office.* Indianapolis: Bobs-Merrill, 1945.

Montgomery, Kathryn C. *Gay Activists and the Networks: A Case Study of Special Interest Pressure in Television.* Diss. U of California, Los Angeles, 1979. Ann Arbor: UMI, 1979.

———. *Target: Prime Time, Advocacy Groups, and the Struggle over Entertainment Television.* New York: Oxford UP, 1989.

Morgan, Michael, Justin Lewis, and Sut Jhally. "More Viewing, Less Knowledge." *Triumph of the Image.* Ed. Hamid Mowlana, George Gerbner, and Herbert I. Schiller. Boulder, Colo.: Westview, 1992.

Moynihan, Daniel Patrick. *The Negro Family: The Case for National Action.* Washington, D.C.: U.S. Department of Labor, Office of Policy Research, 1965.

Mullen, Jim. "Tinky Wink Wink." *Entertainment Weekly* 17 Apr. 1998: 10.

Mulvey, Laura. "Afterthoughts on 'Visual Pleasure and Narrative Cinema' Inspired by *Duel in the Sun*." *Feminism and Film Theory.* Ed. Constance Penley. New York: Routledge, 1988. 69–79.

NCTV News 2.4 (July–Aug. 1981). National Coalition on Television Violence file. ACT Collection.

NCTV News 2.5 (Sept.–Nov. 1981). National Coalition on Television Violence file. ACT Collection.

O'Barr, William M. "The Airbrushing of Culture: An Insider's Look at Global Advertising." *Public Culture* 2.1 (1989): 1–19.

O'Connor, John E. *American Television/American History.* New York: Ungar, 1983.

Ohmann, Richard, ed. *Making and Selling Culture.* Hanover, N.H.: Wesleyan UP, 1996.

Olsen, James T. *Bill Cosby: Look Back in Laughter.* Mankato, Minn.: Creative Education, 1974.

Paley, Vivian Gussin. *Boys and Girls.* Chicago: U of Chicago P, 1984.

Palmer, Edward L. *Children in the Cradle of Television.* Toronto: Heath, 1987.

———. *Television and America's Children: A Crisis of Neglect.* New York: Oxford UP, 1988.

Palmer, Edward L., Milton Chen, and Gerald S. Lesser. "Sesame Street: Patterns of International Adaptation." *Journal of Communication* 26.2 (Spring 1976): 109–123.

Palmer, Patricia. *The Lively Audience: A Study of Children around the TV Set.* Sydney: Allen and Unwin, 1986.

Parker, Sandra J. "L.A. TV Veterans Speak." *Emmy Magazine* Dec. 1991: 54.

Pecora, Norma Odom. *The Business of Children's Television.* New York: Guilford, 1998.

Pekurny, Robert. *Broadcast Self-Regulation: A Participant-Observation Study of the National Broadcasting Company's Broadcast Standards Department.* Diss. U of Minnesota, 1977. Ann Arbor: UMI, 1977.

Penley, Constance. "The Cabinet of Dr. Pee-wee: Consumerism and Sexual Terror." *Camera Obscura* 17 (May 1988): 133–153.

———. "From NASA to The 700 Club (with a Detour through Hollywood): Cultural Studies in the Public Sphere." *Disciplinarity and Dissent in Cultural Studies.* Ed. Cary Nelson and Dilip Parameshwar Gaonkar. New York: Routledge, 1996. 235–250.

Penley, Constance, and Sharon Willis, eds. *Male Trouble.* Minneapolis: U of Minnesota P, 1993.

Phillips, Phil. *Turmoil in the Toybox.* Lancaster, Pa.: Starburst, 1986.

Poggi, Patricia May. *Audience Influence on the Programming of "Sesame Street" from 1969 through 1975.* Diss. Columbia U, 1978. Ann Arbor: UMI, 1978.

Polsky, Richard M. *Getting to Sesame Street: Origins of the Children's Television Workshop.* New York: Praeger, 1974.

Postman, Neil. *The Disappearance of Childhood.* New York: Random House, 1982.

Price, Deb. "Gay Studies Show New Dimensions of the World." *Democrat and Chronicle* 3 Dec. 1992: 4C.

Radecki, Thomas. Letter to Peggy Charren. C. 5 Sept. 1980. National Coalition on Television Violence file. ACT Collection.

Rand, Erica. *Barbie's Queer Accessories.* Durham, N.C.: Duke UP, 1995.

Rieger, Hank. "Editorial." *Emmy Magazine* Fall 1979.

Romano, Carlin. "Between the Motion and the Act." *Nation* 15 Nov. 1993: 567.

Rose, Jacqueline. *The Case of Peter Pan, or, the Impossibility of Children's Fiction.* London: Macmillan, 1984.

Roszak, Theodore. *The Making of a Counter-Culture: Reflections on the Technocratic Society and Its Youthful Opposition.* New York: Anchor, 1969.

"Roundtable on Children's Programming." *Emmy Magazine* Fall 1979: 14–22, 61–68.

Rubinstein, Eli A. "The TV Violence Report: What's Next?" *Journal of Communication* 24.1 (Winter 1974): 80–88.

Sacher, Emily. "Cartoon Power: Are Children Being Brainwashed to Buy Toys?" *Newsday* 17 Feb. 1985: 15.

Sartin, Hank. "Bugs Bunny: Queer as a Three Dollar Bill." *Windy City Times* 24 June 1993, sec. 2: 79.

Scheer, Robert. "Violence Is Us." *Nation* 15 Nov. 1993: 557.

Schneider, Cy. *Children's Television: The Art, the Business, and How It Works.* Chicago: NTC Business Books, 1987.

Schneider, Cynthia, and Brian Wallis, eds. *Global Television.* New York: Wedge, 1991.

Schwarz, Meg, ed. *TV and Teens: Experts Look at the Issues.* Reading, Mass.: Addison-Wesley, 1982.

Scott, Allen J. *Metropolis: From Division of Labor to Urban Form.* Berkeley: U of California P, 1988.

See, Carolyn. "Diahann Carroll's Image." *TV Guide* 14 Mar. 1970: 26–30.

Seiter, Ellen. "Power Rangers at Preschool: Negotiating Media in Child Care Settings." Unpublished paper. 1996.

———. *Television and New Media Audiences.* Oxford: Oxford UP, forthcoming.

Seiter, Ellen, and Karen Riggs. " 'Barney's Better than Jesus': TV and Conflict in the Evangelical Preschool." Conference paper. Console-ing Passions. Madison, Wis. Apr. 1996.

Selig, Josh. "Muppets Succeed Where Politicians Haven't." *New York Times* 29 Mar. 1998, sec. 2: 45.

Selnow, Gary W., and Richard R. Gilbert. *Society's Impact on Television: How the Viewing Public Shapes Television Programming.* Westport, Conn.: Praeger, 1993.

Sesame Street Research: A Twentieth Anniversary Symposium. New York: Children's Television Workshop, 1990.

Shaw, Daniel R. *A Mother's Battle against Trash TV: The Story of Terry Rakolta and Americans for Responsible Television.* N.p.: Dogwood, 1992.

Silverstein, Brett. *Fed Up: The Food Forces That Make You Fat, Sick, and Poor.* Boston: South End, 1984.

Singer, Jerome, and Dorothy Singer. "Come Back, Mister Rogers, Come Back." *Television and American Culture.* Ed. Carl Lowe. New York: Wilson, 1981. 124–128.

Skolnick, Jerome H. *The Politics of Protest*. New York: Simon and Schuster, 1969.

Skovmand, Michael. "Barbarous TV International: Syndicated *Wheels of Fortune*." *Media Cultures: Reappraising Transnational Media*. Ed. Michael Skovmand and Kim Schrøder. London: Routledge, 1992. 84-103.

Smith, Lendon H. *Improving Your Child's Behavior Chemistry*. New York: Pocket Books, 1976.

Smoodin, Eric. *Animating Culture: Hollywood Cartoons from the Sound Era*. New Brunswick, N.J.: Rutgers UP, 1993.

———. "Compulsory Viewing for Every Citizen: Mr. Smith, Film Reception, and the Discourse on Democracy." Conference paper. Society for Cinema Studies. Syracuse, N.Y. Mar. 1994.

———. *Disney Discourse: Producing the Magic Kingdom*. New York: Routledge, 1994.

Solomon, William S., and Robert W. McChesney, eds. *Ruthless Criticism: New Perspectives in U.S. Communication History*. Minneapolis: U of Minnesota P, 1993.

Spector, Bert. "A Clash of Cultures: The Smothers Brothers vs. CBS Television." O'Connor 159-183.

Spigel, Lynn. *Make Room for TV: Television and the Family Ideal in Postwar America*. Chicago: U of Chicago P, 1992.

———. "Seducing the Innocent: Childhood and Television in Postwar America." Solomon and McChesney 259-290.

Spigel, Lynn, and Henry Jenkins. "Same Bat Channel, Different Bat Times: Mass Culture and Popular Memory." *The Many Lives of the Batman: Critical Approaches to a Superhero and His Media*. Ed. Roberta E. Pearson and William Urrichio. New York: Routledge, 1991. 117-148.

Stacey, Jackie. "Textual Obsessions: Methodology, History, and Researching Female Spectatorship." *Screen* 34.3 (Autumn 1993): 260-274.

Stacey, Michelle. *Consumed: Why Americans Love, Hate, and Fear Food*. New York: Simon and Schuster, 1994.

Stern, Sydney Ladensohn, and Ted Schoenhaus. *Toyland: The High Stakes Game of the Toy Industry*. Chicago: Contemporary Books, 1990.

Sutton-Smith, Brian. *Toys as Culture*. New York: Gardner, 1986.

Tashman, Billy. "E-Z Street: Twenty-five Years and Still Counting." *Village Voice* 23 Nov. 1993: 55-56.

Thomas, Anna. *The Vegetarian Epicure*. New York: Vintage, 1972.

Thompson, Kristin. "Implications of the Cel Animation Technique." *The Cinematic Apparatus*. Ed. Teresa de Lauretis and Stephen Heath. New York: St. Martin's, 1980. 106-120.

Toy, Steve. " 'Suspended' Animation: Hard Times for Cartoonists as TV Webs Taper Off." *Variety* 3 Apr. 1974: 1+.

Toy Manufacturers of America. *Toy Industry Fact Book.* New York: Toy Manufacturers of America, 1990–1991.

Transcript the MacNeil/Lehrer Report 5/10/78." To Be Integrated ACT Speeches filing cabinet. ACT Collection.

"TV Cartoon Plans Are Dropped." *New York Times* 31 Mar. 1992: D7.

U.S. Commission on Civil Rights. *Window Dressing on the Set: Women and Minorities in Television.* Washington, D.C.: U.S. Commission on Civil Rights, 1977.

———. *Window Dressing on the Set: An Update.* Washington, D.C.: U.S. Commission on Civil Rights, 1979.

Varis, Tapio. "Trends in International Television Flow." Schneider and Wallis 95–107.

Vizzard, Jack. *See No Evil: Life inside a Hollywood Censor.* New York: Simon and Schuster, 1970.

Washington, Valora, and Ura Jean Oyemade. *Project Head Start: Past, Present, and Future Trends in the Context of Family Needs.* New York: Garland, 1987.

Watson, Mary Ann. *The Expanding Vista: American Television in the Kennedy Years.* New York: Oxford UP, 1990.

Wertham, Frederic. *Seduction of the Innocent.* New York: Rinehart, 1954.

West, Mark I. *Children, Culture, and Controversy.* Hamden, Conn.: Archon, 1988.

White, Theodore H. *The Making of the President 1960.* New York: Pocket Books, 1961.

Wilkinson, Alec. *Big Sugar.* New York: Knopf, 1989.

Williams, Anna. "Domesticity and the Aetiology of Crime in *America's Most Wanted.*" *Camera Obscura* 31 (Jan.–May 1993): 97–118.

Williams, Linda. *Hard Core: Power, Pleasure, and the Frenzy of the Visible.* Berkeley: U of California P, 1989.

Williams, Raymond. *Television: Technology and Cultural Form.* Hanover, N.H.: Wesleyan UP, 1992.

Willis, Susan. *A Primer for Daily Life.* New York: Routledge, 1991.

Winn, Marie. *The Plug-In Drug: Television, Children, and the Family.* New York: Viking, 1977.

Winston, Michael R. "Racial Consciousness and the Evolution of Communications in the United States." *Daedalus* Fall 1982: 178.

Woolery, George W. *Children's Television: The First Thirty-Five Years, 1946–1981. Part 1: Animated Cartoon Series.* Metuchen, N.J.: Scarecrow, 1983.

Yudkin, John. *Sweet and Dangerous.* New York: Bantam, 1973.

Index

ABC, 38, 210

Action for Children's Television, 10, 26, 31, 55–59, 61, 64, 66, 69, 71, 95, 108, 111–112, 116, 123, 148, 198, 208, 210, 219; and advertising, 82; and advocacy, 62; and annual symposium, 73; and anticensorship image, 74; and antisugar campaign, 62, 81, 82, 84–90; and boycotting, 74, 78, 81; and censorship, 61, 92, 94; vs. Coalition for Better Television, 76; and commercialism, 79, 130, 133; and content-based research, 130; and corporate media, 64, 78; and disciplining the child's body, 84; and effective reform, 72–73; vs. FCC, 80; and food consumption, 83; and good culture, 85; and indecency legislation, 79–80; and maternalism, 66–68, 80; and media education, 80; and NCTV, 77; and nutritional activism, 81, 88, 90–91, 128; and puritan dental campaign, 83; vs. radical feminists, 67; and resource library, 81

Adults: and advertising, 83; and censorship of children's television, 9; and criticism of children's media, 6–7, 22, 58–59, 100–101, 137; protesting for children, 217–218; theorizing child reception, 207; as viewers, 109, 158; as viewers of *Fat Albert and the Cosby Kids*, 211; as viewers of *Mister Rogers' Neighborhood*, 148–149; as viewers of *Sesame Street*, 150–151

Advertising, 23, 56, 80; and anti-Communist boycotts, 23

Advertising Age, 124–127

African Americans, 34, 63, 102–106, 141, 143, 155; and cultural icons, 202–203; and education, 155; on television, 216. *See also* Blacks

AIDS activists, 62

Aiken, Joan E., 100

Ambrosino, Lillian, 68

American Academy of Pediatrics, 73

American Civil Liberties Union, 93

American Dental Association, 83

American Greetings Corporation, 105, 128

American Revolution of 1963, The, 63

American Society of Toy Manufacturers (ASTM), 19

Amos 'n' Andy, 105, 207, 216

Anglos, 144, 206–207

Animation, 100–111; art of, 61; and commercials, 86; and ethnically stereotyped animals, 102–103; history, 37, 230–231 n.9; limited, 257 n.11. *See also* Cartoons

Animation industry, 42; and class inequities, 44; and gender bias, 43–44; and racial politics, 47

Animators, 36, 39–40, 99; and unskilled laborers, 3, 43–44, 47

Antitrust, 75

Arabic viewers, 172

Arsenio Hall Show, 103

Asians, 71, 102, 106, 206–207; and cartoon labor, 48; as characters in cartoons, 106; and health-food movement, 87

Audiences, discourses of multiple, 9

Averill, Gage, 171, 174

Heather Hendershot is Assistant Professor of Media Studies at Queens College.

Library of Congress Cataloging-in-Publication Data
Hendershot, Heather.
Saturday morning censors : television regulation before the
V-chip / Heather Hendershot.
p. cm. — (Console-ing passions)
Includes bibliographical references and index.
ISBN 0-8223-2211-0 (alk. paper). — ISBN 0-8223-2240-04
(pbk. : alk. paper)
1. Television programs for children. 2. Television and
children. 3. Television—Censorship. I. Title. II. Series.
PN1992.8.C46H46 1999
303.3'76'083—dc21 98-33581 CIP